Ancient Rome on the Silver Screen

Ancient Rome on the Silver Screen

Myth versus Reality

Gregory S. Aldrete and Graham Sumner

Foreword by Lindsay Powell

ROWMAN & LITTLEFIELD
Lanham • Boulder • New York • London

Published by Rowman & Littlefield
An imprint of The Rowman & Littlefield Publishing Group, Inc.
4501 Forbes Boulevard, Suite 200, Lanham, Maryland 20706
www.rowman.com

86-90 Paul Street, London EC2A 4NE, United Kingdom

Copyright © 2023 by the Rowman & Littlefield Publishing Group, Inc.

British Library Cataloguing in Publication Information Available

Library of Congress Cataloging-in-Publication Data

Names: Aldrete, Gregory S., author. | Sumner, Graham, author.
Title: Ancient Rome on the silver screen : myth versus reality / Gregory S. Aldrete and Graham Sumner.
Description: Lanham : Rowman & Littlefield, [2023] | Includes bibliographical references and index. | Summary: "A fascinating examination of films set in Ancient Rome that assesses their historical accuracy in terms of plot, costumes, sets, and characterizations and leaves the reader with a deeper understanding of Roman history and modern cinema"—Provided by publisher.
Identifiers: LCCN 2022033706 (print) | LCCN 2022033707 (ebook) | ISBN 9781538159514 (cloth) | ISBN 9781538159521 (epub)
Subjects: LCSH: Rome—In motion pictures. | Civilization, Ancient, in motion pictures. | Historical films—History and criticism. | Peplum films—History and criticism.
Classification: LCC PN1995.9.R68 A54 2023 (print) | LCC PN1995.9.R68 (ebook) | DDC 794.43/65837—dc23/eng/20221220
LC record available at https://lccn.loc.gov/2022033706
LC ebook record available at https://lccn.loc.gov/2022033707

Contents

~

Illustrations

the famous *caligae*-type boot worn by Roman soldiers. (E) A brass legionary helmet and *lorica segmentata* body armor. *Photographs and props from The Terry Nix Collection*

This and other films have memorably promoted an ahistorical but indelible image of Roman warships being propelled by gangs of harshly abused slaves. *United Archives GmbH/Alamy Stock Photo*

Reconstruction of rowers on a Roman warship. Although employed in an arduous profession, the oarsmen on both Greek and Roman galleys were actually free men who were paid for their service. *Illustration by Graham Sumner*

The thrilling chariot race from *Ben-Hur* (1959). While the chariots are a bit heavier in construction than Roman ones likely would have been, most details are fairly accurate and the scene ably captures the excitement and danger of such races. *Screen Prod/Photononstop/Alamy Stock Photo*

(A) Roman charioteer costume from *Ben-Hur* (1959). (B) Reconstruction of a Roman charioteer of the Green faction based on a Roman mosaic. He wears a protective leather harness on his chest and a helmet, probably of leather as well. (C) Rather fanciful Roman charioteer ensemble from *Ben-Hur* (2016). The only accurate aspect is the curved knife. *Illustrations by Graham Sumner; photograph and props from The Terry Nix Collection*

(A) Roman sword, dagger, and scabbards used in *Spartacus* (1960). The sword appears to be the general shape of a Roman *gladius* but is not based on any specific archaeological find. (B) Roman "Captain" from *Spartacus* (1960) in an unusual combination of a leather jerkin over mail armor. (C) Roman legionary from *Spartacus* (1960) with leather muscle cuirass and "Italic-style" helmet. *Illustrations by Graham Sumner*

(A) Legionary from *King of Kings* (1961). (B) Marching legionary from *Ben-Hur* (2016) with odd ammo-pouch-like bags across the chest. (C) Reconstruction of a first-century AD legionary on the march, with accurate equipment. *Illustrations by Graham Sumner*

and (C) are reliefs featuring the banded armor known as *lorica segmentata*, a staple of Roman movies. (D) and (E) are helmets found at Heddernheim, Germany, that were copied in *The Fall of the Roman Empire* and other films. *Illustrations by Graham Sumner*

From the silent era onward, filmmakers loved to portray Vestal Virgins in rather skimpy ahistorical attire. A typical example is (A) this Vestal from *Carry On Cleo* (1964/1965 US). Real Vestals (B) wore considerably more modest outfits befitting their role as revered priestesses charged with tending the sacred flame of Rome. *Illustrations by Graham Sumner*

First-century AD legionaries from (A) *Quo Vadis* (1951) and (B) *Masada* (1981). Both soldiers wear body armor of a type used at this time, but (A) is missing the chest and back plates, while (B) is of leather rather than metal. Both their shields are too small and of the wrong shape. (C) Reconstruction of a first-century AD legionary showing the correct form of this armor and proper shield. *Illustrations by Graham Sumner*

First-century AD centurions from (A) *Ben-Hur* (1959) and (B) *Masada* (1981). Neither has the distinctive transverse helmet crest that was one of the identifying hallmarks of centurions, as shown in the (C) reconstruction of a first-century AD centurion. *Illustrations by Graham Sumner*

Maximus versus Tigris from *Gladiator* (2000). Although it is a thrilling sequence, there is little that is historically accurate in this combat between champion gladiators. The equipment, the presence of tigers, and the conical pillars on the amphitheater floor are all unhistorical additions of the filmmakers. *Lifestyle Pictures/Alamy Stock Photo*

Reconstruction of a bout between two historical types of Roman gladiators, a Thracian and a *hoplomachus*. Romans enjoyed watching combats pitting different types of gladiators against one another. The man with the stick is the bout's referee. *Illustration by Graham Sumner*

~

Acknowledgments

Greg Aldrete would like to thank his wife, Alicia Aldrete, who watched all the movies in this book with him, contributed comments and analysis of them, and edited and proofread the entire manuscript. He dedicates this book to her, in memory of innumerable happy hours spent together across four decades watching and discussing films and their creators, from Kurosawa to Coppola, Werner Herzog to Wong Kar-wai, Leone to Lee, the Coen brothers to the Shaw brothers.

Both Aldrete and Sumner would like to thank Lindsay Powell for his thought-provoking and kind foreword, which for Sumner additionally brought back memories of life in "The Guard."

Graham Sumner would like to offer thanks to the following: First of all, his partner, Elaine Norbury, who helped with scanning, layouts, and photographs and gave her unstinting daily support. To Clive Constable, Peter Johnson, and Chris Jowett for their assistance with photographs, in particular Clive, who went out of his way to help. To Cate Tren, curator of the River and Rowing Museum, Henley on Thames, UK, for her help with photographs of the museum's trireme diorama. To Colchester's Roman Circus Visitor's Centre, UK; Ursula Rothe; John Peter Wild; Lloyd Llewellyn-Jones; Terry Nix, for his assistance with photographs from his extensive collection and generous advice; François Gilbert, for his research on gladiators; and Thomas Kurtz, for allowing the use of some of his paintings from the Mules of Marius exhibition, https://mules-of-marius.com/de/home-2/. Graham dedicates this book to his dearest Elaine.

~

Foreword

By Lindsay Powell

For me, it all started with *Spartacus*—Stanley Kubrick's film starring Kirk Douglas in the lead role. I watched enthralled as a motley gang of gladiators fought disciplined Roman legionaries—and won! I was studying Latin in school at that time, and the movie catalyzed my interest in ancient Rome, which has stayed with me for my entire life. The film may be different, but your interest in Roman history may well have been sparked by watching a movie too.

When the lights dim in a movie theater and the silver screen glimmers, for a while we suspend our belief and enter another world of breathtaking buildings and brutal battles. Yet it is a world created by producers, directors, screenwriters, costume designers, actors, and many other trades and crafts. When the credits roll and the lights are turned on, the first question one often ponders is: Did it really happen like that? In this book, Gregory S. Aldrete sorts modern myth from ancient reality.

Does it matter if the movies accurately reflect the past? A lot of people think so. Many filmgoers believe they are watching accurate depictions of historical events. Teachers use movies to inspire students in classrooms. A favorite activity of historians and period reenactors is debating the accuracy of films and TV miniseries set in ancient Rome. History professors or bloggers review them based on their insights from years of research and scholarship; history buffs or Roman-period interest groups debate them on Facebook or Roman Army Talk. We argue over the accuracy of the historical characters, the timeline of events, the sets, and the choices costume designers make for the legionary helmets or *lorica segmentata*, because we care.

In a recent thread on Facebook, an author of a post remarked that he thought there was great discontent among "educated people" about the historical accuracy of Sir Ridley Scott's *Gladiator* (2000). One contributor answered how it had always been for him a "Spaghetti Western" in which actors dressed in Roman clothes, adding that they were rather poor attempts at Roman clothes as well. Coming to the defense of the director, another replied that it was entertainment, not a documentary, a sentiment echoed by another commentator, while a third who agreed with them added the caveat that it was nevertheless a horrible Roman history movie. One of those "educated people" then pointed out that the source material was inherently biased anyway and was highly likely to be inaccurate on a range of matters simply because history was not written by ancient historians the way modern historians write ancient history. If you are one of these enthusiasts, you will enjoy *Ancient Rome on the Silver Screen.*

The errors in characters, costumes, and chronology notwithstanding, we are a loyal audience. We want to escape to the time in human history that captures our imagination and to experience the grandeur and glory that was Rome. We get very excited when word of a new film is in production. Despite its shortcomings, *Gladiator* almost by itself reinvigorated the public's appetite for historical films and books: thank you, Sir Ridley!

Should we reasonably expect film producers to pay attention to historical accuracy? The phrase *based on true events* that appears in many film intros sells them as factual, even if loosely. But, bottom line, the movie business is a for-profit industry. Studios expect a return on their investment (ROI). Movies are "products" crafted to pull in viewers at the box office—or "content" to bring new subscribers to a streaming service—that drive top line. Moviemaking is a dynamic, entrepreneurial, technology-based industry. Aldrete charts its changing fortunes starting with *Cabiria* produced in 1914. He shows how audiences' tastes, and the movies we are served up, have changed in five distinct periods over the century since. To drive demand, directors have sought to awe the public with ever more grandiose sets or bigger battle scenes. Some of Aldrete's findings are shocking. In the early days, special effects (SFX) were real and dangerous. He describes how, in *Ben-Hur* (1925), "the most expensive silent film ever made," Fred Niblo used ships and oarsmen: incredibly, he was filming an actual sea battle off the Italian coast, complete with onboard fires! Today, ROI—and health and safety regulations—dictate that productions are increasingly filmed against a greenscreen with computer-generated SFX added in postproduction.

The movie business's imperative is to build profitable products and franchises. To compete in a market for discretionary dollars, ancient Rome must be branded and merchandised. Managing the budget of a ninety-minute film or eight-part TV series forces artistic compromises: timelines are compressed, historical characters are combined or eliminated, generic costumes or props are rented. Cinecittà Studios has re-created a portion of the Roman Forum, which has featured in many films and TV dramas. In a city of ancient monuments, the modern set itself has become a tourist attraction.

The combination of Greg Aldrete's historical knowledge and Graham Sumner's fine illustrations makes this a go-to book when watching a Roman-themed film or series. I have known Graham since we were in The Ermine Street Guard, a registered charity that re-creates—as accurately as possible—the arms and equipment of the Roman army of the mid-first century AD. Now as news editor of *Ancient History* and *Ancient Warfare* magazines, I regularly see Graham's art in feature articles, some illustrating popular pieces about "Hollywood Romans." In this book, his comparisons of gear worn in the movies and how it should have looked if historically accurate to the period are particularly striking. The images also suggest that over the years the accuracy of arms and equipment made for film and TV has improved. I hope that up-and-coming directors and costume designers study this book to learn about the industry they work in and to help them to continually improve their craft.

So, "History or Hollywood"? Grab yourself a soda and a bag of popcorn, turn the page, and prepare to be informed every bit as much as entertained.

Lindsay Powell
Historian and Author
Austin, Texas
Memorial Day 2022

Introduction

Have you ever wondered how accurate your favorite movie set in ancient Rome really is? Or whether the eye-catching costumes and heroic deeds of Hollywood's legionaries, emperors, and gladiators are invented fictions or historical reality? If so, then this book is for you. It examines fifty films set in the Roman world and assesses their historical accuracy in terms of plot, costumes, sets, and characterizations. We'll progress chronologically, moving from classics of the dawn of cinema in the early twentieth century, through the great Golden Age of sword-and-sandal flicks in the 1950s, up to contemporary depictions in both traditional cinema and on premium television. Along the way, you will gain insights into the process of making each movie and learn about the challenges that the filmmakers faced in bringing the Roman world to vivid cinematic life.

The coauthors of this book are a Roman historian (Aldrete) and a professional artist specializing in ancient military history (Sumner), and from an early age, we have both been passionate fans of cinema, and especially films about the ancient world. Whenever we encounter students and members of the general public, one of the most common queries directed at us is how true to history their favorite Roman movie is. To answer those questions while also sharing our love for antiquity and film was the motivation for writing this book. A special feature is Sumner's paintings depicting, first, the costumes actually worn by actors in these films, and then reconstructions of what historically accurate versions of the same attire would look like—in other words, both what was worn and what should have been worn. While the entries on each film are designed to be read individually, the book can also be enjoyed as a continuous narrative that traces the history and development of the ancient Roman epic over time.

No sooner had the dazzling new technology of cinema been invented near the end of the nineteenth century than filmmakers immediately turned to ancient history for inspiration and subject matter. Within the first decade, many of the conventions and topics of the ancient epic genre were already being established. In 1896, Georges Hatot made a feature titled *Nero Trying Out Poisons on His Slaves* (*Néron essayant des poisons sur des esclaves*). Available on YouTube, this earliest ancient costume drama shows the despotic emperor majestically seated on a throne surrounded by his lackeys.[1] Two slaves are brought in. The first is made to drink from a cup, after which he expires with histrionic convulsions while Nero cranes forward, watching his death with fascination. Before the corpse is even cleared away, the second slave comes forward, drinks, and dies, with even more thrashing about. This was the first instance of a filmmaker exploiting the lurid possibilities of Nero's cruelties, but it would certainly not be the last.

A few years later, cinema pioneer Georges Méliès introduced to audiences another figure that would become a staple of historical epics. His short film *Cléopâtre* (1899) depicted a grave robber plundering the ancient Egyptian queen's tomb and arousing her vengeful spirit. While this film belongs more to the genre of horror than history, at least four conventional biographies of the Egyptian queen would soon follow in 1912, 1917, 1928, and 1934. In 1906, another titan of early cinema, the prolific director Alice Guy-Blaché, spectacularly launched one of the most popular ancient genres, the Bible film, with *The Birth, the Life and the Death of Christ* (*La vie du Christ*). Prefiguring characteristics of later Bible epics, not only did it boast lavish sets and a cast of hundreds, but in an era when films were typically less than five minutes long, it had a suitably epic running time of thirty-three minutes. Cecil B. DeMille would soon enthusiastically follow her lead with his own Bible epics, such as *The Sign of the Cross* (1932). Popular novels would prove another perennial source of inspiration, with versions of Lew Wallace's tale *Ben-Hur* appearing in 1907 and 1925. Unsurprisingly, Italian filmmakers looked to antiquity, producing historical epics like *Cabiria* (1914) and *Scipione l'Africano* (1937).

After this promising start, the ancient epic languished for a few decades while other film genres took their turns in the spotlight, but by the 1950s, the time was ripe for its recrudescence. The triumphant commercial and critical success of 1951's *Quo Vadis* initiated a craze for cinematic antiquity, and the 1950s became the "Golden Era" of the ancient epic. Also around that time, Hollywood felt threatened by television's rapid rise in popularity, and countered with the strategy of making big budget movies using the very latest film and sound technologies and showing them on extra-large screens to win back audiences. Among the highlights of this period were *The Robe* (1953), *Ben-Hur* (1959), *Spartacus* (1960), and the Jesus biography *King of Kings* (1961). Not only were a number of these films among the top box office performers of that decade, but they achieved a new level of critical acclaim as well. Before 1950, only a single film set in antiquity had been nominated for a Best Picture Oscar, but from 1951 to 1963 six were.

This phase also embodied a characteristic that would become a long-term attribute of the genre: these films, although set in the remote past, frequently functioned as a mirror to reflect and comment upon contemporary concerns, fears, and aspirations. For example, in the United States, the Cold War was perceived by many as a life-and-death ideological battle between the "West," representing freedom and traditional Christian values, and the "godless" totalitarian menace of the Soviet Union. Films such as *Quo Vadis* echoed this cultural struggle though its portrayal of the conflict between an authoritarian Roman Empire and oppressed groups such as Christians and slaves.

The success and popularity of these movies inevitably prompted an outpouring of low-budget imitators looking to cash in on the fad. By the early 1960s, the status of the ancient epic had been eroded by a horde of cheesy, low-budget sword-and-sandal flicks (sometimes called "peplum" films) made in Italy and crudely dubbed into English. Meanwhile, the big-budget Hollywood productions were becoming stilted and clichéd, and audiences seeking sensation and spectacle were drawn to newer and trendier action genres such as the "Spaghetti Western."

Three star-studded and hideously expensive films, *Cleopatra* (1963), *The Fall of the Roman Empire* (1964), and *The Greatest Story Ever Told* (1965), were all disastrous financial flops that marked the end of the Golden Era. So catastrophic was this trio of movies that no more big-budget, mainstream ancient epics would be made for almost three decades.

In the interim, filmmakers nevertheless found creative new ways to depict the Roman world. One of the most significant of these, parody, took advantage of the very staleness of the genre, which made it ripe for caricature. A number of clever parodies of the ancient epic soon appeared: *Carry on Cleo* (1964/1965 US), which providentially made use of some of the sets from *Cleopatra; A Funny Thing Happened on the Way to the Forum* (1966), an adaptation of the farcical musical; and the witty and intelligent send-up of the biblical film genre, *Monty Python's Life of Brian* (1979). Another path to success for onscreen portrayals of antiquity emerged, not in the traditional venue of the movie theater, but in people's homes on television screens. The structure of the TV miniseries proved a fertile ground for telling stories set in the Roman world, as exemplified by *I, Claudius* (1976/1977 US), the BBC's literate ancient soap opera, as well as *Jesus of Nazareth* (1977) and *Masada* (1981), about the Roman siege of a Jewish fortress.

During the 1970s and 1980s, there were also quirky films shaped by the unique visions of their creators. In 1969, eccentric Italian director Federico Fellini came out with *Fellini Satyricon*, a surreal film that owed much to the ethos of the late 1960s, while a decade later in 1979, porn king Bob Guccione somehow enlisted a group of A-list actors to appear in his X-rated flick *Caligula*. Finally, in 1988, acclaimed director Martin Scorsese offered his distinctive take on a Bible movie, *The Last Temptation of Christ*. Thus, while the period between the Golden Era of grand ancient epics in the 1950s and their revival in the early 2000s is often regarded as a gap in the historiography of cinematic depictions of antiquity, this was actually a time of considerable creativity and innovation, during which onscreen stories about ancient Rome evolved to encompass a variety of new formats and genres.

The year 2000 initiated not only a new century and millennium, but a new era for films set in the Roman world. This was due to the huge and unexpected commercial and critical success of director Ridley Scott's *Gladiator*, which was released in that year and single-handedly resuscitated the big-budget ancient history epic. The first two decades of the twenty-first century brought a slew of films set in Roman Britain, such as *King Arthur* (2004), *The Last Legion* (2007), *Centurion* (2010), and *The Eagle* (2011). In a reversal of the Golden Era tendency to portray members of the Roman military as oppressive villains, the heroes in all of these movies are Roman soldiers who, even if the empire is corrupt, are themselves noble-minded and virtuous. Many of these films also seem to have been influenced by recent wars, such as Vietnam and the conflicts in Iraq and Afghanistan, in their sympathetic depiction of the legionaries as combat-weary men who only want to return home, fighting a seemingly intractable war in a strange foreign land.

One of the biggest media developments of the twenty-first century has been the rise of networks outside the traditional Hollywood studio system producing movie-quality shows for pay television. As part of this trend, HBO and STARZ created expensive and well-received series about ancient Rome. Taking place during the transition from Roman Republic to Empire, HBO's *Rome* (2005–2007) offers one of the most realistic portraits of life in the Roman world ever realized, while STARZ's *Spartacus* (2010–2013) is a sensationalistic but popular fictionalized melodrama featuring the rebellious gladiator. Filmmakers continued to produce projects driven by their personal interests, among them *The Passion of the Christ* (2004), a controversial film about Jesus made by Mel Gibson; *Agora* (2009–2010 US), a biography of the late antique female philosopher Hypatia; and *The First King* (2019), a creative Italian-made reinterpretation of the story of the semi-mythical founders of Rome, Romulus and Remus.

Over the first 120 years of cinema's existence, the genre of the ancient Roman epic, despite being set in the remote past, has consistently proved popular with modern audiences. While certain subjects, such as Cleopatra and gladiators, have demonstrated enduring appeal, filmmakers have repeatedly found ways to put new twists on old themes. The tendency to infuse ancient epics with contemporary resonances and allusions has often provoked sharp controversy, but it has also kept the genre fresh and relevant. While it is impossible to predict exactly how the ancient Roman epic will evolve over the coming decades, it seems likely that antiquity will remain an inspiration for filmmakers. We hope that you enjoy this survey of movies set in the Roman world and come away from it with a greater knowledge and appreciation of both film history and Roman history.

∼

CHAPTER ONE

The Early Years of Cinema

Film's First Forays into the Roman World

From the dawn of cinema, filmmakers turned to the Roman world for subject matter. During the first phase, which encompassed the silent era and early sound years, many of the most enduring figures that would feature in films for the next 120 years had already made their way onto movie screens. Cleopatra was one such popular character, with directors cranking out cinematic portrayals of her life in 1912, 1917, 1928, and 1934. Early Christianity and the life of Jesus proved another fruitful source of inspiration for early directors, as exemplified by Cecil B. DeMille's *The Sign of the Cross* (1932). Film versions of popular novels about the ancient world, most notably Lew Wallace's bestseller, *Ben-Hur*, also appeared on the silver screen (1907 and 1925). In Italy, filmmakers looked to dramatic moments in Roman history to produce epics such as *Cabiria* (1914) and *Scipione l'Africano* (1937), both set during the Punic Wars.

Cabiria (1914)

Director: Giovanni Pastrone
Producer: Giovanni Pastrone
Production Company: Itala Film
Cast: Umberto Mozzato (Fulvio Axilla), Bartolomeo Pagano (Maciste), Lidia Quaranta (Cabiria), Italia Almirante-Manzini (Sophonisba), Vitale Di Stefano (Massinissa), Dante Testa (Karthalo), Gina Marangoni (Croessa), Raffaele di Napoli (Bodastoret), Emilio Vardannes (Hannibal)

Although not the first film ever to be set in ancient Rome, *Cabiria* was the first truly great Roman historical epic. It exerted enormous influence over subsequent historical movies and established numerous precedents for what became standard components of both the historical epic and filmmaking itself. Among the technical innovations either invented for or popularized by *Cabiria* are the use of multiple cameras, artificial lighting, on-location filming, the camera dolly, and extensive three-dimensional sets as opposed to simpler backdrops derived from theater. Its huge sets and lavish costumes forever linked the historical epic with the expectation of spectacle, and it also created the enduring muscleman and sword-and-sandal tropes. Among its thrilling action scenes are the dramatic volcanic eruption of Mt. Aetna, buildings crumbling in an earthquake, Hannibal crossing the Alps complete with elephants, the sieges of Syracuse and Cirta, child sacrifice in the Temple of Moloch at Carthage, and even the brilliant Greek inventor Archimedes roasting a Roman fleet by concentrating the sun's rays with giant mirrors.

The movie is set during the Second Punic War (218–201 BC), which was a struggle for dominance in the Western Mediterranean between the two young, expanding rival empires of Rome and Carthage. As the film opens, the title character is a young girl of an aristocratic Roman family living at a villa in Sicily. When Aetna erupts, she is saved by her nurse, but the two are then kidnapped by pirates and taken to Carthage. There, Cabiria is sold to the high priest to be sacrificed in the Temple of Moloch. At the last moment, she is rescued from this fate by Fulvio, a Roman spy, and his enormous hyper-muscular slave, Maciste, but she is recaptured and becomes a servant to Sophonisba, the daughter of a Carthaginian general. Further adventures ensue, and these characters become intertwined with the historical events surrounding Rome's North African campaign against Carthage, in particular the issue of whether the powerful North African kingdom of Numidia will side with Rome or Carthage. The two men contending for the Numidian throne, who represent competing pro-Roman and pro-Carthaginian factions, are also conveniently rivals for the hand of Sophonisba, and, as this struggle plays out, other famous historical figures, including Hannibal and Scipio Africanus, make appearances in the film.

At the time, *Cabiria* was the most expensive film yet produced, and director Giovanni Pastrone spared no effort in making it as spectacular as possible. It was shot on location in Italy, Sicily, North Africa, and the Alps, and noted Italian poet Gabriele D'Annunzio was recruited to write the intertitle cards, which consequently are rather flowery in their diction. The costumes and sets are extensive and elaborate, with those depicting Carthage and the Numidian capital of Cirta especially impressive. The filmmakers clearly drew upon ancient art and architecture for inspiration, and copies of many famous statues, reliefs, paintings, and structures can be identified among the sets and costumes. While all this makes for pleasing and impressive visuals, these ancient details are not derived from the appropriate cultures. For example, the buildings and décor of Cirta owe far more to Egyptian and Assyrian art and architecture than they do to actual Numidian culture. Similarly, the sets and costumes of Carthage are composed of a grab bag of artistic and architectural references lifted from various civilizations of the ancient Near East and even India. Scholars such as Annette Dorgerloh have convincingly argued that the film's consistent use of these Eastern visual elements for Rome's enemies was a deliberate choice by the filmmakers to "orientalize" them and enhance the visual and cultural contrast between them and the Romans, with their Greco-Roman architecture.[1] Much as with the sets, the costumes tend to fairly accurately reflect ancient examples, if not always derived from the correct culture or era. Thus, the armor of the Roman troops is modeled on real Roman armor, but of a type that was worn by legionaries several centuries after the film was set.

Probably the most famous and imitated sequence is the one in the Temple of Moloch. The temple entrance consists of a huge demon-like face with a gaping fanged mouth that recalls (and was likely inspired by) medieval depictions of the Mouth of Hell or the famous "Mouth of Hell" sculpture located in the Renaissance-era garden of Bomarzo near Rome. Inside, children are placed on a hatch in the chest of another hideous statue, which is a giant oven, and each time the hatch snaps shut, a child is immolated and flames flare from the creature's nostrils. While the murder of children at the Temple of Moloch is one of *Cabiria*'s most memorable scenes, the occurrence of both child sacrifice and Moloch-worship at Carthage is questionable from a historical standpoint. The actual primary Carthaginian deities were Tanit and Baal, and this episode seems to have been inspired mainly by Gustave Flaubert's novel *Salammbô*, which is set during the Punic Wars and contains just such a child sacrifice to Moloch.

As for other historical components of the film, the basic facts of the Roman campaign against Carthage and the role of Numidia are true, as is the triangle between Sophonisba and her two suitors. Also as portrayed in the film, although Massinissa, the pro-Roman Numidian, eventually wins both her and the kingship, he is then ordered to turn her over to Scipio, the conquering Roman general, who fears that the Carthaginian woman will suborn Massinissa into turning against Rome; but rather than obey, she drinks poison. The choice to focus on ancient Rome's invasion of North Africa was not a random one but instead reflected contemporary politics, since in 1911

Italy had invaded Libya, the site of ancient Carthage. Therefore, a film about ancient Romans invading and conquering the very same territory made this film, which ostensibly depicted a third-century BC war, into a statement of political propaganda justifying twentieth-century Italian colonialism.

Worth mentioning are the film's physical stunts, which are still thrilling today, such as Roman legionaries athletically and creatively scaling a city wall by building a human pyramid of men standing atop their shields, and Fulvio dramatically leaping from a high cliff into the ocean. Many of the stunts center around feats of strength by the muscle-bound Maciste, played by Bartolomeo Pagano, who, prior to his casting in the film, was a Genoese dockworker. In one scene, the captive Maciste is shackled to a massive millstone and forced to trudge in a tight circle, grinding grain for ten years until eventually freed by Fulvio—an episode that would be copied verbatim in *Conan the Barbarian* (1982), with Arnold Schwarzenegger taking on the captive grain-grinding muscleman role. So charismatic and popular was the character of Maciste that Pagano would go on to star in no fewer than twenty-six Maciste spin-off films over the next thirteen years, and the series was revived again in the 1960s, with a new brawny actor stepping into the muscleman sandals and cranking out another two dozen films with titles such as *Maciste versus Hercules* and *Maciste versus the Vampire*.[2]

Cabiria was a commercial and critical success that cast a long shadow over the subsequent development of the historical epic. One of its most lasting legacies was to popularize the alluring notion that cinema can provide a kind of window into what the ancient world looked like, a notion expressed by critics from the time of its release through the present. Thus, in 1920, a German critic wrote that when we watch *Cabiria*, "Antiquity with all its charms arises before us, fitting and true to life as we have never seen it before," and eight decades later, famed director Martin Scorsese described his reaction to first seeing *Cabiria* thus: "It was as if I'd found a secret door that led right to the heart of the ancient world."[3]

Cleopatra (1917)

Director: J. Gordon Edwards
Producer: William Fox
Production Company: Fox
Cast: Theda Bara (Cleopatra), Fritz Leiber (Caesar), Thurston Hall (Antony), Alan Roscoe (Pharon)

The Egyptian queen's life has been one of the most popular topics for ancient epics, and by the time this 1917 silent film was shot, there had already been multiple earlier versions (1911, 1912). This was the longest, most expensive one yet attempted. A commercial success, it caused a scandal due to the revealing nature of star Theda Bara's costumes. Today, it is perhaps best known as one of the most coveted of the "lost films," for which no copies exist because the last prints were destroyed by fires.

A few seconds of footage and hundreds of still images are extant, however, which illustrate the impressive scale of the production and confirm that the elaborate Art Nouveau-influenced costumes and sets were indeed visually striking.[4] Bara supposedly wore fifty different costumes—a record that may have remained unbroken until the 1963 remake starring Elizabeth Taylor. The text for the intertitle cards, which also survives, suggests that this version presented Cleopatra as a seductive temptress, keeping with both Bara's established screen persona as a "vamp" who preyed upon men and the prevailing "orientalist" stereotypes of that era. In historical terms, in order to promote its predatory concept of Cleopatra, the plot seems to have played loose with the facts, and it drew heavily on a novel penned by lurid adventure fiction specialist H. Rider Haggard. Even in its extremely fragmentary form, the film has been influential, due to the arresting nature of the surviving images and for serving as one of the main inspirations for the 1963 version.

Ben-Hur: A Tale of the Christ (1925)

Director: Fred Niblo
Production Company: Metro-Goldwyn-Mayer
Cast: Ramon Novarro (Judah Ben-Hur), Francis X. Bushman (Messala), May McAvoy (Esther), Frank Currier (Quintus Arrius), Claire McDowell (Princess of Hur), Mitchell Lewis (Ilderim)

This version of Ben-Hur was the most expensive silent film ever made, costing nearly $4 million. It is an important film, not only because it was a commercial and critical success, but also because it established patterns that would be emulated by many future historical epics and served as direct inspiration for the more famous, and even more successful, 1959 version. From today's perspective, however, it is an uneven film, with passages that can seem dated or are narratively disjointed or unconvincing. The handling of the religious scenes was considerably hampered by the contemporary convention dictating that Jesus, or at least his face, should never appear. Thus, although Jesus figures in many episodes, his actual onscreen presence always takes the form of a glowing arm that often seems disconcertingly disembodied.

The source material for the movie was the massively popular 1880 novel of the same title written by General Lew Wallace, which sold millions and was hailed by *Life* magazine as "one of the most important books ever written in America." Further amplifying the story's popularity was a stage adaptation that played to rapturous audiences in theaters around the world for decades and boasted dazzling special effects such as horses running on a huge treadmill during the chariot-racing scene. As has been demonstrated by the classical scholar Jon Solomon, *Ben-Hur* quickly attained the status of a true cultural phenomenon.[5] In addition to the novel and play, there were Ben-Hur pantomime shows, tableaux vivants of famous scenes, and numerous poems and songs that had been inspired by the story. Composer John Philip Sousa was moved to write a musical piece titled "Ben-Hur's Chariot Race," which employed galloping drums played "furioso," trumpets, and simulated hoof beats. Businesses looking to cash in named every imaginable commercial product after the film—you could smoke Ben-Hur cigars, cook with Ben-Hur flour, and bathe with Ben-Hur soap. It was such a fundamental part of pop culture that it became the target of parodies and vaudeville skits, and there was even a saucy burlesque show featuring whip-brandishing female charioteers that was leeringly called "Bend Her."

It was therefore not surprising that filmmakers were eager to create cinematic versions of this cultural sensation. The first was a fifteen-minute film made in 1907 by the Kalem Company that depicted just a few key scenes from the novel, including a rudimentary chariot race. However, because it was made without obtaining proper permission, it provoked a lawsuit that helped to establish the principle of copyright for literary properties. After an eight-year legal wrangle, Metro-Goldwyn-Mayer obtained the rights, but the production was troubled. The initial attempt to film in Italy culminated in the firing of the director and the recasting of most of the major roles. Following this false start and the expenditure of millions of dollars, Fred Niblo was ultimately hired as director, Mexican American actor Ramon Novarro was tapped to play the Jewish protagonist, Judah Ben-Hur, and production was eventually completed in California.

Niblo's film adheres more closely to Wallace's novel than does the 1959 version. It includes more of the book's explicitly religious scenes, such as several episodes from the life of Jesus. Although there is a brief mention that the Jewish prince Judah Ben-Hur and the Roman aristocrat Messala were childhood friends, as adults, they almost immediately become hostile antagonists, without any of the initial comradely interaction found in the 1959 remake that fleshes out their relationship and gives greater poignancy to the story. While the religious segments of the film and the sections concerning the tribulations of Judah's family are serviceable, the film's claim to fame really rests on just two famous action sequences: the naval battle and the chariot race. Taking up one-fifth of the movie's length, these two episodes are genuinely thrilling spectacles.

Judah is sentenced by Messala to serve in the Roman navy as a galley slave and endures three years of degradation and cruelty, chained to a rowing bench and whipped by sadistic overseers. When the Roman squadron fights a pirate fleet, the viewer is treated to a dramatic ancient naval battle. We alternately see interior shots of triple ranks of slaves straining to pull the oars in unison as a brawny *hortator* beats out the rhythm on a giant drum, and exterior views of triremes hurling flaming missiles at one another with catapults and then smashing their bronze rams into the sides of enemy vessels. Swarms of boarders clambering over the decks flail at one another with a variety of weapons, and shattered, flaming hulls sink into the sea as their crews try to swim clear of the wrecks. Made in the pre-code era of Hollywood, it is surprisingly violent even by modern standards. The pirate leader brandishes a severed Roman head skewered on his sword and has a captive Roman strapped to the end of his ship's ram, and we get a close-up of his terrified screaming face just before the ram plunges into a Roman vessel.

This is arguably one of the best ancient naval battles ever captured on film, largely because much of it was real. Whereas today the scene would almost certainly be entirely composed of computer-generated special effects, this naval battle did not even employ the old Hollywood trick of using model ships, as the 1959 version would. Instead, the filmmakers had seven full-size warships constructed, as well as about a dozen partial-scale ones. Two thousand eight hundred extras were hired to man the ships, and the battle was shot with an unprecedented twenty-eight cameras off the coast of Italy on the waters of the Mediterranean Sea. When the Roman flagship catches fire and panicked crewmen leap into the sea, it is not just playacting—the onboard fires actually got out of control, and the extras had to jump in order to save their lives. A rumor claims that when the prop masters did their accounting at the end of the day, they discovered that three sets of armor were missing and found three unclaimed suits back at the site where the extras were clothed, suggesting that three men had drowned. A counter-rumor asserts that the three missing extras were rescued by a fishing boat and showed up the next day, but which story (if either) is true remains uncertain.

Although there are fanciful, invented touches, such as when the pirates fling glass spheres filled with hissing snakes onto the deck of the Roman vessel, the naval battle is well done from a historical standpoint, and effectively conveys the basic tactics of an ancient naval engagement. There is, however, one major problem with the entire sequence. This is the fundamental issue that the oarsmen aboard Roman warships were not actually slaves, and that being sent to the galleys was not a standard punishment in the Roman world. Instead, during all eras of Roman history, free men were paid to serve as oarsmen in the galleys. This was not a prestigious job, but it was not a dishonorable one either, and there is a huge difference between being a salaried employee and being a slave. In fact, pretty much all ancient galleys, including those of Greek states such as Athens during the Persian and Peloponnesian Wars, employed free men as rowers.[6] (See Figure 2.6 for a reconstruction of what actual rowers on a Roman warship would have looked like.)

In representing the rowers as brutalized slaves, the filmmakers were simply following Wallace's book, and all subsequent cinematic and theatrical versions did likewise. So memorable were these depictions of the Romans using slaves as rowers that this trope has entered the public consciousness as one of the few "factoids" that nearly everyone knows about the Roman Empire. This tidbit of information has become a staple of other movies, books, and even jokes and cartoons, such as Gary Larson's *Far Side* comics, in which ancient galley slaves regularly appear. Even supposedly accurate and dependable history-themed nonfiction books and websites repeat this false "factoid."

So, where did Lew Wallace get the notion that the Romans used galley slaves? It turns out that there was an era in the Mediterranean when slaves were indeed commonly put to work on galleys, but this was over a thousand years later than Roman times, beginning during the Renaissance and extending into the early modern period. Ironically, galley slaves first seem to have been utilized on a widespread basis not by pagan Rome, but by Christian states such as Genoa and Venice in the sixteenth and seventeenth centuries. The practice was then adopted by all the maritime powers of the day, including the kingdoms of France, Spain, and the Ottoman Empire. While Mediterranean war galleys of this era no longer rammed one another but instead fought with cannons, in appearance, they still had much in common with those of antiquity and were similarly propelled by hundreds of rowers pulling heavy oars. It was these much later galleys, crewed by gangs of chained and abused slaves, which clearly served as an inspiration for Wallace and were so memorably depicted in *Ben-Hur*. Astonishingly, such slave galleys were still being used by some Mediterranean powers as late as the 1800s.

The other big action scene is the chariot race that takes place in the circus of Antioch, which pits Judah and Messala against one another as rival charioteers. It is another amazing piece of filmmaking that, like the naval battle, was shot in a realistic way, with the actors and stunt men actually driving four-horse chariots at breakneck speed around a full-size reconstruction of a Roman circus. As with the naval battle, although a number of details are in-

Figure 1.1. *Ben-Hur* Legionaries. Roman legionaries from (A) *Ben-Hur* (1925) and (B) *Ben-Hur* (1959), both in Hollywood versions of the banded *lorica segmentata* body armor and carrying smallish rectangular shields. For comparison, (C) is a reconstruction of a historically accurate early first-century AD legionary wearing the same armor and with a standard *scutum* shield. *Illustrations by Graham Sumner.*

Figure 1.2. *Ben-Hur* Props. (A) Brass legionary helmet from *Ben-Hur* (1925) that was reused in *Quo Vadis* (1951). (B) Fabric jerkin worn under armor in *Ben-Hur* (1925). (C) Assortment of Roman prop swords manufactured in Germany that were used in *Ben-Hur* (1925) and other early films. (D) Aluminum legionary shield used in *Ben-Hur* (1925) and reused in the 1959 version. *Props and photograph from The Terry Nix Collection.*

correct, the movie does an excellent job of illustrating the basic elements and overall feel of an ancient chariot race. The chariot race in this film served as a kind of rough draft in terms of equipment, sets, staging, and plot points for the one in the 1959 version. The latter one is probably slightly superior, but the two are so similar that we refer you to the entry on the 1959 film for specific details about the good and bad points of the scene from a historical perspective.

Quite a few costumes were made for the movie, many of which were subsequently reused in MGM films for decades. Figure 1.1 shows Roman legionaries from the 1925 film (A) and the 1959 version (B). For comparison, (C) represents what a legionary of that era should have looked like. The segmented metal body armor worn by all three figures was a type used during the early empire known as a *lorica segmentata*. Both the 1925 and 1959 costumes are missing the chest plates, and their shields are somewhat too small, although the wings-and-lightning-bolt design is historically attested. Neither of the spears carried by (A) and (B) are types commonly carried by legionaries, while (C) bears a correct legionary spear of the *pilum* design. Figure 1.2 depicts actual surviving props used in the 1925 *Ben-Hur*, including the shield and helmet of a legionary (A) in Figure 1.1, as well as a tunic and a variety of swords.

As a final note, there is an interesting link between this *Ben-Hur* and the 1959 version that goes beyond the films simply sharing the same novel as source material and that further explains the similarity of their chariot races. William Wyler, a young assistant director on the 1925 movie, was chosen, more than three decades later, to be the director of the 1959 version. One of his assignments in the earlier movie had been to film the chariot race, so he is directly responsible for having created both of these extremely exciting action sequences.

The Sign of the Cross (1932)

Director: Cecil B. DeMille
Producer: Cecil B. DeMille
Production Company: Paramount
Cast: Fredric March (Marcus Superbus), Charles Laughton (Nero), Claudette Colbert (Poppaea), Elissa Landi (Mercia), Ian Keith (Tigellinus)

The Sign of the Cross cemented in place what would become an irresistible and long-lasting formula for ancient epics. This was a plot that centered around the depiction of two stereotyped groups: a set of arrogant, decadent Romans who reveled in every sort of indulgence and vice, and a band of virtuous and devout Christians. Typically, the Christians were the objects of cruel and imaginative persecutions at the hands of the Romans, although the story usually focused on one of the Romans ultimately being converted to Christianity through the love of a beautiful yet chaste Christian woman. An essential element was sequences that re-created—often on a colossal scale and in sensational fashion—the violent spectacles of the ancient world, such as gladiator combats, chariot races, and beast hunts. Best of all, with this formula, even though you had just spent several hours being titillated by the lurid behavior of the ancient pagans, you could walk out of the theater feeling virtuous by identifying with the noble Christians.

The film was based on a highly popular play written by Wilson Barrett that director Cecil B. DeMille had seen in his youth, and, for the most part, it closely follows the play's plot. It was made employing the new technology of sound, which had only come into use a few years earlier. DeMille was working with a relatively tight budget, but creatively squeezed every cent to provide filmgoers with a lavish visual feast. For example, the film opens with a dramatic portrayal of the emperor Nero gleefully strumming his lyre and singing while the city of Rome is consumed by a raging inferno. While giving the impression of an expensive special effects extravaganza, in reality, the entire sequence is achieved with only one small set of the imperial palace balcony where Nero performs and some good incendiary work with miniatures to represent the burning metropolis.

The Sign of the Cross was made just before the Motion Picture Production Code of 1934 cracked down on licentious behavior in films, and it took full advantage of this greater freedom, tantalizing viewers with spectacles of violence and sexual suggestiveness. The most famous of these features a sultry, topless Claudette Colbert as the depraved empress Poppaea cavorting in a bath of ass's milk and ordering one of her attending noblewomen to strip and join her for an implied lesbian romp. The blatant eroticism of the scene is intermingled with witty comic touches, such as a pair of cats opportunistically lapping at the edge of the milk bath, and a bucket brigade of servants outside the building industriously milking a herd of braying asses and passing the buckets up to the roof to fill the bath's holding tank. Meanwhile, Charles Laughton's foppish and pudgy Nero, who spends most of the movie lolling languidly on overstuffed cushions while being fed fruit by a nearly naked pretty-boy attendant, was plainly intended to evoke the negative stereotypes of the 1930s regarding homosexuals and to depict Nero as a representative of "deviant" sexuality in contrast to the strict moral virtue embodied by the young Christian heroine, Mercia. The film's use of homosexuality as a signifier for Roman decadence and immorality reaches a sort of climax with a banquet/orgy scene in which the Roman officer Superbus attempts to seduce Mercia. When she rebuffs his advances, Superbus enlists the aid of an exotic dancer, played by Joyzelle Joyner, who attempts a lesbian seduction of Mercia by performing the lascivious "Dance of the Naked Moon." Not surprisingly, this would be one of the scenes edited out in a cleaned-up 1944 re-release of the film.

In terms of historical accuracy, the movie has both good and bad moments. An early street scene is an excellent depiction of daily life in ancient Rome. It accurately renders a typical Roman street as bustling but rather dirty and chaotic, teeming with beggars, porters, and pack animals. There are idlers dicing on the steps with knucklebones, densely graffitied walls, busy street-side taverns, revolving hourglass-shaped grain mills, bakeries hawking bread loves shaped exactly like those found at Pompeii, and people filling jugs at public fountains—all historically attested details. The long final sequence in the amphitheater has some good elements, beginning with an advertisement on a wall touting the day's entertainments that replicates the language found in ancient examples, such as "the awnings will be employed for shade." The equipment of the gladiators is very well done, precisely emulating gladiator helmets excavated at Pompeii and accurately portraying several historical types of gladiators, such as the *retiarius*, who fought with a net and a trident. The film also captures the sense of a long day's worth of entertainments of various kinds, including wild beast hunts of exotic animals, a category of bloody spectacle of which the Romans were inordinately fond. The film gives us bears, bulls, lions, elephants, and crocodiles, all of which are well documented as having featured in Roman games. The violence and cruelty of these games is vividly presented in a succession of vignettes, such as an elephant stepping on a man, and sundry skewerings and impalements.

On the negative side, all the gladiators battle en masse rather than being divided up into pairs who fight successive individual duels. While criminals or untrained fighters might appear in groups, highly trained (and valuable) gladiators always fought one on one. Also, the Flavian Amphitheater (commonly known as the Colosseum), where the action unfolds, was not actually built until several decades after the events of the film. The slaughter of a group of Christians who are fed to wild animals is presented as the absolute highlight of the day's entertainments, when in reality such executions would have been regarded as one of the least interesting acts and were often staged during the Roman equivalent of halftime or intermission. In general, the film portrays Romans at all levels of society, from the poorest citizens up to the emperor himself, as being far more aware of Christians, and obsessed with their persecution, than they likely would have been at this point in time. After the Great Fire of AD 64, Nero did indeed order a particularly cruel

Figure 1.3. Empress Poppaea. (A) One of the typically racy, yet wholly unhistorical outfits worn by Empress Poppaea in *The Sign of the Cross* (1932). **(B)** A more historically plausible reconstruction of the attire of a Roman empress based on a statue thought to represent Poppaea from the Temple of Hera at Olympia. *Illustrations by Graham Sumner.*

and widespread persecution of Christians in the city, but at that moment in history, such actions were the exception rather than the rule. Given the plot of the film, its focus on Christian persecution is understandable, but it established an influential pattern that would be followed by subsequent Roman movies.

While a lot of the set dressings and the costumes of the background characters are decently done, the clothing of the main protagonists is another matter. Poppaea's outfits are outrageously risqué for a Roman noblewoman and reflect modern fashion trends instead of ancient ones. These outfits were crafted by costume designer Travis Banton, and Figure 1.3.A illustrates a typically racy example with exposed stomach and bra-like top. While visually striking, neither the dress nor the elaborate harness/belt-like contraption around her waist bear any resemblance to the attire of an upper-class Roman noblewoman. Perhaps the most accurate aspects of the ensemble are Poppaea's hairstyle and the elaborate tiara. Upper-class Roman women did indeed arrange their hair into extremely elaborate coifs with curls and braids, and surviving coins of Poppaea almost always show her wearing a tiara-like object. Figure 1.3.B portrays a more historically plausible outfit that a Roman empress might have worn during the first century AD. This image is based on a statue found in the Temple of Hera at Olympia that may depict Poppaea in the guise of a priestess of the temple. Her heavy woolen dress and mantle are of a type often portrayed on statues of imperial women, while her jewelry is modeled on actual examples recovered from various archaeological sites. As for other characters in the film, Mercia's demure waist-belted gowns seem to have been inspired more by medieval nuns than any ancient attire. Most problematic is the costume sported by Superbus, which contains practically no element that is accurate. He resembles some sort of fantasy vision of an Art Deco Arabian sheikh more than a Roman military officer.

The film did well at the box office, and together with his earlier Bible epics *The Ten Commandments* and *The King of Kings*, it solidified DeMille's reputation as the preeminent Hollywood maker of ancient epics. *The Sign of the Cross* was helped by an aggressive marketing campaign by Paramount. The pressbook highlighted the film's mix of piety and salaciousness and clearly identified the intended audiences, urging promoters to target three groups: "the masses," with "drama and thunder and sex"; "Church-Goers," with "religious appeal"; and "schools," with "educational appeal" and the promise that "DeMille's great spectacles are always historically accurate." It ended with the exhortation, "DON'T MIX YOUR APPROACHES! . . . HAMMER EACH APPROACH FOR ALL THEY'RE WORTH! THEY'RE WORTH PLENTY!"[7]

The Sign of the Cross is an uneven movie, boasting some sequences that are undeniably visually powerful and historically sound, but others that are less successful either as storytelling or as history. Its influence on the historical epic, however, is undeniable and wide ranging. Many later films would emulate its formula of decadent Romans versus noble Christians as well as its uneasy stance of breathlessly reveling in depictions of Roman vice and debauchery while allegedly condemning them.

Cleopatra (1934)

Director: Cecil B. DeMille
Producer: Cecil B. DeMille
Production Company: Paramount
Cast: Claudette Colbert (Cleopatra), Warren William (Julius Caesar), Henry Wilcoxon (Marc Antony), Ian Keith (Octavian), Joseph Schildkraut (Herod), Gertrude Michael (Calpurnia), C. Aubrey Smith (Enobarbus)

Cecil B. DeMille followed up the success of *The Sign of the Cross* with another ancient epic just two years later featuring the same star, Claudette Colbert: *Cleopatra* (1934). Although the Egyptian queen had already been the subject of quite a few films, this was the first with sound. It was also the first big-budget Cleopatra flick made since the discovery of King Tut's tomb in 1922, which had sparked a fresh round of Egyptomania. Today, the film is famous for its stylish Art Deco–influenced sets and costumes, which are sometimes seen as giving it a modernistic feel; however, this sensibility is not totally inappropriate from a historical perspective because the Art Deco style was itself heavily influenced by ancient Egyptian art and incorporated many of its iconographic elements and motifs.

In terms of their physical resemblance to the historical figures that they play, some of the casting choices were outstanding. Warren William is one of the best onscreen Julius Caesars, sharing the Roman general's domed forehead, aristocratic nose, and sharp cheekbones. William's terse, impatient, no-nonsense Caesar also captures something essential of the man's personality. We first meet him busily multitasking, reviewing models for siege engines while simultaneously negotiating terms with Egyptian ambassadors. In later scenes, he is always energetically perusing and answering correspondence, studying maps, and devising strategies. All of this accords nicely with the accounts of ancient authors such as Plutarch, which emphasize Caesar's qualities as a decisive and energetic administrator who was such a workaholic that he dictated letters to his secretaries even while riding his horse. William's Caesar speaks in clipped, to-the-point sentences and employs colloquialisms, as when he acknowledges a gift with a curt, "Thanks." At the time of the film's release, the casual speech patterns of Caesar and other characters were harshly mocked by film critics, who thought they were too "modern-sounding" and apparently wanted characters in a historical epic to speak only in flowery Shakespearean cadences or in the sort of stilted, faux-archaic English often found in the later epics of the 1950s. However, it could be argued that the plain language of William's Caesar is much closer to the historical mark, since Caesar's writings, such as *The Gallic Wars*, are renowned for the direct and simple style of their prose. Similarly, a scene of a party at Caesar's villa, where gaggles of patricians engage in lively gossip, incurred widespread criticism, with *Variety* scoffing that it was "like a modern bridge night."[8] However, ancient Rome of this era was an arena in which rumor and gossip played a significant role in politics as a form of propaganda. Their importance is attested to by the actions of wily political operators like Cicero, who, whenever he was away from the city, peppered his friends with letters demanding that they relate to him the latest gossip.

As Marc Antony, Henry Wilcoxon was also a great casting choice, in terms of both physical appearance and demeanor. With his broad face, curly hair, blunt nose, and burly build, Wilcoxon recalls the portraits of Antony on Roman coins. Whereas William captures Caesar's coldly calculating intelligence, Wilcoxon's Antony embodies a kind of bluff, open virility that corresponds with ancient accounts of Antony's personality. Crucially, the film gives us both sides of Antony's character: the pleasure-loving hedonist, but also the dynamic and charismatic man of action. When he hears that the Roman senate has declared war on them, he springs up from the couch where he had been lolling with Cleopatra and commandingly barks out a string of precise orders to muster his troops for battle. At this moment, we can well believe that this is a man who has fought his way to the top of the hyper-competitive Roman political pyramid. Even Cleopatra, no slacker in the leadership department herself, is so awed by this alpha male display that she drops to her knees before him and declares, "I've seen a god come to life!" This is the aspect of Antony that is absent from the more famous 1963 film, where Richard Burton's Antony comes off as alternately ineffectual and petulant.

Less successful is the film's Octavian, played by Ian Keith, also recycled from the cast of *The Sign of the Cross*. Partly, this is simply due to age, since at the time of Caesar's assassination in 44 BC, Octavian was just eighteen years old, whereas Keith was nearly twice that age when he played the role. His Octavian is demonstrably peevish at being in Antony's shadow, which is somewhat at odds with the real Octavian, who was a master at manipulating his public image, but it is a serviceable performance overall. As for Colbert's Cleopatra, surviving coins and portraits suggest that she was not the glamorous beauty that Hollywood prefers, but Colbert imbues her with both a playful wit and a smoldering vampiness that do not seem excessively out of place. More importantly, she projects both intelligence and determination, which were certainly qualities of the historical Cleopatra. There are also some effective scenes where she expresses the tension between fulfilling her own wishes and the weight of responsibility to do what she thinks is best for Egypt. The real Cleopatra, despite not being a native Egyptian (she was a descendant of Ptolemy, a Macedonian general of Alexander the Great), did seem to closely identify and sympathize with the Egyptians.

Cleopatra deliberately seduces Caesar and then Antony, but the strategies she employs reflect the differences in their characters. When her physical charms and girlish flirtations fail to distract Caesar from his work, she switches tactics and appeals to his strategic mind by pointing out that a union with Egypt would give him geographic access to the wealth of India in order to fund his conquests. After this gets his attention, she completes her seduction by impressing him with her composure and cold-bloodedness when she calmly hefts a spear to skewer an assassin hiding behind a curtain. While this scene is an invention of the filmmakers, it succinctly conveys a truth about Cleopatra's character. Whereas Caesar is attracted and won over by her intelligence and the political opportunities she dangles before him, Antony requires a different approach. The historical Antony was infamous for his love of revelry—once when presiding at a formal public political assembly, he had to vomit into a fold of his toga because he was so hungover from his debauchery. The film's Antony follows this tradition of susceptibility to self-indulgence; but since he has already seen and done everything, how will Cleopatra appeal to his jaded tastes? The answer is the film's most famous sequence, Cleopatra's seduction of Antony aboard her pleasure barge.

This eight-minute-long visual extravaganza makes the argument that DeMille deserves his reputation as a master of movement and pageantry. To receive Antony, Cleopatra reclines in a form-fitting dress, framed against a colossal, gently pulsating arch of feathers arranged in Art Deco curves. She treats him to various spectacles, beginning with a troupe of scantily clad women performing a saucy dance whose theme is the mythological seduction of Europa by Jupiter in the form of a bull. This is followed by a banquet of exotic tidbits, musical performances, and yet more dancing girls—some hauled up dripping wet from the sea in a net, writhing across the floor to present Antony with clamshells overflowing with precious jewels, while others, dressed in leopard skins, gyrate, wrestle with one another, and leap through flaming hoops, all while being literally whipped into a frenzy by a leather-clad man wielding a bullwhip. This pageantry overcomes Antony's initial hostility, and by the end, he is leering delightedly while stuffing roasted birds into his mouth. The scene concludes with a slow pull-back from the couple, as attendants sweep in from the sides to obscure the lovers behind billowing curtains, wave palm fronds, and hold aloft golden boat-shaped censers that fill the air with clouds of perfumed smoke. As the camera continues to recede through the ship's interior, a *hortator* begins pounding out a slow, sonorous drumbeat and ranks of brawny rowers rhythmically heave huge rams-head-tipped oars back and forth in unison—an image clearly intended to suggest the lovemaking taking place behind the curtains. It is an astonishing tour-de-force piece of filmmaking, and the film's marketing materials breathlessly promoted it, promising that those who purchased a ticket would witness "Cleopatra's Paradise: A Love Boat 500 feet long, where Antony is wafted to unknown delights by the sloe-eyed Temptress of Egypt!"[9] DeMille himself stated that his goal was that "this entire barge sequence should be the most seductive, erotic, beautiful, rhythmic, sensuous series of scenes ever shown."[10] Amazingly, rather than being an example of over-the-top Hollywood fantasy, this episode is actually rooted in historical fact. Plutarch describes Cleopatra traveling to Tarsus in her barge in order to meet and seduce Antony, and dwells at length on the opulence of her ship. The golden canopies, silver oars, clouds of perfumed incense, array of exotic delicacies, swarms of musicians, and even the bevies of female attendants dressed in mythological costumes are all specifically mentioned.

Some of the less historical aspects of the film include its portrayal of the war between Antony and Octavian, which is conveyed through a brief montage of battle scenes. In the film, all of Antony's Roman supporters and generals, as well as his legions of Roman soldiers, immediately desert him when he chooses to stay loyal to Cleopatra, so that he is forced to fight using only Egyptian troops, but in reality, Antony commanded over twenty Roman legions and had the support of nearly half the Roman senate during this conflict. The montage prominently and erroneously features battle scenes of massed Egyptian chariots, which are only included because DeMille was frugally reusing combat footage from his earlier film *The Ten Commandments* (1923). To fit everything into its brisk 101-minute running time, the movie significantly compresses events and leaves out people, most notably the multiple children that Cleopatra had with both Caesar and later Antony, all of whom are entirely omitted. Also, some of the scenes dealing with the assassination of Caesar owe more to Shakespeare's play than to historical reality, although Caesar being slain at the base of a statue of his old rival Pompey the Great is entirely correct.

The military attire is a mixed bag, with some armor being reused from earlier films. One of the strangest costumes appears on a messenger who is apparently intended to be a Gaul but is bizarrely dressed in a clichéd version of a Viking outfit, complete with horned helmet and heavy furs (although his presence does provide a wonderful little nonverbal interaction when his impressive physique earns him a frankly admiring appraisal from Colbert). The sets for Cleopatra's palace, although not always accurate as ancient architecture, are glorious Art Deco constructs. Likewise her dresses, while

Figure 1.4. Three Cleopatras. Unhistorical versions of casual palace outfits worn by Claudette Colbert in (A) *Cleopatra* (1934) and Elizabeth Taylor in (B) *Cleopatra* (1963). For comparison, (C) is a historically plausible reconstruction of the sort of Hellenistic attire Cleopatra may actually have worn. *Illustrations by Graham Sumner.*

visually arresting, owe rather more to 1930s Art Deco style than antiquity. Nevertheless, quite a few of the props and decorations, as well as individual elements of Colbert's dresses and jewelry, are clearly based on real antique Egyptian models. A significant historical error is that all of these sets, costumes, and props are purely Egyptian in inspiration and completely omit any hint of Hellenistic Greek influence, which would have been very strong at this time, at least in the attire and dwellings of the ruling Greco-Macedonian family of the Ptolemies. Figure 1.4 depicts one of the rather risqué and wholly unhistorical outfits designed by Travis Banton and worn by Colbert (A) in scenes in which she is lounging around the palace, as well as an outfit (B) worn by Elizabeth Taylor in similar scenes in the 1963 *Cleopatra*. For comparison, (C) is a reconstruction of the considerably more modest sort of Hellenistic apparel that the historical Cleopatra would likely have worn in such circumstances. The clothing of the reconstructed historical Cleopatra is based on ancient statues and images of elite women of that era, while the jewelry emulates extant examples uncovered by archaeologists.

The film contains some first-rate minor details of Roman culture, such as a scene in a Roman bath during which the senators discuss politics while rubbing olive oil from a flask on their bodies and then scraping it off with a curved bronze implement called a *strigil*. This is precisely how Romans cleaned themselves, and it was an important part of bathing rituals. Another praiseworthy moment occurs when Caesar is preparing to depart from his house, and two slaves carefully wrap a long toga around his body as he stands between them. In films, the Roman toga is rarely depicted in a realistic fashion, but Caesar's toga and the complicated procedure by which the slaves carefully wind and fold it around his torso and arms are exactly how ancient Romans actually wore them. When they are done, Caesar looks just like surviving statues of toga-clad senators. Togas were complex garments that probably required at least one attendant to wrap correctly, and there is no other film that illustrates this process so clearly.

All in all, DeMille's *Cleopatra* is perhaps the best of the many cinematic versions of this story. Its portraits of the main characters are plausible and its deviations from history are not overly egregious. The film hums along with a vitality and wit too often absent from the well-known but rather bloated 1963 version, covering the same territory in one-third the time. Its mix of breezy, colloquial dialogue and elegant Art Deco style somehow makes it seem less dated than most films of its time, or even compared to those of the much later Golden Age of ancient epics in the 1950s and 1960s. As a bonus, you get some truly dazzling spectacles.

The Last Days of Pompeii (1935)

Director: Ernest B. Schoedsack
Producer: Merian C. Cooper
Production Company: Merian C. Cooper Production/RKO Pictures
Cast: Preston Foster (Marcus), Basil Rathbone (Pontius Pilate), Alan Hale (Burbix), John Wood (Flavius), Wyrley Birch (Leaster)

After completing *King Kong* (1933), the creative team behind that film looked around for a subject as spectacular as a giant ape rampaging through New York for their next project. While on his honeymoon, Producer Merian Cooper had recently visited the ruins of Pompeii and, stimulated by this, they settled on a movie that would culminate with the dramatic destruction of that Roman city by the eruption of Mt. Vesuvius in AD 79. They called their film *The Last Days of Pompeii*, which was the title of a bestselling 1834 novel written by Edward Bulwer-Lytton that was so popular during the nineteenth century that it inspired an opera, numerous paintings by famous artists such as Lawrence Alma-Tadema, long-running theatrical adaptations, and outdoor "pyrodramas" that thrilled crowds with elaborate reenactments complete with full-size collapsing buildings and exploding fireworks to simulate the volcano's eruption.

By 1930, this cultural phenomenon had already led to at least five movie versions of the novel, in 1900, 1908, 1913 (Pasquali), 1913 (Ambrosio), and 1926. Several of these that were made in Italy meticulously re-created actual Pompeian structures. For their film, Cooper and his team jettisoned almost all the familiar plot elements and characters from the novel, replacing them with a stew of disparate ingredients. As scholar Maria Wyke has pointed out, the story ultimately featured not only the spectacular natural disaster, but also a gladiator subplot, a romance between young lovers, a criminal's rags-to-riches storyline lifted from the then-popular gangster movie genre, and a pious religious parable with persecuted Christians and conversions. They even somehow contrived for the protagonist, a Pompeian blacksmith, to make a quick round trip to Judea, where he hobnobbed with Pontius Pilate, fortuitously had his ill son healed by Jesus, witnessed Jesus's crucifixion, and engaged in some lucrative horse rustling.

It's an awkward mix, and the parts don't totally gel, but they result in a quick-moving film with some entertaining episodes. There are good daily life scenes showing the people of Pompeii buying, selling, eating, working, socializing, and bustling around on sets that were clearly modeled after the actual streets and buildings of Pompeii. Basil Rathbone contributes an engaging performance as a rather thoughtful and sympathetic Pontius Pilate. His elegantly draped and carefully folded toga closely emulates those on surviving statues of Roman magistrates. The climactic volcanic eruption and subsequent devastation of the city, with crumbling buildings, screaming, fleeing mobs, and gouts of spewing lava, are genuinely exciting.

In terms of historical authenticity, the biggest problem is that, in order to squeeze both the death of Jesus and the destruction of Pompeii into the same film, the eruption of Vesuvius had to be shifted about five decades earlier. The gladiator section also contains some oddities. Instead of representing them as the highly trained slaves that they were, in this cinematic Pompeii, any brawny free man can walk in off the street, volunteer to be a gladiator, and immediately find himself fighting in the arena. Also, the film bizarrely portrays gladiators earning their fees by having individual members of the audience literally fling cash at them during bouts to determine whether defeated opponents should be killed or spared.

Made in the shadow of the Great Depression, the film's depiction of poor people driven to a life of crime by bad luck and economic circumstances may have hit a bit too close to home, since it was a failure at the box office.

I, Claudius (1937)

Director: Josef von Sternberg
Producer: Alexander Korda
Production Company: London Films
Cast: Charles Laughton (Claudius), Merle Oberon (Messalina), Flora Robson (Livia), Emlyn Williams (Caligula)

In 1934 and 1935, author Robert Graves published the historical novels *I, Claudius* and *Claudius the God*, which presented the history of the first family of Roman emperors, the Julio-Claudians, as a sensational tale of familial intrigue and (sometimes literal) backstabbing. This was excellent dramatic material for a movie, and it did not take long for filmmakers to snap up the rights and attempt one. The British filmmaking industry was feeling somewhat eclipsed by the flashy big-budget Hollywood productions, and London Films resolved to create a grand historical epic of their own based on the novels. Acclaimed director Josef von Sternberg was enlisted to helm the project and a high-wattage cast was assembled, including Flora Robson, Merle Oberon, Emlyn Williams, and, in the central role as the emperor Claudius, Charles Laughton, fresh off his triumphant performance as Nero in *The Sign of the Cross*. Large-scale, lavishly decorated sets were constructed, and all the pieces seemed in place for the creation of a serious historical epic that would also be visually dazzling and emotionally engaging.

It was not to be, however. Filming began in 1937, but after several weeks, Laughton still struggled to find the right tone for the complicated character of Claudius, there was feuding among the director, producer, and actors, and then Merle Oberon was injured in a car accident. The production was canceled, and the film has acquired a reputation as one of the great missed opportunities for a potential cinematic masterpiece. About twenty minutes of footage survives, including several compelling scenes, most notably one in which the unbalanced emperor Caligula announces to the Roman senate his intention to appoint his favorite racehorse to the highest office in the Roman government. In another, Claudius lays out to the senate the terms under which he will assume the throne and, in doing so, reveals that there is much more to his character than most people had assumed.

The extant footage features impressive sets, such as a fine replica of the Ara Pacis reliefs. Some of the costumes are more fanciful than historical, however, and an anecdote recounted in an interview with the costume designer, John Armstrong, offers insight into why this is the case. Producer Alexander Korda came to Armstrong and asked, "Have we any Vestal Virgins?" Armstrong responded that there would be six (the historically correct number) and showed Korda the sketches for them, which he had based on ancient statues and which accurately depicted the Vestals swathed in concealing robes. Korda replied, "This won't do, I want sixty, and I want them naked!" In the footage of the resulting scene, there are indeed sixty Vestals provocatively draped in transparent veils. As Armstrong dryly comments, "It looked lovely, but it had nothing to do with the Roman religion." For a realistic reconstruction of Vestal attire, see Figure 4.1, which also includes a typically skimpy cinematic rendering from *Carry on Cleo* (1964).

The Korda interview, as well as the surviving footage, can be viewed in a 1965 documentary about the star-crossed project called *The Epic That Never Was*. The misfortunes of this production scared filmmakers away from Graves's novels for nearly four decades, until the BBC returned to them as the source for the much acclaimed and beloved television miniseries *I, Claudius* (1976).

Scipione l'Africano (1937)

Director: Carmine Gallone
Producer: Frederic Curiosi
Production Company: Consorzione Scipio l'Africano/Ente Nazionale Industrie Cinematografiche (ENIC)
Cast: Annibale Ninchi (Scipio), Camillo Pilotto (Hannibal), Francesca Braggiotti (Sophonisba), Fosco Giachetti (Massinissa)

In 1936, Italian Fascist dictator Benito Mussolini established Cinecittà Studios on the outskirts of Rome. One of the first films produced there was *Scipione l'Africano*, an ambitious, expensive, and rather pompous military epic about the Roman Republic's struggle against the Carthaginian general Hannibal. It is a significant early historical epic, but it is impossible to evaluate it as a film without taking into account the fact that it was intended as a work of political propaganda and was deliberately made in order to justify Fascist Italy's recent aggressive colonial invasion of Ethiopia.

Scipione l'Africano is set during the Second Punic War, fought between the Roman Republic and its main rival for control of the Western Mediterranean, the North African city-state of Carthage. The Carthaginian army was commanded by the military genius Hannibal, who invaded Italy and inflicted three crushing defeats on the Romans, including the Battle of Cannae in 215 BC, at which over fifty thousand Romans were killed. Eventually, the Romans found a good general of their own, Scipio. The two generals met at the Battle of Zama in 202 BC in the desert outside Carthage, and despite Hannibal's deployment of a contingent of war elephants, he was vanquished by Scipio. This film, which tells the story of Scipio's invasion of Africa, would be the most expensive made up to that point in Italy, utilizing thirty-two thousand extras from the Italian army and forty elephants.

The story of how and why this enormous epic came about is inextricably linked with dictator Benito Mussolini and Fascism. In the 1920s and 1930s, Mussolini founded the international Fascist movement, eventually gained political control over Italy, and established an Italian Empire with colonial territories in Africa. He explicitly portrayed himself and his regime as a modern revival of the ancient Roman Empire. All the Fascist states of the time, including Hitler's Germany, were keenly aware of the value of propaganda and its ability to inspire and motivate their followers. Both Mussolini and Hitler adroitly deployed propaganda across a wide range of media and contexts, such as art, architecture, clothing, film, symbols, rituals, and language. In the realm of cinema, all of these elements came together in well-known propaganda movies of the era, such as Leni Riefenstahl's frighteningly effective 1935 documentary *Triumph of the Will*, which glorified the Nazi party rallies at Nuremberg. Mussolini wanted the Italian filmmaking industry to similarly support his regime, and to encourage this, he pushed for the establishment of Cinecittà Studios.

The most important way in which Mussolini hoped to emulate ancient Rome was by conquering a great empire, and he aimed his efforts in this direction at Africa. By 1934, Italy had managed to acquire territories in Libya, Somalia, and Eritrea, and was next targeting Ethiopia. Mussolini was particularly keen to subjugate this country because, forty years earlier in 1896, Italy had invaded Ethiopia and suffered a humiliating defeat at the Battle of Adwa. He at last realized his ambition in the Second Italo-Ethiopian war of 1935–1937, during which his army occupied and annexed Ethiopia. Even before the conquest of Ethiopia, Fascist officials had been lobbying for a film about Scipio Africanus and ancient Roman imperialism in Africa, as a way to assert a sort of historical Italian claim to the region and thereby justify the current invasion. A strongly negative international reaction to Italy's attack on Ethiopia gave further impetus to the project, as a means of combating the criticism with positive propaganda. The Fascist state was involved in every stage of the planning, production, filming, and distribution of the movie, and a special fund of 12.6 million lire was created to pay for it.

An experienced director, Carmine Gallone, was chosen, and those working on the movie were under no illusions as to its propagandistic motivation. As the then-head of the Directorate-General for Cinematography, Luigi Freddi, explained, "*Scipione* was conceived on the eve of the African undertaking, and was begun soon after the victory. It was desired because no theme for translation into spectacle seemed more suited than this, to symbolize the intimate union between the past grandeur of Rome, and the bold accomplishments of our epoch."[11] To further this aim, LUCE, the Union of Educational Cinematography, which was a state-sponsored media institute, churned out a constant stream of propagandistic newsreels and documentaries about the making of the epic. These show Mussolini and other Fascist dignitaries visiting the sets at Cinecittà Studios and observing the process. The final battle was filmed in the Pontine Marshes situated between Rome and the coast, the draining of which had been another of Mussolini's pet projects. During one scene in the newsreels, Mussolini climbs to the top of a tall camera tower and the actors gather around him, shouting Fascist slogans and performing the Fascist salute with outstretched right arms and open hands. In a case of fiction imitating real life, many of these extras were conscripts to the Italian army, who were to embark shortly thereafter on military service in Africa.

In the movie, many scenes depict the ancient Romans hailing Scipio by anachronistically using this same Fascist salute. The word *Fascist* itself is derived from an ancient Roman symbol, the *fasces*, which was a bundle of sticks tied together with an axe that was carried by the attendants of Roman magistrates as an emblem of their authority. Because of its association with power, the *fasces* was adopted by Mussolini as well. In the film, *fasces* feature prominently, constantly being carried around preceding Scipio, and the camera often lingers lovingly on them—a not-very-subtle nod to contemporary Fascism that everyone would have understood. Scipio makes a number of speeches during which his body language and delivery style are clearly modeled after the well-known oratorical mannerisms of Mussolini himself. Even the way in which the actor playing Scipio was filmed, often from angles emphasizing his profile, imitates how Mussolini liked to be viewed.

Other references to current events include a scene of Scipio's wife removing her elaborate jewelry and placing it in a box to be donated to the war effort. This mirrors the situation in 1935, when the cost of the Ethiopian war was putting a strain on the Italian economy, and a call went out for patriotic Italian women to contribute their jewelry—even their golden wedding rings—to help pay for the war. The film characterizes the Carthaginian soldiers as animalistic brutes in a similar manner to how Italian Fascist propaganda represented the Ethiopians, thus advancing the argument that the invasion of Ethiopia was necessary to bring civilization to these alleged "savages." In the movie, not only are many of Hannibal's troops portrayed as having black or dark skin, but many are even dressed in the clothing of contemporary African tribesmen of the 1930s.

The most famous sequence is an extended re-creation of the Battle of Zama. The movie does deserve praise as a very rare instance of trying to accurately represent the different stages of a historically attested battle. We see the initial Carthaginian elephant charge and its failure, Hannibal holding his veterans in reserve, the infantry clash in the middle, the cavalry battle on the wings, the routing of the Carthaginian cavalry, and the encircling flank attacks by the Roman horsemen that ultimately won the battle. It is also the only cinematic example of a large-scale charge by dozens of war elephants performed by real animals rather than computer-generated effects. It is an exciting sequence, but be warned that if you are sensitive to violence against animals, there is suspicion that some of the elephant spearings were genuine.

The 1930s conquest of Ethiopia was seen by Italians as avenging the earlier defeat at Adwa and restoring lost Italian honor. The film explicitly makes this connection as well, drawing a parallel with Rome's initial defeat at Cannae followed by its eventual victory at Zama. In fact, the very first shot of the film is a sea of Roman dead littering the battlefield in the aftermath of Cannae. The movie then ends, after the triumph at Zama, with a soldier exultantly exclaiming, "You have avenged Cannae!" The movie was so heavy-handed in its presentation of this argument that even young schoolchildren could connect the dots. In 1939, an Italian film journal held a writing contest about the movie for third and fourth graders, and a majority of the submissions were about this theme. For example, one child wrote, "I liked the scene where Scipio announces the victory to the Romans with the words 'You have avenged Cannae.' In that moment, my thoughts turned to the fallen soldiers at Adwa, in the same Africa, avenged by the Italians in the conquest of the Empire." Another offered an even more succinct summary: "Scipio avenged Cannae, just like Mussolini avenged Adwa."[12]

When evaluating the film, it is hard to separate it from its propagandistic intent and close association with the Fascist regime. The acting is stilted and the characterizations simplistic, and much of the camerawork is unimaginative. It cannot be denied, however, that some of its more spectacular moments, such as the Battle of Zama and the crowd scenes in the Roman Forum, are impressive simply due to their scale. Despite vigorous promotion by the Italian government and being awarded the Mussolini Cup for Best Italian Film at the 1937 Venice Film Festival, the movie has not proved enduringly popular. It can be hard even to find a copy to watch. There is a version dubbed into English titled *Scipio Africanus: The Defeat of Hannibal* that is a half hour shorter than the original. Although not a great movie, it is worth seeing as a fascinating case study of a film that is very much the product of the specific era and propagandistic context in which it was made.

Caesar and Cleopatra (1945/1946 US)

Director: Gabriel Pascal
Producer: Gabriel Pascal
Production Company: The Rank Organization
Cast: Claude Rains (Caesar), Vivien Leigh (Cleopatra), Flora Robson (Ftatateeta), Stewart Granger (Apollodorus)

Playwright George Bernard Shaw and producer/director Gabriel Pascal repeatedly teamed up to turn Shaw's plays into films, most notably *Pygmalion* in 1938, which was a hit at the box office and earned four Oscar nominations, winning Best Screenplay. Soon after, they decided to do a film version of Shaw's 1898 play *Caesar and Cleopatra*. Riding high on their successes, they were able to round up a star-studded cast featuring Claude Rains as Julius Caesar, Vivien Leigh as Cleopatra, and Stewart Granger as Apollodorus, as well as a big budget that would balloon even further by the time it was finished, making it the most expensive British film up to that point.

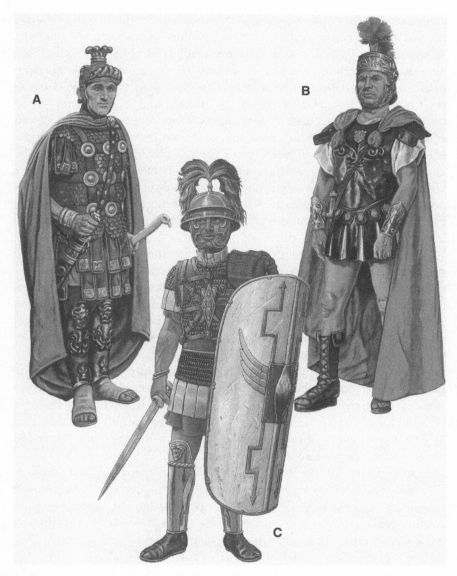

Figure 1.5. Centurions. (A) Centurion from *Caesar and Cleopatra* (1945/1946 US). The harness bearing discs (*phalerae*) given as awards is attested for centurions of the early empire. (B) Centurion from *King of Kings* (1961) in a leather cuirass. Very little of this outfit is authentic. (C) Reconstruction of how a centurion of the late Roman Republic would more likely have looked. *Illustrations by Graham Sumner.*

In terms of the sets, props, and costumes, they got their money's worth, because these are spectacular and show evidence of research. For example, during the Pharos scenes, several Roman artillery machines are visible that are reasonably accurate versions of a *ballista*. The legionaries' armor also suggests they studied the ancient sources. One issue is that, although the film is set in the last days of the republic, the military equipment is clearly based on later imperial evidence; in particular, soldiers depicted on the Column of Marcus Aurelius. Figure 1.5 shows a centurion from the film (A) whose equipment seems to have been directly derived from this source. He can be compared with (C), a reconstruction of a late Republican centurion. Of note are the film centurion's award discs (*phalerae*) displayed on his chest, his decorated greaves, and a vine stick topped with an eagle's head. Similarly, Figure 3.4 illustrates a legionary (A) from the film along with a reconstructed late Republican legionary (C).

While the costumes were a good effort for the time when they were made, some of the script's artificially stilted diction and its nineteenth-century gender dynamics have aged less well. Shaw offers an atypical take on Cleopatra, portraying her at the outset as utterly air-headed, impulsive, petulant, and extremely naive, as opposed to the rather savvy political operator that she actually seems to have been, even at a young age. Under Caesar's paternal guidance, she begins to develop "queenlike" virtues, which typically seem to be expressed by an eagerness to put people to death. The plot deviates considerably from history, almost entirely eliminating the romantic relationship between Caesar and Cleopatra (including the multiple children they had together), having her stay in Egypt rather than follow him to Rome, and, most curiously, representing her as being totally infatuated with Mark Antony before she even meets Caesar.

Filmed during World War II, the production was beset with difficulties, including hostility among the principals of the cast and crew, a tragic miscarriage suffered by Leigh, and a V2 rocket strike that demolished the costume-making workshops. Despite its often impressive visuals, the film was not a success critically or commercially, as it permanently broke up the Pascal/Shaw partnership and left the studio in a deep financial hole.

~

CHAPTER TWO

The 1950s

The Golden Era of the Ancient Epic

After its early flourishing during the silent film era through the dawn of sound, the ancient epic declined in popularity during the late 1930s and the 1940s, as other movie genres became dominant. For over a decade, few films set in antiquity appeared. This allowed a new generation to come of age so that, by 1950, the time was ripe for a revival, and the subsequent decade became the Golden Age of the ancient epic. The remarkable run of high-profile movies set in the Roman world that managed to be both commercial and critical successes began with 1951's *Quo Vadis* and continued with films such as *The Robe* (1953) and *Ben-Hur* (1959). Although released in the first year of the next decade, *Spartacus* (1960) properly belongs to this 1950s Golden Era string of solid successes. However, it also marked its end, since by then, the formula was starting to grow stale, audiences were becoming jaded, and mainstream Hollywood epic film budgets were ballooning out of control, while at the same time, a swarm of cheaply made, campy sword-and-sandal flicks sapped the prestige from the genre.

Quo Vadis (1951)

Director: Mervyn LeRoy
Producer: Sam Zimbalist
Production Company: Metro-Goldwyn-Mayer
Cast: Robert Taylor (Marcus Vinicius), Deborah Kerr (Lygia), Peter Ustinov (Nero), Leo Genn (Petronius), Patricia Laffan (Poppaea), Finlay Currie (Peter), Buddy Baer (Ursus)

The film that ushered in the 1950s Golden Era and really established its template was MGM's *Quo Vadis* (1951). It revived the sure-fire formula established by 1932's *The Sign of the Cross*, which ostensibly presented a wholesome and pious message about the persecution of early Christians but actually spent most of its time lovingly dwelling on the supposed depravities of the Romans. Like the earlier movie, *Quo Vadis* offered a story about a Roman officer converted to Christianity by the love of a virtuous woman. It starred Peter Ustinov, who delivered a delightfully wicked performance as the tyrannical emperor Nero, Deborah Kerr as the Christian girl Lygia, and Robert Taylor as the Roman general Vinicius, who begins the film as an enthusiastic and dedicated defender of the empire but is gradually won over to the Christian cause through his love for Lygia. The movie follows the plot of an 1896 novel of the same title written by Polish author Henryk Sienkiewicz. It was a huge international bestseller, translated into over fifty languages, which brought Sienkiewicz to the attention of a global audience. Sienkiewicz was even awarded the 1905 Nobel Prize in Literature. There had been several earlier cinematic versions of the novel, one as early as 1901, as well as an ambitious 1913 Italian silent film.

MGM went all out for its take on the novel, committing to one of the largest, most expensive films made up to that point. It was filmed over six months at Cinecittà Studios at Rome and in the Italian countryside around the city. The project had an unprecedented for-the-time budget of seven million dollars, employed a veritable army of thirty thousand extras dressed in some thirty-two thousand custom-made costumes, and entailed the construction of a series of colossal sets, such as the sumptuous interiors for Nero's palace, a section of the Circus Maximus that could seat tens of thousands of spectators for the gladiator scenes, and a 1/12 scale model of the entire city of Rome that would be immolated by three hundred alcohol burners emitting twenty-foot-high flames for a scene re-creating the Great Fire of Rome in AD 64. The massive scale of the production necessitated the procurement of extra electric generators, with one even being opportunistically obtained from the recently decommissioned Italian World War II battleship *Vittorio Veneto*.

In terms of historical accuracy, the pair of lovers at the center of the story, the Christian girl Lygia and the Roman general Vinicius, are both fictional. There is evidence of a Roman legionary commander of the same name who fought in Britain and was executed by the emperor Claudius prior to the time when the film is set, so in theory, the film's protagonist could be intended as his son. Lygia and Vinicius are reasonably representative idealized types. Lygia embodies a core set of Christian virtues, especially modesty, devotion to her faith, and chastity, while Vinicius personifies the perfect Roman general, exuding military competence, decisiveness, and dedication to the Roman state.

The real star of the film is Peter Ustinov as Emperor Nero. Ustinov's Nero is vain, peevish, insecure, cruel, grandiose, and temperamental, all at the same time. He revels in self-absorbed pomposity, as when he repeatedly subjects the members of his court to his dreadful musical performances on the lyre (an ancient stringed instrument) accompanied by his horribly sung renditions of his even-more-wretched poetic compositions. This behavior is drawn straight from ancient Roman authors such as Tacitus and Suetonius, who depicted Nero as being obsessed with singing and acting. Nero apparently fancied himself a supremely gifted musician, especially on the lyre, and loved to enter musical contests where, out of fear, he was always awarded first place. He traveled to Greece in order to participate in the most prestigious festivals, where, competing in multiple categories, as an actor, musician, and charioteer, Nero happily collected no fewer than 1,808 prizes. It does not seem to have dimmed his enthusiasm that many of these trophies were bestowed before he had actually performed, or even when he had completely botched the performance; for instance, during an Olympic chariot race, Nero clumsily fell out of his chariot and was unable to finish, yet, absurdly, was still presented with the victor's crown.

Ustinov's cinematic Nero constantly seesaws between ludicrous displays of overweening egotism during which he proclaims his own greatness and boundless talents, and moments of abject insecurity and self-doubt. This seems not so far off the historical mark. The film also accurately portrays Nero's infamous cruelty and sadism, showing him chortling gleefully as he watches victims in the arena being torn apart by wild beasts, and blithely ordering his minions to set fire to the city of Rome to clear space for his planned reconstruction on a more grandiose scale. The historical Nero was indeed an avid fan of violent spectacles who delighted in viewing people being tortured and killed. If anything, the film shies away from presenting some of his worst behavior in this regard. Not only did he have innumerable people killed, ranging from senators to slaves, but he also had almost every member of his immediate family, including his mother, his stepfather, his stepbrother, his aunt, his sister, and his wife, either murdered or slain.

It is worth noting that *Quo Vadis* is part of a pronounced tradition in 1950s historical films whereby upper-class British actors are invariably cast as characters who are either outright evil, or who are arrogant and domineering agents of totalitarian power structures, typically the Roman state itself. Thus, in *Quo Vadis*, the evil emperor Nero is played by the English Ustinov, who attended one of the most prestigious upper-class English boarding schools.

On the other hand, it became a 1950s historical film convention for American actors to be cast as the antagonists to these poshly-accented villains. With their no-nonsense American accents, these heroes usually represented a freedom-loving and persecuted group. Although Vinicius starts out with his allegiance to Rome, because he ends up on the Christian side, it is appropriate that he is played by American actor Robert Taylor, with a down-to-earth midwestern accent derived from his Nebraska upbringing. In keeping with his Americanization, the film also makes Vinicius far more clean-cut and agreeable than the corresponding character in the novel. The consistent casting of American actors as the heroes in these historical films was plainly the product of a 1950s Hollywood ideology in which the United States was justifiably viewed as having nobly defended the causes of freedom and justice against totalitarian dictators during World War II. *Quo Vadis's* portrait of devout Christians struggling against a frightening militaristic and pagan totalitarian state also neatly dovetailed with the Cold War American self-image as the defender of freedom locked in a death match with the implacable threat of "godless" Soviet Communism.

As for the secondary characters, a commendable number are based on actual historical figures. Foremost among these is Nero's chief courtier, Petronius, played by Leo Genn. Note that as he is portraying an aristocratic Roman, it is no surprise to discover that Genn was an upper-class British actor who attended tony Cambridge University. The historical Petronius was a sophisticated literary man who wrote the novel the *Satyricon* and functioned as a kind of cultural advisor at Nero's court. The cinematic Petronius is a somewhat sympathetic character who is fully aware of how terrible Nero's artistic efforts are, but, out of fear for his life, is forced to incessantly praise them. In the film, Petronius deftly uses flattery to try to steer Nero away from some of his more destructive impulses, but is ultimately forced to commit suicide, leaving behind a memorable note in which he at last gives Nero an honest evaluation of his awful poetry and singing. The real Petronius was in fact eventually driven to suicide, and he did indeed leave a posthumous note to the emperor denouncing his activities. Other characters at least loosely based on historical figures include the Praetorian Prefect Tigellinus, Nero's mistress Acte, the Stoic philosopher Seneca, the Apostles Peter and Paul, and Nero's second wife, Poppaea. Although only briefly appearing onscreen, these characters more or less conform to their supposed historical personalities, with the possible exception of Poppaea, whom the filmmakers have transformed into an unabashedly stereotypical Hollywood vamp: slinking around the palace in ahistorically flimsy garments, casting come-hither looks at any brawny man who crosses her path, and—as if all this were not enough to clearly signal her nature as a sexual predator—constantly accompanied by two large cheetahs on leashes.

One of the most exciting sequences is a depiction of the worst fire ever to strike Rome, an event known as the Great Fire of AD 64. This catastrophe resulted in the complete destruction of three-quarters of the city of Rome as the inferno raged unchecked for a week. In the movie, Nero is unambiguously portrayed as having deliberately ordered that the fire be set in order to make room for the newer, more elaborate version of the city that he planned to build as a monument to himself—an ambition reflected in the fact that he also intended to rename Rome as Neropolis. While the historical Nero shared his cinematic counterpart's plans to build a grander Rome that would be named after himself, there is no credible evidence that he was responsible for starting the fire. However, it is true that, in the aftermath of the blaze, some people voiced this suspicion, and that, in order to deflect blame, Nero spread a counter-rumor that the fire had been set by Christians. That the Christians actually ignited the fire is even less likely than that Nero did; in reality, it almost certainly started by accident. However, at this time, the Christians were an entirely obscure sect that no one knew much about, so Nero's lie proved effective in turning the Christians into scapegoats for the blaze. As depicted in the film, he rounded up a number of Christians and had them executed, some by the especially sadistic method of being tied to posts, covered in pitch, and set alight as a kind of human torch.

The most famous legend associated with the fire is that Nero was inspired by the sight of the burning city to put on his musician's robes and perform a song about the destruction of the city of Troy. This notion has been immortalized in the phrase "to fiddle while Rome burns," which has become shorthand for exhibiting indifference to a crisis. However, fiddles were not invented until much later and, as we've seen, Nero's instrument of choice was the lyre; so this phrase should really be "to strum the lyre while Rome burns." *Quo Vadis* enthusiastically embraces this tradition by showing Nero perched atop the palace, merrily playing his lyre and delivering one of his pretentious and awful singing performances to a crowd of appalled courtiers while, behind him, the city is dramatically engulfed in flames. It is a memorable scene, but unfortunately, it probably never happened. While several ancient authors tell the story of Nero singing while Rome burns, our most reliable source, Tacitus, reports that it was likely just a hostile rumor. Nero was not even in Rome when the fire broke out, but at the coastal town of Antium. He returned to Rome while it was still burning and was especially active in organizing relief efforts for the survivors, demanding that food be

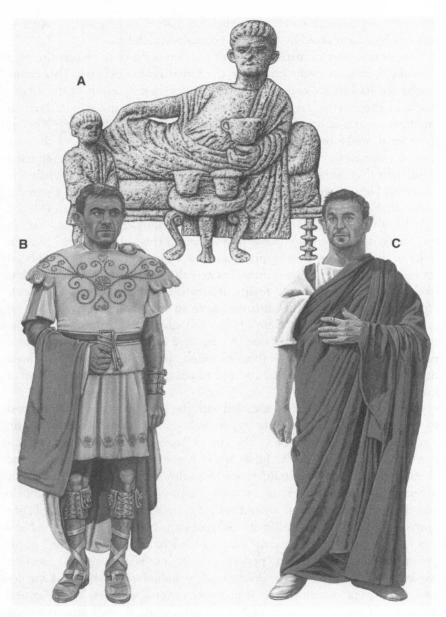

Figure 2.1. Dining. (A) Drawing of a Roman funerary relief from Cologne of a veteran reclining on a dining couch and wearing a tunic and cloak draped loosely in the Greek fashion. Probably the inspiration for (B) the banqueting costume worn by legate Robert Taylor in *Quo Vadis* (1951). (C) Reconstruction of a more historically plausible legate's dining attire. *Illustrations by Graham Sumner.*

brought into the city and opening up state-owned buildings and gardens to provide shelter for the refugees. The Great Fire of Rome occurred in AD 64, but Nero was not deposed until AD 68. The movie compresses time by depicting the failure of Nero's efforts to divert blame onto the Christians as prompting a provincial general, Galba, to stage a coup and march on Rome with his troops, which triggers a general uprising of the city's populace against the emperor. In reality, Nero seems to have succeeded in averting blame for the fire in its immediate aftermath. Eventually, however, his erratic behavior would catch up with him, leading Galba and others to rebel.

In their publicity for the film, MGM stressed the scale of the labor that went into producing the film's many costumes. The *Quo Vadis* souvenir booklet claimed that various local firms were subcontracted to work on the costumes, which were then distributed to housewives throughout Italy. It claimed that thirty-two thousand costumes were made, including fifteen thousand hand-sewn sandals; four thousand helmets of brass, aluminum, or tin; four thousand breastplates; and two thousand shields. However, it is also evident that some shields and helmets were reused from the 1925 MGM production of *Ben-Hur*, including the helmets worn by the rebellious Roman troops at the end of the film and the Praetorian and cavalry shields, which ironically had been carried in the earlier film by the Jewish rebel army. During the movie's triumphal parade, the ordinary legionaries are shown with full armor and weapons. This does not accord with the Arch of Titus, which represents the legionaries marching in the triumph celebrating the victory over the Jewish revolt as wearing only military tunics. (See Figure 4.2, located with the entry on *Masada*, which includes an illustration of a Roman legionary from *Quo Vadis* [A] as well as a reconstruction [C] of a historically plausible mid-first-century AD legionary.)

Many of the details of set, costume, and plot seem to be attributable to the film's historical advisor, Hugh Gray. Gray had studied ancient philosophy and classics at the universities of Louvain and Oxford, and later taught at UCLA. Gray injected several interesting historical touches into *Quo Vadis*, such as incorporating some of the few surviving fragments of ancient music in the film's score. Other uses of ancient sources proved less successful. Figure 2.1 shows the interesting outfit worn by Vinicius in a banquet scene (B), which seems to have been inspired by ancient sculptures such as (A), a funerary relief. At a formal dining event, a Roman would have worn a toga, as shown in the reconstruction painting (C) of a togate Roman nobleman.

Quo Vadis was made only a few years after the conclusion of World War II, and that recent conflict seemed to exert a noticeable effect on how the

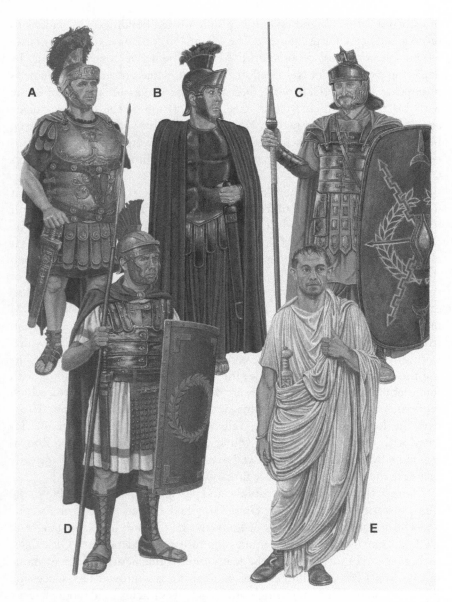

Figure 2.2. Sinister Praetorians. Menacing Praetorian guardsmen are a staple of films set in ancient Rome. Four versions depicted here are from (A) *Quo Vadis* (1951), (B) *Quo Vadis* (1985), (C) *Gladiator* (2000), and (D) *The Robe* (1953). Costume makers' predilection for portraying Praetorians in black is evident, but this is not based on ancient evidence. Within the city of Rome, Praetorians carried a sword, but often wore a toga rather than armor, as shown in (E). *Illustrations by Graham Sumner.*

filmmakers portrayed the Romans, whose behavior and appearance mirror aspects of Nazi Germany. As illustrated in Figure 2.2, the movie's Praetorian guardsmen (A) are identified by their menacing black cloaks and the black plumes on their helmets. This is not historically attested, but obviously recalls the black uniforms of Hitler's Waffen SS soldiers. As demonstrated by the other characters depicted in Figure 2.2, similar sinister black-clad and armored Praetorians became a cinematic cliché, popping up in films such as a remake of *Quo Vadis* (B), *Gladiator* (C), and *The Robe* (D). It should be noted that within the city of Rome, or at least within the palace, actual Praetorians often wore civilian togas, as in the reconstruction of such a Praetorian (E).

In *Quo Vadis*, the Praetorians greet Nero by rigidly extending their right arms with palms open, precisely emulating the Nazi salute. This gesture is not clearly attested as having been used by the Romans as a salute, but for the film's postwar audience, it would have been immediately recognizable as a Nazi gesture from countless wartime newsreels and propaganda films, and thus functioned as an effective shorthand to suggest a totalitarian or repressive state. Visual parallels with Nazism occur throughout the film. Classical scholars have pointed out how the movie's depiction of Vinicius's triumph directly echoes scenes from Leni Riefenstahl's infamous Nazi propaganda film *Triumph of the Will*.[1] Not only do both feature similar images of massed standards and flags and orderly phalanxes of soldiers stomping by a review stand, but even specific moments are replicated, such as when a woman holds up her baby to see the leader—an incident in the Nazi film copied in *Quo Vadis*.

Another fascinating analog transpires when Nero is inspecting the gigantic scale model of the new Rome that he intends to build, featuring a plethora of immense public structures. Hitler similarly planned to completely rebuild Berlin and to adorn it with an array of stupendously sized buildings promoting Nazism. Models of these proposed edifices were created, and surviving photographs show Hitler proudly reviewing them. The scene of Nero examining and flaunting his model of Rome precisely mirrors the photographic images of Hitler doing the same thing, so it seems likely that the filmmakers were aware of and deliberately imitating them. For this scene, the filmmakers used the scale model of ancient Rome from the Museo della Civiltà Romana, a museum and model that appropriately were commissioned by another famous Fascist, Benito Mussolini. Even specific lines in the script suggest conscious parallels with Nazi Germany on the part of the filmmakers. Joseph Goebbels, the Nazi minister of propaganda, famously stated that big lies told with conviction are easily believed by the masses. In *Quo Vadis*, Petronius expresses this sentiment, declaring, "People will believe any lie, if it is fantastic enough."

Throughout the movie, Nero evinces a pronounced fondness for mass spectacles and displays of power, just as Hitler did. Perhaps the most obvious parallel is that just as the Nazis were obsessed with persecuting and murdering the Jews, the film's Romans are fixated on oppressing and persecuting their own religious minority, the early Christians. Although Peter and Paul appear in the film, and there is a nice scene of Peter preaching to the early Christian community of Rome, the titillating revelry of Nero's court gets far more screen time than the sober religious message of Peter and Paul.

Quo Vadis had a particularly aggressive marketing campaign that included the selling of specially made consumer products acting as tie-ins with the film. *Star Wars* is typically pointed to as the movie that began the now-standard practice of high-profile films being accompanied by a slew of thematically-linked toys and other merchandise, but *Quo Vadis* anticipated this phenomenon by two decades. Perhaps most amusing was an ad campaign for men's underwear based around a drawing of an American man in boxer shorts playing a fiddle while his wife gazes at him adoringly. The caption reads: "Make like Nero in *Quo Vadis* Shorts." The text for the ad further boasted: "The gay designs are plucked right out of the dazzling motion picture of spectacular Roman days. Poor toga-clad Nero never knew the smart comfort of these full-cut boxer shorts." The commodification of the film to hawk merchandise to the American public promoted innumerable other items, from raincoats to tablecloths and jewelry to pajamas.

The effort put into making and marketing *Quo Vadis* paid off, as it was both a financial and a critical triumph. It was the highest-grossing film of 1951 and earned eight Academy Award nominations, including Best Picture and Best Supporting Actor for Peter Ustinov as Nero. Perhaps its most important legacy is that it spawned a host of imitators, so that the 1950s and early 1960s witnessed a steady stream of big-budget ancient world epics, notably *Ben-Hur*, *Spartacus*, *The Robe*, and *Cleopatra*, as well as a veritable swarm of cheap sword-and-sandal knock-offs, including an astonishing nineteen films featuring the legendary strongman Hercules and boasting titles such as *Hercules against the Moon Men* and *Hercules and the Captive Women*. *Quo Vadis* established a successful and lucrative template for epic films set in classical antiquity and ushered in an entire decade's worth of sword-and-sandal flicks of varying degrees of quality.

Julius Caesar (1953)

Director: Joseph Mankiewicz
Producer: John Houseman
Production Company: Metro-Goldwyn-Mayer
Cast: Marlon Brando (Mark Antony), James Mason (Brutus), John Gielgud (Cassius), Louis Calhern (Caesar), Edmond O'Brien (Casca), Greer Garson (Calpurnia)

After the success of *Quo Vadis*, Metro-Goldwyn-Mayer moved quickly to follow up with another epic set in ancient Rome. They settled on an adaptation of Shakespeare's play *Julius Caesar*, produced by John Houseman and directed by Joseph Mankiewicz. The resulting film debuted in 1953, just two years after *Quo Vadis*, and is probably the most successful cinematic rendition of one of Shakespeare's plays set in antiquity. From *Quo Vadis*, MGM had accumulated a substantial collection of Roman armor, equipment, and costumes, which they thriftily recycled in *Julius Caesar* as well as in subsequent Roman films made during the decade. The movie had plenty of star power, with Marlon Brando cast as Mark Antony, James Mason as Brutus, and John Gielgud as Cassius. It was planned as a relatively low-budget film, but according to Mankiewicz and Houseman, the decision to shoot it in black and white was not a cost-saving measure, but rather resulted from their belief that color would be a distraction from the sort of serious drama they intended to present, and that black and white would give it the look of a contemporary political thriller.

Since the film is a cinematic version of a play, any discussion of the historical accuracy of its plot points hinges on the historicity of Shakespeare's text. The main source that he used when writing his play seems to have been the biography of Caesar written by the ancient author Plutarch, who lived in the second century AD. Not only the plot, but many of the play's (and movie's) most famous lines are copied word for word from Plutarch; for instance, Caesar's comment that Cassius has "a lean and hungry look . . . such men are dangerous," and a soothsayer's warning to Caesar, "Beware the Ides of March!" The exchange between Caesar and the same soothsayer later in the play—"Well, the Ides of March have come / Yes, but they have not gone"—is also straight from Plutarch.

On the whole, both play and film correspond fairly closely to the historical events described by Plutarch. The main exception is that some of the action is compressed, as when Brutus and Antony address their speeches to the people in the Forum immediately after Caesar's assassination; in reality, Caesar's funeral was held five days later. Similarly, the Battle of Philippi is briefly depicted in the movie as not much more than a skirmish that takes place in a single day, rather than the prolonged and confusing sequence of two clashes spaced three weeks apart that it actually was. None of the actors particularly resemble the Romans that they are portraying, but they make up for it with excellent acting. Brando is a dynamic, seething Mark Antony, and James Mason subtly but effectively conveys Brutus's internal conflict as a man whose conscience compels him to betray a friend.

Unlike many ancient films of the time, it does not incorporate large, spectacular sets. Most of the action is economically and tightly staged on one exterior street corner, in a villa set reused from *Quo Vadis*, and around a series of vaguely classical-looking staircases and foyers. This is in keeping with the filmmakers' intent to direct the viewers' focus to the dramatic performances of the actors rather than to dazzle them with spectacle. The sets are dressed with lots of copies of antique statuary, although sometimes these are from periods much later than when the film takes place. For example, several monologues are delivered by characters standing beside a replica bust of the emperor Hadrian, who lived a good century and a half later. Despite such minor errors, there are some nice visual touches. The street scene at the beginning is quite well done and accurately evokes a busy corner in the ancient city of Rome. There are bustling vendors; a tavern with a counter facing the pedestrians; narrow, crooked streets crowded by overhanging projections from the high-rise brick and concrete apartment buildings; loiterers gambling on the curb; graffiti on the walls; a central fountain; brick vaulting exposed on the structures; and laundry dangling from windows and balconies.

Some of the costume details also reflect knowledge of the ancient world. When we first meet Antony, he is participating in the festival of Lupercalia, a popular Roman holiday during which young men ran naked through the streets performing rituals, and in a nod to this, a youthful Brando makes his entrance shirtless. Later, in the Roman army camp, there are several scenes during which sacrifices are offered, and the garb of the priestly attendants, known as *victimarii*, who performed these is correctly depicted. Throughout the movie, the female characters and extras are clad in suitably modest attire, unlike in the many epics that portray Roman women in ahistorically racy costumes.

On the other hand, the armor of the principal characters seems to be mostly invented, often consisting of leather jerkins copiously peppered with metal studs and paired with leather arm bracers. Both of these elements are quite unlike anything actually worn by Roman military officers. The ordinary soldiers are equipped with an assortment of armor left over from *Quo Vadis* and earlier films going back at least to the 1925 *Ben-Hur*. Some is pure fantasy, and even the authentically Roman bits usually date to later

Figure 2.3.   Cavalry. (A) Drawing of a Roman cavalryman depicted on Trajan's Column in Rome. Although dating to the second century AD, the figures on Trajan's Column have influenced costume designers and artists re-creating Roman soldiers from all eras of Roman history, such as (B) a cavalryman from *Julius Caesar* (1953). (C) Reconstruction of an early imperial Roman cavalryman. *Illustrations by Graham Sumner.*

eras in Roman history. For example, Figure 2.3 depicts a Roman cavalryman from the film (B) who seems to have been inspired by a horseman (A) on Trajan's Column, a monument dating to the second century AD. In combat, a Roman cavalryman would likely have worn a chain mail shirt, as can be seen on the reconstructed early imperial cavalryman (C). The filmmakers' reliance on later sources is understandable, because at the time when the movie was shot, knowledge of Republican equipment remained sketchy, so they had no choice but to use what was available to them.

The highlight of the film is Caesar's funeral, with the rival speeches by Mason's Brutus and Brando's Antony. Both actors are terrific in their delivery, and the staging, with frequent reactions and interjections from the crowd, vividly conveys the power their oratory exerts on the gathered citizenry. Its most disappointing aspect is the Battle of Philippi, which is perfunctory and half-hearted in tone. Mankiewicz supposedly disliked shooting battle scenes, and instead of even attempting to show the large, formal battle that it actually was, he turns it into a small-scale ambush in a narrow canyon that recalls Hollywood cowboys-versus-Indians westerns.

On the whole, with this version of *Julius Caesar*, Mankiewicz and Houseman created a gripping and effective psychological drama with wonderful acting that adheres reasonably closely to the accounts of Caesar's assassination, at least as described by Plutarch and Suetonius. Despite the script consisting entirely of Shakespeare's verse, the skill of those declaiming it ensures that there is no hint of stuffiness, and that the film has a sleek, timeless feel and a strong narrative drive. It is Shakespeare done well.

The Robe (1953)

Director: Henry Koster
Producer: Frank Ross
Production Company: 20th Century-Fox
Cast: Richard Burton (Marcellus Gallio), Jean Simmons (Diana), Victor Mature (Demetrius), Michael Rennie (Peter), Jay Robinson (Caligula), Ernest Thesiger (Tiberius)

Having witnessed the success that MGM had enjoyed with *Quo Vadis* (1951), rival studio 20th Century-Fox soon came out with an ancient epic of its own, *The Robe* (1953). Their rendition did not stray far from the sure-fire formula established by *The Sign of the Cross* and *Quo Vadis* since, like both of those films, it too was based on a bestselling novel, was set during the early empire, featured persecuted Christians and a mad, tyrannical Roman emperor, included a cameo by Jesus, and had as its protagonist a dutiful pagan Roman officer who, motivated by the love of a pious Christian woman, ultimately converts. Also like those other films, it would be a financial and critical success for its studio, and, in addition, it spawned a sequel, *Demetrius and the Gladiators* (1954).

The novel that 20th Century-Fox chose for its big-budget entry in the ancient epic competition was a 1942 bestseller by Lloyd C. Douglas, a Lutheran minister who had written a series of extremely popular religious-themed novels, including *Magnificent Obsession*, which was also turned into a movie. Richard Burton was chosen for the central role as the Roman tribune Marcellus Gallio; Jean Simmons played the virtuous Christian woman Diana; Jay Robinson hammed it up as Emperor Caligula; Victor Mature took on the part of Gallio's brawny slave Demetrius; and Michael Rennie rounded out the cast as a dignified Peter. Further raising the film's profile was 20th Century-Fox's decision to select *The Robe* to be the first movie released in the new, much-touted widescreen CinemaScope format, a process marketed as a revolution in the movie-going experience that the studio hoped would stem the loss of viewers to television.

The film not only followed the well-worn path established by previous Roman epics, but it also entrenched additional tropes of the genre. Not least of these was beginning with a rather pretentious opening statement that represented the early empire as a world in which brutalized, conquered peoples resentfully suffered under despotic Roman rule, and asserted that slavery was both a vital source of Rome's power and a fatal flaw that would ultimately lead to its downfall. *Ben-Hur* and *Spartacus*, both made within the next decade, would also open with solemn declarations of nearly identical sentiments. In all of these films created at the dawn of the Cold War, the Roman Empire became a useful symbol for totalitarianism and corruption. Viewers were clearly invited to identify the United States with the virtuous, freedom-loving, and pious slaves and Christians, while the cruel, authoritarian, godless Romans stood in for the insidious Communist "Red Menace." While one can draw parallels between almost any empire and ancient Rome, these films' insistence that slavery would precipitate Rome's downfall is more of a stretch. While historians are still arguing over which of many possible factors were the principal causes for Rome's collapse, slavery is really not among the main contenders.

The Robe is also typical of many historical epics in that its main characters, Gallio, Diana, and Demetrius, although entirely fictitious, are woven into the narratives of historical figures, such as the emperors Caligula and Tiberius and the Apostle Peter. Burton's turn as Roman military officer Gallio is gruffly convincing, arguably more so than his performance as another Roman aristocrat-soldier, Mark Antony, in *Cleopatra*. As Caligula, Jay Robinson delivers a stridently unhinged performance, depicting the young emperor as an egotistical sadist eagerly craning forward to relish the effects of his cruelties on his victims. While his interpretation might seem over the top, it may not actually be so far from the truth. After all, the real Caligula reportedly delighted in torture and terror and frequently proclaimed, "Let them hate me, so long as they fear me." Although Hollywood usually jumps at any chance to spotlight Roman decadence and depravity, in the case of Tiberius—the other emperor to appear in this film—the filmmakers atypically chose to downplay the negative aspects of his personality. The elderly Tiberius supposedly spent the last decades of his life ensconced in a sumptuous villa on Capri, engaging in all manner of debauchery. In *The Robe*, we are treated to scenes set at the infamous villa, but Tiberius instead acts like a rather avuncular figure who kindly intercedes on Gallio's behalf at Diana's request and philosophically ruminates about fate and destiny. Tiberius's wife, Julia, also shows up, even though she had already been dead for eighteen years by the time the movie begins.

Many of the minor historical errors in the film seem to have been inspired by popular but misguided notions about ancient Rome that have become staples of ancient epics. Among these are the idea that Roman warships were rowed by slaves and that condemnation to the galleys was a common judicial punishment (see also every version of *Ben-Hur*); one of the senators in the film secretly hoping or scheming to restore the Roman Republic (see also *Spartacus*, *The Fall of the Roman Empire*, *Gladiator*); characters referring to one of Rome's eastern provinces as "Palestine" rather than "Judea"; and portraying all Romans of the early imperial era as being both extremely knowledgeable about Christians and totally obsessed with persecuting them (even though the first Roman source to even mention either Christians or Christianity was not written until seven decades after the time when the film is set).

The legionary equipment on the film's Roman soldiers (see Figure 3.2.B) is superior to that in its rival, *Quo Vadis*, and possesses a more realistic and lived-in appearance than that in many other 1950s movies. The Roman centurion played by Jeff Morrow wears a *lorica hamata* (mail shirt) with added shoulder defenses and has *pteruges* (leather strips) hanging from the shoulders and waist. The French artist James Tissot's famous 1897 set of illustrations of scenes from the Bible seems to have been a major source of inspiration for the filmmakers. The helmets are a hybrid of the various types classified as "Imperial Gallic" or "Italic" rather than any particular known archaeological specimen. The Praetorian guardsmen (see Figure 2.2.D) wear the same body armor as the legionaries, but sport dark crimson cloaks befitting their higher status, in addition to the white tunics with a red horizontal band also seen in *Quo Vadis*. Some of the Praetorians carry hexagonal shields, but most have curved rectangular shields, like the legionaries. While most of the equipment is fairly accurate, many of the swords are not, likely being based either on the nineteenth-century French infantry/artillery sword or on Hollywood ideas of medieval swords.

The Robe was the year's top-grossing film, making $30 million on an investment of $4.5 million, and it won two Oscars, for Best Costume Design and Best Art Direction. It was also nominated for Best Picture, as was Burton for Best Actor. So confident was 20th Century-Fox that they had a hit on their hands, they took the unprecedented step of beginning to film a sequel, *Demetrius and the Gladiators*, just three weeks after having completed *The Robe*. Sharp-eyed viewers might notice that they got the most out of their investment by reusing many of the same sets and costumes.

Demetrius and the Gladiators (1954)

Director: Delmer Daves
Producer: Frank Ross
Production Company: 20th Century-Fox
Cast: Victor Mature (Demetrius), Susan Hayward (Messalina), Michael Rennie (Peter), Jay Robinson (Caligula), William Marshall (Glycon), Anne Bancroft (Paula), Debra Paget (Lucia), Ernest Borgnine (Strabo)

Demetrius and the Gladiators has two interesting distinctions: it was an early example of a studio trying to cash in on a hit by making a sequel, even if this meant overcoming the awkward detail that the main characters of the first film had died at the end of it, and many of its scenes involving gladiators constitute a kind of rough draft for later versions of the same in the better-known films *Spartacus* (1960) and *Gladiator* (2000). The plot revolves around Victor Mature's character, Demetrius, a Christian slave freed by the Roman officer protagonist of *The Robe* who inherited Jesus's robe when his former master was martyred. Demetrius is soon captured by the Romans and sentenced to fight in the arena, and most of the film follows his career as a reluctant gladiator. Jay Robinson reprises his role as the deranged emperor Caligula, fixated on identifying and murdering Christians and intent on obtaining the robe, which he believes might magically grant immortality. Many of the historical problems with the first film apply to this sequel as well, in particular that at this very early point in the history of Christianity, it is debatable whether most Romans would have even heard of Christians, let alone be obsessed with persecuting them. Although Michael Rennie repeats his stately performance in the role of the disciple Peter, and there are some nice depictions of early Christian congregations, this film is generally less interested in religious history than its predecessor, and much more focused on offering a rousing gladiator story.

In its representation of gladiators, the training scenes at the gladiator school are fairly well done. The novice gladiators are shown practicing with wooden weapons, which was an established Roman training technique. They are also correctly portrayed as specializing in a particular style of fighting, each utilizing a specific set of weapons and armor. The most well known of these is the *retiarius*, who fought with a trident and net but wore little defensive armor, and we are treated to quite a few scenes of *retiarii* training and fighting. Many of the gladiator helmets are quite accurate copies of examples unearthed at Pompeii, and none of the equipment used in the arena looks badly out of place. There is a good scene when Demetrius arrives at gladiator school and hears an introductory speech delivered by the hard-bitten *lanista*, or head trainer, Strabo, played with a convincingly bluff manner by Ernest Borgnine. Strabo recounts how he was once a gladiator himself, but, after winning fifty-two bouts, was granted his freedom. Such manumissions did happen, and while the number of gladiators who won their freedom in this way was probably small, it is not improbable that such a man would then become a *lanista*. The tough former-gladiator-turned-*lanista* who lectures new recruits was such an appealing figure that he was copied by both *Spartacus* and *Gladiator*, with characters played by Charles McGraw and Oliver Reed, respectively. Finally, despite being slaves, champion gladiators were sometimes admired both for their martial skills and as sex symbols, as attested by multiple surviving examples of ancient Roman graffiti. The film references this when Strabo proclaims, "Dardanius here is the best of netmen. You've seen his name often where the girls have scratched it on the walls of Rome."

On the negative side, characters repeatedly express the erroneous idea that absolutely every gladiator match ended with the death of one of the combatants. We don't know exactly what percentage of fights resulted in death, but the best guess of modern scholars is that fewer than one-quarter ended with a fatality. Another common misconception found in the film is that multiple pairs of gladiators fought simultaneously, when, in reality, bouts of trained gladiators were always a single pair at a time. At one point, Demetrius has to grapple with a trio of tigers, and while it is true that the Romans delighted in witnessing combats that pitted exotic animals both against one another and against human opponents, the men who fought beasts, called *venatores*, were actually a completely different group from gladiators. Still, in a clever touch, Demetrius's success against the tigers is commemorated later in the movie as the subject of a decorative relief on his breastplate when he becomes a tribune in the Praetorian Guard. The dramatic sequence featuring the hero versus tigers is yet another element from this film that would be copied almost exactly by *Gladiator*.

Demetrius and the Gladiators also seems to have established the long-running convention that, when the protagonist arrives at the training school, he has the good fortune to be immediately taken under the wing of an experienced gladiator, who mentors and befriends him. In a kind of ancient world variant on the "magical negro" trope, this helpful figure is always a physically imposing yet modestly noble Black man. Additionally, this character selflessly ends up either risking or sacrificing his own life in order to aid the hero. In *Demetrius*, this character is named Glycon (William Marshall); in *Spartacus*, it is Draba (Woody Strode); and in *Gladiator*, we get Juba (Djimon Hounsou). In all three movies, the respective performances by Marshall, Strode, and Hounsou are some of the most memorable, and the scenes that include them are among the most crucial in establishing the hero's moral complexion.

Besides the gladiator sequences, some of the film's other historical high points include Caligula harboring delusions that he is a god, something that is emphasized in multiple ancient sources, and his uncle Claudius craftily pretending to be less intelligent and more inept than he really was in order to avoid being murdered by Caligula. In the scene where Caligula has Claudius doing research for him, there is also a nod to Claudius's attested genuine interest in scholarship and history. On the negative side, the film shows Caligula being murdered and Claudius being hailed as the next emperor at the games. In reality, Caligula was slain in a basement passageway of the palace and Claudius was discovered hiding behind a curtain before being acclaimed emperor. It is true, however, that both deeds were performed by the Praetorian Guard. Perhaps the most historically improbable moment occurs right at the end, when Claudius's notoriously unfaithful and ambitious wife, Messalina, proclaims—in what the filmmakers apparently intended to be a sincere announcement—that henceforth she will completely renounce her wanton ways and be a loyal and subservient wife to Claudius. Her hairstyles throughout the film are also particularly out of place, all but screaming 1950s-era fashion rather than anything that could be construed as being remotely classical. Another amusing anachronism is that the decoration of the imperial box at the arena appears to include a version of Michelangelo's statue of David, a full 1,500 years before it was sculpted.

Made on the cheap by reusing costumes and sets from *The Robe* (the village of Cana reappears virtually unchanged in this film as a street in Rome), *Demetrius and the Gladiators* repaid its makers by turning a healthy profit, although it was not as big a hit as the earlier movie. While *The Robe*'s religious message marks it as a more serious and somber film, *Demetrius*, which is at heart just an action movie, has perhaps aged better, and is arguably a more enjoyable watching experience. It also cast a long shadow on later gladiator flicks, especially *Spartacus* and *Gladiator*, which imitated many of its elements.

Attila (1954 Italy/1958 US) and *Sign of the Pagan* (1954)

Attila
Director: Pietro Francisci
Producers: Carlo Ponti, Dino De Laurentiis
Production Company: Ponti-De Laurentiis/Lux Film
Cast: Anthony Quinn (Attila), Sophia Loren (Honoria), Henri Vidal (Aetius), Irene Papas (Grune), Colette Régis (Galla Placidia), Ettore Manni (Bleda), Claude Laydu (Valentinian)

Sign of the Pagan (1954)
Director: Douglas Sirk
Producer: Albert Cohen
Production Company: Universal-International
Cast: Jeff Chandler (Marcian), Jack Palance (Attila), Ludmilla Tchérina (Pulcheria), Rita Gam (Kubra), Jeff Morrow (Paulinus), George Dolenz (Theodosius), Allison Hayes (Ildico)

The vast majority of films about the ancient Roman world are set during the late republic or the early empire (first century BC to second century AD), whereas the period of late antiquity (fourth to seventh centuries AD) has been comparatively underrepresented. In 1954, however, not only were two movies made about this era, but both also focused on exactly the same figure—Attila. The Hollywood production, *Sign of the Pagan* from Universal, starred Jack Palance as the barbarian king, while in Italy, Ponti-De Laurentiis Productions made a rival film, *Attila*, with Anthony Quinn in the title role. Both were relatively low-budget efforts with brisk running times of under an hour and a half. By the time of Attila, the Roman Empire had split in two, with one emperor based at Rome ruling the Western Empire, and another controlling the Eastern Empire from the city of Constantinople. While both movies have Attila as the central figure, the surrounding subplots of the Italian film, *Attila*, are mostly derived from occurrences in the Western Empire, whereas Hollywood's *Sign of the Pagan* draws most of its secondary characters from the machinations at the court of the Eastern Empire. Of the two, *Attila* adheres slightly more closely to historical events, so we'll begin with it.

Attila spends a surprising amount of its brief length accurately tracing aspects of the complicated politics in the Western Roman Empire in the mid-fifth century AD, saving its only big battle scene for the end. Thus, viewers are introduced to many of the key personages of the time, including Attila and his brother Bleda, who were appointed co-rulers of the Hunnic nation after the death of their uncle; Flavius Aetius, a loyal and talented Roman general with personal ties to both barbarians and Romans; the foppish and foolish young Roman emperor in the West, Valentinian III; his intelligent and domineering mother, Galla Placidia, who is the real power behind the throne; and Valentinian's ambitious sister, Honoria, who schemes to seize power, even if it means allying herself with Attila. All of these were real people, and their onscreen personas more or less reflect what is known of their historically attested ones. Perhaps the movie's characterization of Valentinian as a whining mama's boy is exaggerated, but the real Valentinian was a weak ruler; and while Quinn's Attila is one-note in his unrelenting bloodthirstiness, the real Attila was indeed an aggressive conqueror. The film even references some relatively obscure historical incidents as motivation for the characters' actions; for instance, the Huns break a treaty with Rome because of resentment that a Roman bishop had supposedly desecrated some Hunnic tombs.

The film simplifies and rearranges some events; for example, it has Galla Placidia living a year or two past the actual date of her death. In the film, Bleda is presented as a strong advocate of peace with the Romans, in contrast to the warlike Attila, but there is no evidence that Bleda advocated such a policy. The film portrays Attila ordering Bleda's murder during a hunting expedition, and although this is not certain, the extant sources do suggest that it may indeed have happened. The final scene, in which Pope Leo confronts Attila on the banks of a river in northern Italy and persuades him to turn back rather than sack Rome, is also based on actual events. The movie ends rather abruptly and prematurely at this point without covering the remainder of Attila's career.

The clothing and jewelry on the Roman characters deserve particular praise as having clearly been based on surviving mosaics from around this time that depict Roman aristocrats, especially those in the Basilica of San Vitale and the Mausoleum of Galla Placidia in Ravenna. The Huns' outfits are less historically authentic and belong more to the tradition of the savage, fur-clad fantasy barbarian. Some of Attila's men sport truly ridiculous helmets adorned with horns, spear points, and tall fountains of feathers.

Turning to *Sign of the Pagan*, we again have a bloodthirsty Attila menacing the Roman world, this time played with gusto by Jack Palance in distractingly heavy brownface. His main antagonist is a Roman soldier, Marcian, stoically played by Jeff Chandler. In the film, Marcian is identified as a humble sandal-maker's son who enlisted in the Roman army and, due to his military prowess, has risen to the rank of centurion in the bodyguard of the Western emperor, Valentinian. While traveling as a messenger to the Eastern emperor, Theodosius II, he is captured by Attila, but he soon escapes. Meanwhile, Attila marries a captive woman, Ildico, even though she despises him. When Marcian finally reaches the Eastern capital of Constantinople, we are introduced to Emperor Theodosius, whose main foreign policy entails paying the various barbarian kings large bribes to prevent them from attacking his empire. We also meet his sister Pulcheria, who aspires to take the throne for herself and adopt a more hard-nosed attitude toward the barbarians. Attila soon shows up at court along with the other barbarian kings, and they all collect their bribes before leaving to attack the Western Empire. During their stay in Constantinople, Attila's warlike daughter, Kubra, is "tamed" by Marcian and drawn to the peaceful Christian religion. Since this is a Hollywood film, Marcian and Pulcheria naturally fall in love. They eventually stage a coup and force Theodosius to resign, whereupon Pulcheria becomes empress. She promptly sends Marcian and her armies to aid the Western Empire against Attila. Attila's army marches to the very gates of Rome, but he is scared off and persuaded not to attack by a meeting with Pope Leo, who has been tipped off as to how to manipulate Attila's superstitious nature by the now fully Christianized Kubra. While retreating, Attila's army is ambushed by Marcian, and in the melee, he is fatally stabbed by the still-resentful Ildico. Pulcheria marries Marcian, who becomes emperor of the Eastern Empire.

How does this stack up against history? Theodosius was indeed the Eastern emperor, and he did make a practice of appeasing the barbarians with bribes. He had a sister, Pulcheria, who took over after him, not through a coup and forced abdication, but because he died when he fell from his horse and broke his spine. Pulcheria then immediately married Marcian, elevating him to the throne, but all of this happened before Attila's attack on Rome, not afterward. In addition, she was over fifty years old at the time, not the young princess depicted in the movie. Marcian had served in the Eastern Empire's army, not the Western, and was a high-ranking general, not a lowly centurion. Also, rather than a poor sandal-maker, his father had been a military officer. Attila never went to Constantinople in person, he had no known daughter (and certainly not a Christian-sympathizing one), and he never actually made it as far as Rome, since he turned back in northern Italy. As for his death, it did not occur during battle; instead, he expired on his wedding night with Ildico, which occurred after his abortive attack on Rome, not before. The most likely cause of his demise was overindulgence in alcohol, although there were some rumors that Ildico might have poisoned him.

The film's costumes are mostly fanciful, particularly those of the barbarian kings, who are dressed in the stereotypical Hollywood barbarian outfit of furs, and several of them wear horned helmets that are Hollywood's equally inaccurate shorthand for Vikings—or apparently for any barbarian tribe. In the scene where Marcian demonstrates Roman fighting techniques by fencing with Kubra, he uses the short sword (*gladius*) of the early imperial period rather than the longer sword typical of the fifth century. The scenes of the Hunnic army on the move were lifted from an earlier Universal film about the Mongols, *The Golden Horde* (1951), and while a number of those extras are quite accurate as fourteenth-century Mongols, they look more dubious as fifth-century Huns.

Ben-Hur (1959)

Director: William Wyler
Producer: Sam Zimbalist
Production Company: Metro-Goldwyn-Mayer
Cast: Charlton Heston (Judah Ben-Hur), Stephen Boyd (Messala), Jack Hawkins (Quintus Arrius), Hugh Griffith (Ilderim), Haya Harareet (Esther), Martha Scott (Miriam)

By the late 1950s, MGM Studios was in dire financial trouble, and its executives decided to gamble everything on one huge movie extravaganza that would hopefully save the studio. Seeking the surest possible hit, they decided to replicate the *Quo Vadis* formula by creating an epic film set in the ancient world, based on a popular novel, that would combine pagan pageantry with Christian moralizing. The book they selected was *Ben-Hur: A Tale of the Christ*, published by General Lew Wallace in 1880. This was a safe choice, as it had been a massive bestseller and pop culture phenomenon; only the Bible had sold more copies in English, until *Gone with the Wind* appeared fifty years later. It had already spawned several earlier cinematic renditions, including MGM's own silent version in 1925, as well as a hugely popular play that toured America to packed houses for twenty years and featured live horses running on treadmills to simulate the chariot racing scene. So admired was the novel that at least three towns in the United States had actually been named Ben Hur.

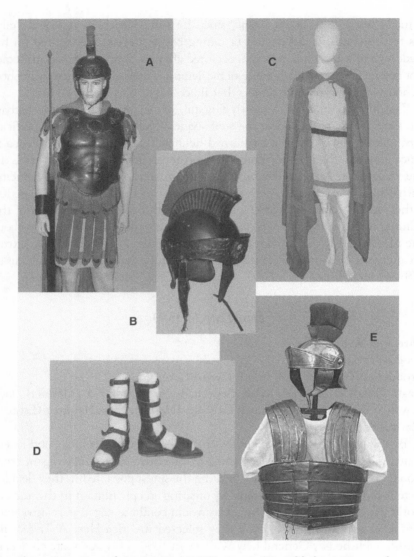

Figure 2.4. Props from *Ben-Hur* (1959). Armor (A) and helmet (B) worn by a Roman galley commander played by Robert Brown. (C) Roman tunic and cloak. (D) A pair of Roman boots. Their closed backs make them very different from the famous *caligae*-type boot worn by Roman soldiers. (E) A brass legionary helmet and *lorica segmentata* body armor. *Photographs and props from The Terry Nix Collection.*

MGM went all in on its gamble, spending $15 million on the film—a sum that made it the most expensive film yet produced. Charlton Heston, fresh off his memorable turn as Moses in *The Ten Commandments*, was recruited to play the title role, and the rest of the cast was filled out with experienced top-rank actors. As director, MGM chose William Wyler, who had been a young assistant director on the 1925 version and had filmed its acclaimed chariot race scene. The epic would be shot in Italy on a lavish scale, utilizing fifty thousand extras, a hundred thousand costumes, and three hundred sets constructed on 148 acres at Cinecittà Studios outside Rome. Figure 2.4 shows some of the props used in the film, including the armor and helmet worn by a Roman galley commander played by Robert Brown.

The film was a big risk for MGM, but it paid off in impressive fashion. Raking in nearly $80 million globally, it not only earned the top place at the box office for 1959, but also second place of all time up to that point. As for critical reception, *Ben-Hur* garnered more awards than any other film in all of cinema history, winning eleven Oscars, including Best Actor, Best Director, and Best Picture. It would hold the record for the most Oscars won by a single film for over forty years, until *Titanic* and *The Lord of the Rings: The Return of the King* each tied its eleven wins.

Most of the action in *Ben-Hur* occurs in the remote frontier province of Judea and the surrounding territories, and much of the plot concerns tensions between the Roman administrators of the conquered province and various indigenous groups, such as the Jews. General Lew Wallace wrote the book while serving as governor of the unsettled frontier Territory of New Mexico and, during his tenure, had to contend with a range war between established Mexican landowners and a new influx of Anglo-white ranchers. This experience of trying to negotiate peace among ethnic groups in a frontier zone seems to have influenced his novel. These tensions are embodied in the central relationship between the characters of the Jewish prince Judah Ben-Hur and the Roman aristocrat Messala, played by Stephen Boyd. The two had grown up together in Judea as best friends before parting and pursuing their respective careers. The film begins when Messala returns to Judea as an administrator and their old friendship becomes strained because Messala wants Judah's aid in suppressing Jewish dissidents.

Novelist Gore Vidal did a late rewrite of the screenplay and controversially claimed that he urged the director to portray the relationship between the two men as if Messala wanted to revive a love affair that had existed when they were boys, thus imbuing the adult Judah's rejection of Messala and his politics with an erotic edge and adding the fury of a spurned lover to the hatred that develops between them. Heston has vehemently denied this homoerotic subtext, but whether or not Heston was in on it, Boyd's performance seems to indicate that he certainly was. Even the dialogue is suggestive, such as Messala's line while arguing with Judah: "Is there anything so sad as unrequited love?" The movie mostly follows the novel, but significantly, one scene that lacks a counterpart in the book depicts Messala urging Judah to name disloyal Jews, and Judah refusing to turn informer—the act that precipitates the collapse of their friendship. For contemporary audiences, this exchange would inevitably have called to mind the recent McCarthy-era hunt for Communists, during which people were pressured to provide names of alleged members of the Communist Party, and a number of prominent Hollywood figures were blacklisted for supposedly being Communist sympathizers.

The film follows the 1950s convention of casting British Commonwealth actors to play upper-class Romans, and Americans as their ethnic or religious antagonists. Thus, Messala is played by Irish actor Stephen Boyd, and Roman general Arrius by English actor Jack Hawkins, while the purportedly Jewish Judah speaks in Heston's broad midwestern American accent. This linguistic paradigm holds for most of the secondary characters as well, with other Romans portrayed by British Commonwealth actors, and the Jews by Americans.

Like *The Robe*, *Ben-Hur* reinforces the impression that Judea was a heavily garrisoned province. It is believed that, at the time of the story, the actual garrison was little more than six auxiliary cohorts strong. However, we first encounter Messala marching at the head of a sizable army that includes legionaries, auxiliary cavalry, and archers. Later, we are informed that Gratus, the new Roman governor, will bring "two more legions" with him. It is also a mystery why the Roman army, presumably traveling to Jerusalem from the ports of Caesarea or Joppa on the coast, would make an enormous detour to go past a certain carpenter's workshop in Nazareth. After being sentenced to the galleys, Ben-Hur is also taken along the same circuitous route. At the time, Nazareth was in Galilee and therefore belonged to the Tetrarchy of Herod Antipas, so it was not even formally a part of Judea.

Ben-Hur famously contains two outstanding scenes of great spectacle: the naval battle and the chariot race. As punishment for a crime that he did not actually commit, Judah Ben-Hur is sentenced to serve in the Roman navy as a galley slave, chained to a bench and doomed to pull a heavy wooden oar. The movie suggests both that this was a standard legal punishment in the Roman Empire and that being condemned to the galleys is tantamount to a death sentence. The shipboard scenes depicting the harshness of the rowers' existence and the cruelty that they are subjected to are among the film's most memorable. The dehumanization of the slaves is symbolized by the fact that, once assigned to their benches, the slaves lose even their names and are simply referred to by the number of their position; thus, Judah is known only as "number forty-one."

The commander of the fleet, Quintus Arrius, functions as a foil to Messala. Both men are arrogant and believe in Rome's greatness and its divine destiny to rule the world. However, Messala's utterly uncritical devotion to Rome causes him to sneer at all non-Romans, and he constantly and rather naively eulogizes the glories of Rome. While just as dedicated to serving Rome, Arrius is more clear-eyed about the costs of imperialism, and although stern, possesses moral virtue. The rituals of naval combat in an oared galley are established in a marvelous scene in which Arrius visits the stinking, inferno-like hold where the rowers dwell, and issues a series of orders that steadily increase the rate of their rowing in order to assess their readiness for battle. As the *hortator* pounds out the rhythm on a massive drum, the ship's velocity is ratcheted up from regular to battle to attack speed, and finally to the frenetically paced ramming speed, causing several slaves to literally drop dead from exertion. The subtext in this scene is a

Figure 2.5. Galley Slave Scene from *Ben-Hur* (1959). This and other films have memorably promoted an ahistorical but indelible image of Roman warships being propelled by gangs of harshly abused slaves. *United Archives GmbH/Alamy Stock Photo*.

Figure 2.6. Real Roman Oarsmen. Reconstruction of rowers on a Roman warship. Although employed in an arduous profession, the oarsmen on both Greek and Roman galleys were actually free men who were paid for their service. *Illustration by Graham Sumner.*

battle of wills between Arrius and Judah, as the admiral attempts to break the defiance that he detects in the slave's eyes. This accurately conveys how exhausting such labor could be for the rowers, and how the maximum effort required for ramming speed could only be sustained for brief periods.

Figure 2.5 is a still from the film showing Heston and the other slaves hard at work at the oars. Figure 2.6 is a painting of how the interior of a Roman warship may have appeared. The exact arrangement of the rowers' seating is a perennial topic of contention among scholars, and there have been a number of experimental archaeology projects, including a full-size reconstruction of a Greek trireme, aimed at testing various theories.

When the enemy Macedonian fleet is sighted, we are treated to a spectacular naval battle. As the two fleets close on each other, there is an exchange of missiles, with catapults hurling explosive flaming pots, and archers shooting clouds of arrows. Such incendiaries were a part of ancient naval warfare and could be effective against wooden ships. However, they were nearly as dangerous to the user as to the target, and it is not clear whether they were employed quite so profligately as portrayed in the film. The climax of the naval battle occurs when an enemy vessel plunges its ram into the unprotected side of Arrius's flagship. We witness the strike from the perspective of the rowers, as the ram bursts through the hull in a shower of splinters and displaced planks. The enemy warriors swarm aboard, and hand-to-hand fighting ensues on deck, while below in the hold, water pours in. The slaves, who cannot escape the rising waters because they are shackled to their benches, start to drown. Just before the battle began, Arrius had ordered that Judah be unchained, and now, in the chaos, Judah manages to strangle a guard, steal his key, and release the other slaves.

These scenes offer a reasonable depiction of naval warfare and do a good job of capturing the horror and panic undoubtedly experienced by the men aboard a sinking vessel that has been rammed. The ships are a bit larger and of heavier construction than they would have been in reality, but this is a minor point. There is, however, one gigantic historical problem with this otherwise exciting sequence in the film. The men who pulled the oars aboard Roman warships were not slaves, and being condemned to serve in the galleys was not a standard judicial punishment in the Roman world. (For a detailed discussion of this topic, including the actual inspiration for galleys being rowed by slaves, see the entry for the 1925 Ben-Hur.)

The centerpiece of the movie and its most famous and most spectacular scene is the chariot race pitting Judah and his Roman rival Messala against one another, driving four-horse chariots. This contest takes place in Jerusalem in an arena shaped like an elongated horseshoe, which is obviously modeled on the great Circus Maximus chariot racing stadium at Rome. The Circus Maximus was an awe-inspiring venue a third of a mile long that could seat a quarter of a million spectators. The chariots raced around an oval track that had a divider known as the *spina*, or spine, down the middle. At each end of the *spina* were three tall cones known as the *metae*, which were the posts around which the chariots turned. On the *spina* were golden dolphins, which served as lap counters, with one dolphin being tipped or lowered as each lap was completed. The *spina* was adorned with various statues, obelisks, and fountains. All these features of the Circus Maximus are faithfully re-created in the movie's fictitious Jerusalem Circus. Historically, the starting signal for the race was the presiding magistrate dropping a cloth known as the *mappa*, a detail that the movie nicely replicates. The drama of the chariot race is captured in Figure 2.7, a still from the movie showing the four-horse chariots driven by Boyd

Figure 2.7. Chariot Race. The thrilling chariot race from *Ben-Hur* (1959). While the chariots are a bit heavier in construction than Roman ones likely would have been, most details are fairly accurate and the scene ably captures the excitement and danger of such races. *Screen Prod/Photononstop/Alamy Stock Photo.*

and Heston racing down the side of the *spina*. The cone-shaped turning posts (*metae*) are visible in the upper left-hand corner.

Some minor errors are that the movie's race consists of nine laps around the *spina*, there are nine chariots in total competing, and the starting line is near the center of the track in front of the magistrate's box. In a standard Roman chariot race, there would actually have been seven laps, not nine; twelve chariots instead of nine; and the racers would have begun inside a set of starting stalls called *carceres* at one far end of the arena. The film's chariots are also a bit heavier in construction than the very light and flimsy ones driven by Roman charioteers. Where the movie really shines is in communicating the drama, speed, and danger of a chariot race. The cinematographers magnificently capture the chariots flying at breakneck speed down the long straightaways on either side of the *spina*, accompanied by the pounding of the horses' hooves, and how the chariots bunched dangerously together as they slewed around the 180-degree turn at each *metae*, their wheels raising thick clouds of dust.

Real Roman chariot racing involved frequent, and often fatal, crashes, and the movie vividly portrays this, with over half the competitors failing to finish the race—smashing into the *spina*, colliding with each other, or losing wheels—with the result that the drivers are gruesomely trampled, a fate that was a common occurrence in ancient chariot racing. A number of Roman charioteers' tombstones record the cause of death as a crash in the Circus. It is worth emphasizing that *Ben-Hur*'s chariot race sequences were not achieved through CGI, miniatures, or other special effects trickery; instead, a full-size Circus was constructed at Cinecittà Studios in Rome, and stuntmen drove replica chariots drawn by teams of real horses. This immense Circus set occupied eighteen acres, cost $1 million, was excavated out of a rock quarry, boasted sides that were five stories high, featured straightaways that were fifteen hundred feet long, and used forty thousand tons of imported sand for the surface of the track. Fifteen thousand extras were employed as spectators in the Circus. Seventy-eight specially trained horses were imported from Sicily and Yugoslavia, and Heston, Boyd, and the stuntmen had to take an elaborate course on how to drive a chariot. Creating this lavish sequence required a full year of construction and practice, and then another three months to film. Incidentally, for nearly fifty years, the huge, crouching statues that decorated each end of the *spina* in the Circus set could still be seen rotting away in a field next to Cinecittà Studios. On a visit to Cinecittà in 1996, they were still there, but unfortunately, they have since been demolished.

There is no doubt that the sequence is a thrilling feat of moviemaking, and accurately captures many details of chariot racing; however, there are

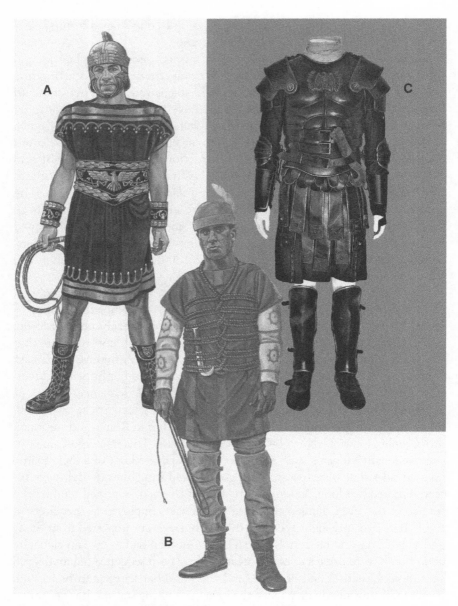

Figure 2.8. Charioteers. (A) Roman charioteer costume from *Ben-Hur* (1959). (B) Reconstruction of a Roman charioteer of the Green faction based on a Roman mosaic. He wears a protective leather harness on his chest and a helmet, probably of leather as well. (C) Rather fanciful Roman charioteer ensemble from *Ben-Hur* (2016). The only accurate aspect is the curved knife. *Illustrations by Graham Sumner. Photograph and props from The Terry Nix Collection.*

two major unhistorical aspects of this scene. In the movie, the different chariots represent various geographic places. Thus, Judah is identified as racing on behalf of the region of Judea, while Messala races for Rome, and the other charioteers are named as competing for Athens, Carthage, Corinth, Phrygia, Alexandria, Messenia, and Cyprus. In reality, like pro athletes today, Roman charioteers performed as representatives of professional teams. The four main chariot racing teams of the Roman world, known as factions, were distinguished by the colors each wore and thus were called the Blues, the Greens, the Reds, and the Whites.

In a standard Roman chariot race, there was a total of twelve chariots in the race, with each of the four factions entering three chariots. The three chariots of a given faction would work together, attempting to clear a path for their star driver and obstructing or hindering the chariots of the other factions. The interplay among the chariots of each team and the strategies they deployed against their rivals would have been one of the most important and exciting characteristics of ancient chariot racing, and it is a shame that no movie has yet attempted to re-create this feature of Roman entertainment. Figure 2.8 portrays the chariot driver ensemble worn by Boyd (A) consisting of a simple cloth tunic and a metal helmet. For comparison, the reconstruction painting (B) shows a driver of the Green faction as pictured in a surviving ancient mosaic now in the Palazzo Massimo in Rome. He is attired in a protective leather chest harness and skullcap-like helmet in his faction's color.

Romans would pick one of these factions to follow, and much like sports fans today, dress in the appropriate colors, sit in blocks with other enthusiasts of their faction, and exchange verbal taunts and abuse with the adherents of rival teams. While current fans like to boast about how passionately they support their team, ancient Roman fans were just as enthusiastic, if not more so. For example, when a star charioteer of the Red faction named Felix was killed in a crash, one distraught fan flung himself onto the pyre at his funeral, immolating himself along with his hero.

A second notable inaccuracy is that Messala's chariot wheels are equipped with long blades that viciously spin as the wheels revolve, with which he intimidates his opponents and slices apart their chariots. There is no attested instance of such blades being employed in any Roman chariot race, although similar weapons are known to have been used on ancient battlefields. For example, at the Battle of Gaugamela fought between Alexander the Great and the Persian King Darius III in 331 BC, the Persian army included a large number of chariots with blades attached to their wheels.

In the end, *Ben-Hur* not only saved MGM Studios, but became perhaps the most famous of all ancient epic films. Recently, the American Film Institute ranked it second among the Top Epics of all time. It was both a commercial and a critical triumph. It was even a merchandising sensation since, in the two years following its release, $20 million of *Ben-Hur* themed merchandise was sold to the public, ranging from toy chariots and armor to candy and gasoline to matching towel sets labeled "Ben-His" and "Ben-Hers." Its success ensured that Hollywood would make more historical epics, and the next few years experienced a glut of high-profile, big-budget films set in the ancient world.

Spartacus (1960)

Director: Stanley Kubrick
Producer: Edward Lewis
Production Company: Universal-International
Cast: Kirk Douglas (Spartacus), Laurence Olivier (Crassus), Jean Simmons (Varinia), Peter Ustinov (Batiatus), Tony Curtis (Antoninus), Woody Strode (Draba), John Ireland (Crixus), Charles Laughton (Gracchus)

Although technically released in the first year of the next decade, *Spartacus* (1960) is most appropriately categorized as part of the Golden Era string of 1950s epics that were both commercial and critical successes. *Spartacus* was Universal Studios' attempt to match the triumph that MGM had enjoyed with *Ben-Hur* (1959), and the core plot of the film is based on famous actual events. In 73 BC, a slave named Spartacus was being trained at a gladiator school run by Lentulus Batiatus located near the southern Italian city of Capua. This Spartacus led the gladiators in a rebellion, and about seventy escaped into the countryside and took refuge on Mount Vesuvius, from which they raided nearby plantations, freed more slaves, and built a slave army that ultimately numbered more than one hundred thousand. For several years, they roamed Italy, defying repeated attempts by the Romans to suppress their insurrection. Eventually, one of the leading Roman politicians of the time, Marcus Licinius Crassus, led a concerted effort by several Roman armies against the rebels and defeated them. As a deterrent against future rebellion, six thousand captured slaves were crucified along the Appian Way. Since the movie conforms to these historically attested facts, one can say it is accurate to that extent.

So where are there differences? One concerns the background and experiences of Spartacus himself. In the film, it is explicitly stated that he was born a slave in the region of Thrace to a mother who was also a slave, and that before the age of thirteen, he was sentenced to labor in the mines of Libya. Later in the movie, when at the gladiator school, he meets and falls in love with a fellow slave, a woman named Varinia, who is identified as being from Britain. While this life story effectively dramatizes the genuinely horrible nature of slavery as an institution, it is invented. The real Spartacus was born a free Thracian who, upon reaching adulthood, fought for Rome as a paid auxiliary. He seems to have deserted from the army and become a bandit, but was captured and, as punishment, sentenced to slavery and sent to the gladiator school. The ancient author Plutarch notes that Spartacus did have a wife, but says she was a Thracian from the same tribe as he was and mentions the interesting detail that she was a prophetess, given to pronouncing oracles in an ecstatic frenzy—certainly not something shown in the movie. Unfortunately, Plutarch does not record her name, but we can be sure that it would not have been Varinia since, rather than being a Thracian name, it is the feminized version of a traditional Roman family name, Varinius. The moviemakers probably changed her nationality from Thracian to British for no better reason than that Jean Simmons, the actress who plays her, was British.

By the way, Jean Simmons's Britishness is an unusual exception to the standard "aural paradigm" found in almost all ancient Hollywood epics made during the 1950s, whereby Romans were played by actors with upper-class British accents, while their oppressed antagonists, usually either Christians or slaves, were portrayed by Americans. The three main Roman roles—Crassus, his political rival Gracchus, and gladiator school owner Batiatus—were all performed by esteemed British thespians with aristocratic demeanors: Laurence Olivier as Crassus, Charles Laughton as Gracchus, and Peter Ustinov as Batiatus. In contrast, the male slaves are a thoroughly American crew including Kirk Douglas as Spartacus, John Ireland as his lieutenant, Crixus, and Tony Curtis as slave boy and singer-of-songs, Antoninus. Both in attitude and accent, Curtis makes a particularly unconvincing Roman; as the reviewer for *Time* magazine commented, his performance "suggests that the ancient Tiber is a tributary of the Bronx River."[2] Initially a German actress, Sabine Bethmann, was to play Varinia, but when her performance proved unsatisfactory, she was replaced at the last minute by the British Simmons, who had already appeared in a number of ancient epics.

The film also misrepresents Spartacus's goals and historical legacy. In the movie, he is repeatedly depicted as a freedom fighter whose objective is not merely to escape servitude but to destroy the entire institution of slavery. This is established right at the outset in the narrated prologue, which states that "under whip and chain and sun he lived out his youth and young manhood, dreaming the death of slavery two thousand years before it finally would die."

In addition to being the star of the film, Kirk Douglas was the producer as well, and had been responsible both for initiating the project and selecting Spartacus as its subject. In his autobiography, Douglas reveals that the idea of Spartacus as a kind of proto-abolitionist was what drew him to the topic in the first place: "I was intrigued with the story of Spartacus the slave, dreaming of the death of slavery, driving into the armor of Rome the wedge that would eventually destroy her."[3] In reality, Spartacus never seems to have harbored any such grand ambitions, but rather was much more narrowly focused on gaining freedom for himself and his immediate companions.

Douglas's words also expose an even more grandiose thesis promulgated by the filmmakers: the Roman Empire's collapse was due to its reliance on slavery, and that Spartacus's revolt directly contributed to that fall. The prologue suggests this when it describes the Roman Republic as "fatally stricken" with the disease of slavery, and Stan Margulies, the director of publicity for the film, clearly revealed the filmmakers' intent in a memo that proclaimed: "Our conclusion . . . is that Spartacus set in motion a chain of events that led to the fall of Rome, and that is why he is remembered."[4] This is a heroic interpretation that both ennobles Spartacus and makes him a pivotal figure in history. Unfortunately, the reality is less inspirational. Slavery does not seem to have been one of the key factors in the collapse of the empire, nor did Spartacus's rebellion initiate a growing movement challenging slavery. To the contrary, rather than representing the beginning of resistance, Spartacus's revolt marked the end of organized opposition. In the decades prior to Spartacus, there had been several other major slave rebellions, which clearly served as models for him; but after Spartacus, there were no more large-scale slave revolts ever again in Roman history. Perhaps the cruel execution of the six thousand captured rebels did indeed deter future uprisings. There is no doubt that Spartacus became an important symbol of freedom and opposition to slavery for later civilizations, but his effect on subsequent Roman history seems to have been fairly negligible.

The scenes in the gladiator school shamelessly copy quite a lot from 1954's *Demetrius and the Gladiators*, but they are nevertheless memorable and enthralling, and, on the whole, they provide a reasonably plausible re-creation. We don't know exactly how such training was conducted, but the use of wooden practice weapons is likely, since this exercise was attested for training Roman army recruits. Two inaccuracies are that the Romans did not brand their slaves as shown, nor was a short curl of hair worn at the back of the head as the mark of being a gladiator. When a private bout between Spartacus and an experienced gladiator named Draba is staged for the amusement of Crassus, we are treated to a display of combat techniques and weapons that are also authentic. Gladiators were trained to battle in one of several dozen specific styles, with equipment unique to each. Appropriately, Spartacus fights in the style of a Thracian, with a very small metal shield, a short sword, and minimal armor. His sword is not quite right, but otherwise the details are well done. The Thracian style favored speed and dexterity, and the athletic Douglas does a good job with the role. See Figure 5.3 for a reconstruction of the equipment used by a Thracian-style gladiator. Draba is a *retiarius*, who wields a trident in one hand and a net in the other. This was one of the most unusual styles, and Draba, as played by former professional football player Woody Strode, skillfully and realistically employs the net, repeatedly attempting to trip up Spartacus and then impale him with the trident. Draba ultimately defeats Spartacus, but when Crassus and his companions call for his death, Draba refuses and defiantly hurls the trident at them before being slain by a guard.

The real-life Spartacus fought over a dozen skirmishes and battles against Roman military forces, winning most of them, and looted four large cities, but almost none of this makes it into the movie. Other than a very brief night assault on a Roman camp, we see none of Spartacus's very impressive military victories. The only battle portrayed in detail is the final one against Crassus, in which the slave army is decisively defeated. For this scene, filmed in Spain, director Stanley Kubrick was able to employ ten thousand soldiers from the Spanish army. The best element of this spectacular sequence is not the warfare itself, but the lead-up to it, where we witness the slave army and the Roman legions facing off on opposite sides of a valley. Spartacus's troops are assembled in a resolute but disordered mass, and a series of pans along the line emphasizes the diversity of the rebels, including old and young, men and women. The slaves are realistically armed with a wide range of weapons and armor that they have scavenged from one source or another over the course of their rebellion.

By comparison, the Roman troops are always seen from a distance as orderly masses of identically equipped and faceless soldiers. The manner in which these scenes are shot transforms the Roman army into an impersonal machine of oppression, in contrast to the obvious humanity of the slaves. One of the best sequences in the entire movie occurs when the Roman army begins to march methodically across the valley while maintaining its perfect formations. Kubrick filmed this deployment from the slaves' side of the valley at a distance of half a mile, with the cameras mounted on towers a hundred feet tall. One of the primary characteristics of the Roman military was discipline, and no scene in any movie has better illustrated this quality than this image of thousands of men arrayed in precise blocks slowly, impla-

Figure 2.9.   Foes of Spartacus. (A) Roman sword, dagger, and scabbards used in *Spartacus* (1960). The sword appears to be the general shape of a Roman *gladius* but is not based on any specific archaeological find. (B) Roman "Captain" from *Spartacus* (1960) in an unusual combination of a leather jerkin over mail armor. (C) Roman legionary from *Spartacus* (1960) with leather muscle cuirass and "Italic-style" helmet. *Illustrations by Graham Sumner.*

cably, relentlessly moving forward, then smoothly shifting formation into a battle line as they approach the enemy. There are no sounds other than the heavy tramping of their massed feet and the jingle of their armor, an effect sound effects wizard Jack Foley allegedly produced by shaking a set of keys. Saul Bass, who worked on the film and choreographed the movements of the soldiers, has stated, "I wanted to suggest a certain precision, a mechanization and geometry. . . . The slaves had a lack of precision. They had no precise uniforms, they lined up, but were never straight. We were trying to project the soulless Roman army against the soulful slave army."[5]

Military historians have correctly pointed out the many flaws in this scene. At this period, Roman soldiers were supplied by the state, and the limited sources available suggest that they would have worn a mail shirt (*lorica hamata*) and a simple bronze helmet and carried a large rectangular shield (*scutum*). Since this was not generally considered by Hollywood as looking distinctively "Roman," movies usually equipped Roman legionaries of all periods in a version of the *lorica segmentata* body armor, formed of rigid strips of metal, which was worn by Roman soldiers during the early imperial period. As illustrated in Figure 2.9, the legionaries in *Spartacus* wear a completely unhistorical leather muscle cuirass with leather strips (*pteruges*) hanging from shoulders and waist, and what appear to be helmets of the later imperial "Italic" type. Also, they are embarrassingly holding their shields the wrong way (horizontally rather than vertically). Finally, those wonderful-looking formations are actually totally incorrect. If they resemble anything historically Roman, they are perhaps closer to formations used by the Romans several hundred years earlier, rather than the ones employed during the late republic. Despite all this, the deployment sequence is still a spine-tingling one that conveys something essential about the implacable nature of the Roman war machine.

Once the fighting starts, all realism goes out the door. First, the slaves unleash a series of flaming logs on the advancing Romans, which is visually exciting but completely unattested, and seems to have been included to satisfy the usual Hollywood insistence on adding some sort of pyrotechnics to any pre-gunpowder-era depiction of warfare. Much worse is that, as soon as contact occurs between the two forces, the Romans promptly abandon their wonderfully precise formations and instead fight as a disorderly mob, with the rest of the battle deteriorating into a chaotic free-for-all. While turning every combat scene into a random melee seems to be a Hollywood convention, just once it would be nice to see a professional ancient army act like one onscreen, maintaining its discipline and formations. Oddly, during his final battle, the real-life Spartacus behaved more like a fictitious Hollywood hero than his movie counterpart does. In the film, Spartacus fairly passively observes the initial skirmishes, calmly orders the fire log attack, and then leads an ineffectual mounted charge, with the viewer eventually losing sight of him in the confusion. As described by Plutarch, however, the historical Spartacus comes off more like a true action movie hero. He delivers an inspiring speech that ends with him dramatically plunging his sword into his own horse's neck, thus demonstrating his commitment to live or die with his men, who do not have horses. He then boldly charges into battle on foot, with the goal of personally attacking Crassus, but is slain before reaching him.

Despite its ancient subject matter, *Spartacus* became embroiled in contemporary American politics and marked an important moment in the McCarthyist anti-Communist movement. Additionally, although the film seems to espouse a very pro-American message advocating freedom, it became the target of conservative and religious groups who boycotted it and condemned it as being anti-American. To understand how this came about, one must look at the post-classical reputation of Spartacus. He remained a minor figure in Roman history up until the era of the Enlightenment, when intellectuals interested in individual human rights began to praise him as an early example of a freedom fighter and as an embodiment of the eternal struggle against totalitarian states and repressive governmental forces. Voltaire, for example, effused over Spartacus and wrote that his rebellion was "a just war, indeed the only just war in history."[6] By the nineteenth and twentieth centuries, Spartacus had been transformed into a catch-all symbol for fighting oppression generally. Spartacus's admirers spanned a wide political spectrum; in addition to individuals such as America's Founding Fathers, they included Karl Marx, who stated that Spartacus was "the most excellent fellow in the whole history of antiquity. A great general . . . of noble character, a real representative of the proletariat of ancient times."[7]

In the aftermath of World War II, spurred on by leaders like Senator Joe McCarthy, anti-Communist fervor resulted in the House Un-American Activities Committee investigating alleged Communists in the United States. Hollywood was decried as a hotbed of supposed Communist sympathizers, and in 1947, the committee held hearings interrogating prominent members of the film industry suspected of Communist leanings. When they refused to answer questions, a group of them known as the "Hollywood 10" was imprisoned and blacklisted by the industry, meaning that the major film studios would not hire them. Although the Communist affiliation of some of the "Hollywood 10" was debatable, one person who legitimately harbored Communist sympathies was popular novelist Howard Fast. While in prison, Fast got the idea of writing a novel about Spartacus, but since he was blacklisted by the publishing industry, he ended up self-publishing the book in 1951. It turned out to be a huge success and a bestseller. In Fast's novel, Spartacus is a true proto-Marxist hero fighting against capitalism and imperialism as embodied by the corrupt Roman Republic. In one speech, Fast's Spartacus echoes Marxist rhetoric, proclaiming, "And to the slaves of the world, we will cry out, Rise up and cast off your chains!"[8] The book was even awarded the Stalin Peace Prize of 1954. Meanwhile, having been passed over for the role of Ben-Hur, Kirk Douglas was eager to make his own ancient epic, and chose Fast's popular novel as its basis. Douglas opposed the Hollywood blacklisting, and because his film originated outside the studio system, he was able to hire Dalton Trumbo, one of the original blacklisted "Hollywood Ten," as the scriptwriter. Trumbo had been writing under pseudonyms, but Douglas intended to credit Trumbo under his own name, defying the blacklist.

Elements of the screenplay could be viewed as vaguely Communist. Thus, there are a number of scenes depicting the harmonious society that the slaves form on Mt. Vesuvius, in which collective action and equality are stressed. Recalling the Marxist adage of "from each according to his ability, to each according to his need," newcomers to the slave army are given roles that best suit their talents, such as when actor Tony Curtis is quizzed by Spartacus to ascertain whether he has any practical skills. On the other hand, the same scenes could just as well be interpreted as representing an idealized early Christian community, such as a medieval monastery, where all property and possessions were shared and tasks were accomplished communally. Nevertheless, the involvement of Fast and Trumbo drew the ire of anti-Communist groups of the time. The influential American Legion called for a boycott of *Spartacus*, and some right-wing and religious groups organized pickets of the film. A key turning point came when President John F. Kennedy, instead of watching the new movie at a private viewing in the White House as was common, attended a showing at a public theater in Washington, crossing a picket line to do so. Afterward, he commented favorably on the film. His actions, combined with the movie's commercial success, did much to legitimize it in the public eye, and these developments effectively ended Hollywood's blacklist era.

If this was not enough politics for one film, it also got embroiled in some controversies concerning gender and race. As one might expect, Hollywood films of the era tended to reflect a fairly conservative social outlook when it came to gender roles and sexuality. Previous films set in the ancient world embodied these cultural mores, with the "good" female characters portrayed exclusively as being virginally chaste, modest, and submissive, while only the "bad" women displayed overt sexuality or aggressiveness. *Spartacus*, however, controversially depicted the character of Varinia as both much more sexually experienced than Spartacus and as unapologetically enjoying her sexuality, as in a famous scene in which she bathes naked and openly invites Spartacus to look at her. Since this was occurring within the context of a genuinely loving, committed, and mutually respectful relationship, from a current perspective, one might wonder why it was considered so transgressive, but it was something novel for ancient epics of that time. Upon viewing an early edit of the film, the ratings board was horrified, demanding that the line about Spartacus's inexperience be removed and declaring the bathing scene "unacceptable." Nonetheless, these elements managed to stay in the movie.

Another scene vigorously condemned by the board was an infamous one in which Crassus, who is being bathed by his slave Antoninus, delivers a suggestive speech during which he propositions him. Known as the "oysters and snails" monologue because Crassus expresses his bisexuality through the metaphor that his tastes include both "oysters and snails," this scene was purged from the film entirely, although later restorations have reinstated it.

Finally, the film touched on race in its (for the time) atypically positive representation of the Black gladiator Draba, who spares Spartacus's life. This was an era when Blacks in film were often presented as either savages or comic relief, but Draba, as portrayed by African American actor Woody Strode and the filmmakers, is a figure of great nobility and dignity. It is Draba's act of self-sacrifice and defiance against his masters that awakens Spartacus's political consciousness and directly inspires him to rebel and seek freedom for the slaves.

Despite all of this controversy, *Spartacus* was a solid hit both commercially and critically; it won four Oscars, including Best Supporting Actor for Ustinov's delightful turn as gladiator school owner Batiatus. It also produced an unforgettable meme in the scene where Crassus is seeking Spartacus among the survivors of the battle in order to torture him, but before Spartacus can reveal himself, all of the slaves stand up and shout, "I am Spartacus!" in a show of solidarity. However, *Spartacus* would be the last of this era's ancient epics to achieve such success, as the genre's excesses would soon precipitate its downfall.

CHAPTER THREE

~

The Early 1960s

The Ancient Epic Veers into Cliché and Hits an Indulgent Pinnacle

By the late 1950s and early 1960s, the Golden Age of the Hollywood big-budget, high-prestige, ancient epic was drawing to a close. Nevertheless, this era gave birth to several spin-off variants. One was the campy "sword-and-sandal" or "peplum" film, characterized by musclemen and monsters and often filmed on the cheap in Italy, then dubbed into English. While many were pure fantasy, a few, such as *The Last Days of Pompeii* (1959/1960 US) and *Hannibal* (1959/1960 US), were at least loosely grounded in actual history. The 1960s also saw a resurgence of epics based on the Bible and early Christianity. Among these were two reverent big-budget biographies of Jesus, *King of Kings* (1961) and *The Greatest Story Ever Told* (1965), as well as *Constantine and the Cross* (1961/1962 US), a rare attempt to tell the story of the first Roman emperor to convert to Christianity. The era came to a crashing halt with three lavish productions—*Cleopatra* (1963), *The Fall of the Roman Empire* (1964), and *The Greatest Story Ever Told* (1965)—that were so self-indulgent, and lost so much money, that one studio was driven into permanent bankruptcy, a second was nearly destroyed, and the career of a once-hot director was effectively ended.

The Last Days of Pompeii (1959/1960 US)

Directors: Mario Bonnard, Sergio Leone
Producer: Paolo Moffa
Production Company: Cineproduzioni/Procusa/Transocean

Cast: Steve Reeves (Glaucus), Christine Kaufmann (Ione), Fernando Rey (Arbaces), Barbara Carroll (Nydia), Anne-Marie Baumann (Julia), Ángel Aranda (Antoninus)

Yet another cinematic rendering of Edward Bulwer-Lytton's immensely popular nineteenth-century novel, this was an international coproduction filmed in Italy that blended elements of the book with various clichés of the peplum/muscleman genre. Like the 1935 film of the same name (see chapter 1), it takes considerable liberties with the novel, using many of the same character names but giving them different identities and introducing completely new plot strands. The most bizarre of these involves a mysterious marauding band of hooded raiders who conduct home invasions of the villas of Pompeii's wealthy citizens, murdering the inhabitants and plundering their riches, then scrawling the Christian cross on the walls. This results in persecution of the city's improbably large Christian population, who are subjected to sadistic cruelties in an elaborate torture chamber that seems lifted straight from a lurid film about the Spanish Inquisition. Of course, in the end, it is revealed that the raiders are actually agents of the cult of Isis masquerading as Christians, who are plotting a massive rebellion against Rome in order to reestablish Egypt as an independent kingdom. None of this bears any resemblance whatsoever to actual Roman history.

The film then piles on the standard components of a peplum flick, with a muscle-bound hero played by American bodybuilder-turned-actor Steve Reeves, fresh off his audience-pleasing performances as legendary strongman Hercules in *Hercules* (1958) and *Hercules Unchained* (1959). As the burly Roman centurion Glaucus, Reeves unravels the mystery of the hooded gang while performing sweaty feats of strength: wrestling a crocodile, breaking thick iron chains and bars to escape from prison, heaving aside massive beams to save accident victims, stopping a runaway chariot, slaying a lion, and dueling against sundry villains.

Films set in the ancient world often garble Roman titles and ranks, but this one is particularly bad in this regard. "Praetorians," who were the emperor's personal bodyguards stationed at Rome, are erroneously used as local police in Pompeii. One character is labeled as a "tribune," but he does not seem to exercise the duties of either a military tribune or a tribune of the plebs. Glaucus has far too much authority and status for any centurion, which was a relatively low rank in the Roman military. One oddity of the film is that, whereas the set designs are pretty decent, the costumes are atrocious. There are a faithfully replicated Pompeian street corner and reasonably accurate props in the interior scenes, as well as copies of actual Pompeian wall paintings adorning the villas. However, Reeves and the other main male leads cavort about in ridiculous, skimpy, off-the-shoulder tunics clearly inspired by his stint as Hercules; the military attire is wrong (especially Glaucus's "centurion" outfit); and the clothes on the other characters are pure fantasy.

There was actually a Temple of Isis at Pompeii, though not on as grand a scale as the one in the film, nor presumably did it have a lever-activated trap door in front of the altar to precipitate unwelcome visitors into a basement den of crocodiles. The film takes a somewhat more historical turn at the very end, when Vesuvius finally erupts (conveniently timed to save the Christians from death in the amphitheater), and the last twenty minutes present standard disaster movie fare as the volcano spews, the city crumbles, and the inhabitants run screaming. These scenes are entertaining in a cheesy way, and the special effects are serviceable, with some convincing moments of extras dodging collapsing walls, flying sparks, and flaming debris. The final scene of the refugees fleeing in boats is a nice touch, attested in ancient sources.

Reeves would star in numerous low-budget sword-and-sandal films over the next few years before retiring due to injuries suffered while performing stunts. Director Mario Bonnard fell ill after only a few days, so most of the film was shot by assistant director Sergio Leone, who would go on to greater fame once he shifted genres and began making Spaghetti Westerns several years later. The sensationalist flavor of this film—and really of the entire peplum genre—is perfectly summed up by a promotional poster, which deserves to be quoted in full, breathlessly exclaiming: "SEE! SEE! SEE! The Yawning Jaws of the Flesh-Ripping Alligator Death Pit! The Martyred Christians Thrown to the Gaping Fangs of Hungry Lions! The Centurion Colossus in Battle with the Blood-Hungry Beasts! The Shameless Orgy As Drunken Pompeii Abandons Itself to the Goddess Isis! The Pillaging, Plundering Black-Hooded Death Riders! The Awesome Eruption of Mt. Vesuvius as it Avalanches Down into a Boiling Inferno! The Dungeon of a Thousand Tortures for the Shrieking Damned! The Slave Girls at the Mercy of Their Bestial Conquerors! Pompeii! City of the Pagan Hordes . . . City of Beasts and Battles . . . of Revels and Orgies . . . of Spectacle and Splendour! The City That Lived in Sin and Died in Flame!"

Hannibal (1959/1960 US)

Director: Edgar Ulmer
Producer: Ottavio Poggi
Production Company: Liber Films
Cast: Victor Mature (Hannibal), Rita Gam (Sylvia), Gabriele Ferzetti (Fabius Maximus), Mario Girotti (Quintilius), Rik Battaglia (Hasdrubal)

This low-budget Italian-made film awkwardly combines stereotyped elements of the peplum genre with plot points drawn from one of the more dramatic episodes in Roman history, the invasion of Italy by the Carthaginian general Hannibal during the Second Punic War (218–201 BC). The title role is played by that beefy staple of ancient epics Victor Mature, Rita Gam is his love interest, and the rest of the cast is rounded out with Italian actors. The movie is an uneasy concoction of a bit of accurate history, a lot of rather wooden acting, an extremely contrived and unconvincing love story, and some visibly cheap effects.

On the positive side, the opening scenes of Hannibal's army crossing the Alps are quite thrilling. We see long lines of heavily burdened troops and pack animals struggling up narrow, treacherous trails through the majestic ice- and snow-covered mountains. The hazards of the journey are emphasized, and more than one shot features unfortunate soldiers losing their footing and dramatically plummeting off the cliffside to their deaths below, where their corpses are scavenged by opportunistic wolves. One of the most impressive aspects of Hannibal's crossing was that he brought along about forty war elephants and managed to get at least some of them to Italy. The filmmakers rented half a dozen elephants, which are prominently showcased being coaxed up the slopes by their handlers. The transit of the Alps is a largely nonverbal sequence that effectively conveys the scale of Hannibal's achievement as well as its dangers and difficulty, and it is one of the best parts of the movie.

Another good part of the film is the scenes set in the senate, where Roman senators clad in historically accurate togas engage in lively debates, shouting and gesticulating at one another in an animated but dignified way that rings more true than in many more "serious" films. The script contains a number of details that reveal a knowledge of history: Hannibal lists the diverse peoples who make up his army, including Numidians, North African cavalry, various tribes from the Iberian Peninsula, and Carthaginians; Hannibal notes that, when crossing the Alps, he lost almost half of his army; Hannibal remarks that strategic victory in the war will depend on persuading Rome's allies to switch sides; and one of Hannibal's generals criticizes him by saying, "You know how to win victories, but you don't know how to follow them up"—a line taken directly from the ancient Roman historian Livy. Some other historical episodes include the Romans tossing the head of Hannibal's brother, Hasdrubal, over the wall of Hannibal's camp to prove that Hasdrubal's army had been defeated; the double-envelopment strategy that Hannibal employs against the Romans at the Battle of Cannae, which Mature illustrates in the film using wine cups; and a reference to the traditional Roman punishment of burying alive priestesses of Vesta who have broken their vows of chastity.

The big battle scenes are a mixed bag. The Battle of the Trebia, at which the elephants did indeed play a key role, is energetically and correctly staged on the banks of the river, and the stunt men gamely do their best to make it look like the elephants are furiously rampaging about, but it is a little too obvious that they are just good-naturedly ambling along beside their handlers. When they seize soldiers with their trunks or pretend to stomp on them, this comes across more like circus tricks rather than deadly warfare. While these scenes are fun to watch, they don't quite live up to the breathless catchphrase repeated in all of the film's promotional material: "Hannibal and his crazed elephant army are coming! Half a world gets trampled!" The elephants also hang around a bit too long in the movie, since in reality, just after the Battle of the Trebia, all but one of the remaining pachyderms froze to death.

On the negative side, the filmmakers apparently felt obliged to invent a truly absurd and improbable love story between Hannibal and Sylvia, a fictitious niece of the real Roman politician and general Fabius Maximus. The ridiculous love story takes up an inordinate amount of the film, and there isn't much chemistry between Mature and Gam. The climactic Battle of Cannae, which was a large set-piece clash between two armies on an open field, is scaled down and transformed into a smallish ambush that quickly degenerates into a chaotic free-for-all of wildly hacking soldiers. This is the complete opposite of what actually happened at Cannae, which was a carefully planned battle involving precise formations and movements. After the tragic resolution of the love story, the movie comes to an abrupt and unsatisfying conclusion, leaving both Hannibal's invasion of Italy and the war itself unresolved.

The career of Hannibal is one of the most dramatic in all of ancient history, so it is surprising that there has not yet been a big-budget attempt to capture it on film. If one keeps expectations low, this rather campy but intermittently knowledgeable movie can be entertaining.

King of Kings (1961)

Director: Nicholas Ray
Producer: Samuel Bronston
Production Company: Metro-Goldwyn-Mayer
Cast: Jeffrey Hunter (Jesus), Siobhan McKenna (Mary), Hurd Hatfield (Pontius Pilate), Ron Randell (Lucius), Robert Ryan (John the Baptist), Rip Torn (Judas), Harry Guardino (Barabbas), Frank Thring (Herod Antipas), Viveca Lindfors (Claudia), Rita Gam (Herodias), Brigid Bazlen (Salome), Royal Dano (Peter)

During the early 1960s, Samuel Bronston set up a production company in Spain to take advantage of lower costs and churned out a rapid succession of notable historical films, such as *El Cid* (1961) and *55 Days at Peking* (1963), which mingled heroic adventure with at least some concern for historical accuracy. Bronston's foray into the ancient world was *King of Kings* (1961), an ambitious attempt to tell the story of the life of Jesus. Although Jesus frequently made cameos in the ancient epics of the 1950s, such as *Quo Vadis* and *Ben-Hur*, he appeared only briefly and indirectly, as a shadow or an arm; no major studio movie since Cecil B. DeMille's silent-era *King of Kings* (1927) had based an entire film on his life or shown his face onscreen. Whereas the earlier *King of Kings* had just focused on Jesus's final days, Bronston aspired not only to cover the major episodes of his entire life, but also to set his life and ministry within their larger historical context. The film thus begins with Pompey the Great's siege and conquest of Jerusalem in 63 BC and contains sequences dealing with Jewish rebels and political intrigue among the Jewish priests, Herod the Great, and the members of Herod's family who ruled as Roman client kings or tetrarchs over Judea and Galilee.

Pompey's capture of Jerusalem and his desecration of the Temple by entering its sanctuary are dramatically portrayed. The filmmakers have his troops massacre a line of silently protesting Jewish priests in order to gain entrance, and it is true that thousands of Jews were killed during this siege. One inaccuracy is that the voice-over narration places great emphasis on Pompey being primarily motivated by greed for the Temple's fabled treasures, only to be disappointed when the Sanctuary holds nothing but a Torah scroll. The ancient Jewish historian Josephus informs us that, in reality, the Temple did indeed contain golden objects as well as two thousand talents of money—an enormous sum—but that Pompey took none of it due to his respect for religion.

Another interesting historical moment occurs when Pontius Pilate greatly offends the Jews by placing Roman imperial images on the walls of the Temple. Josephus and another ancient Jewish historian, Philo, both mention this incident, although the images were actually mounted on the walls of Herod's palace rather than in the Temple. In *King of Kings*, the images take the form of colossal coins of Emperor Tiberius, whereas in reality they were either gilded shields or military standards. The film appropriately highlights the demonstrations against these images, and the fact that Pilate stubbornly refused to remove them. What the film fails to show is that Jewish leaders then sent a petition directly to Tiberius himself, who ordered Pilate to transfer the objects to the less inflammatory location of the Temple of Augustus in Caesarea, the provincial capital. These are relatively minor issues, however. More problematic is that the film greatly enhances Pilate's status by depicting him as being married to the daughter of Tiberius. Not only was Pilate a very unimportant figure in the empire, but Tiberius did not even have a daughter.

As usual, the film suggests that Rome had far more troops stationed in the region than it did, and also that they took a more active role in events than was probably the case. For example, the massacre of the innocents is portrayed as having been carried out by Roman legionaries, but at that time, there were no Roman legionaries stationed in the area; thus, the troops involved would almost certainly have been Herod's own mercenaries. While notionally a biography of Jesus, the film nevertheless manages to include two rather large battles between Jewish rebels and the Roman army. In order to insert these action sequences, the filmmakers take the biblical figure of Barabbas and invent an entire plot line around him, in which he serves as a Jewish leader who advocates violent action against the Romans. In the gospels, Barabbas is described as a "murderer" or "rioter" being held in prison at the same time as Jesus, and when Pilate gives the people of Jerusalem the opportunity to free one prisoner, they choose Barabbas instead of Jesus. That is pretty much all the Bible says about him, but in the film, he is the leader of a large group of Jewish rebels, whom the narrator labels the "Messiah of War" in contrast to Jesus, the "Messiah of Peace." Early in the movie, Barabbas and his men ambush Pilate's army in the countryside, and he later leads a combined force of Zealot warriors and local civilians in an all-out assault against the Roman fortress of Antonia in Jerusalem. There certainly were insurrections by Jews against Roman rule, but the insertion of these violent battle sequences among the episodes of Jesus's ministry seems jarring. During the ambush, the rebels realistically employ slings to pepper the legionaries with rocks—a welcome inclusion of an important weapon of the ancient world that is often omitted from movies.

As can be seen in Figure 3.1, which contrasts a legionary from the film (A) with a reconstructed legionary (C) of this era (as well as one [B] from the 2016 *Ben-Hur*), there are significant problems with the equipment of the film's Roman soldiers. They completely lack the plates that should protect the chest and upper back, leaving them rather vulnerable looking. They also carry very odd heart-shaped shields that are quite unlike the distinctive rectangular *scutum* borne by legionaries. These shields have likely been recycled from an earlier MGM movie, *Solomon and Sheba*, in which they were carried by Egyptian troops, and have been repurposed by simply painting them with the Roman wings-and-thunderbolts design. Both films were shot in Spain, and many of the Jewish forces are shown using a *falcata*, a type of curved sword that was popular in ancient Spain, but not in Judea. Equally problematic are the costumes of the film's centurions (see Figure 1.5.B), who wear leather

Figure 3.1. Marching Through Judea. (A) Legionary from *King of Kings* (1961). (B) Marching legionary from *Ben-Hur* (2016) with odd ammo-pouch-like bags across the chest. See Figure 5.7 for photographs of props carried by marching legionaries in this film. (C) Reconstruction of a first-century AD legionary on the march, with accurate equipment. *Illustrations by Graham Sumner.*

cuirasses and completely unhistorical large metal arm guards rather than the chain mail shirts and other equipment (see Figure 1.5.C) that they probably would have had.

When we turn to the actual events of Jesus's life as described in the Bible, they are faithfully and reverently presented, and include all the scenes of Jesus preaching, healing the sick, and instructing his disciples that one would expect. Jesus is played by Jeffrey Hunter, whose curly auburn locks and bright blue eyes are striking, if perhaps not typical of the inhabitants of that region. His matinee-idol looks led critics to derisively refer to the film as "I Was a Teenage Jesus," but to be fair, attempting to portray Jesus is a rather thankless task in which you are never going to please everyone. While Siobhan McKenna gives a dignified performance as Mary, in appearance and accent she is so obviously Irish that it is distracting. As for the rest of the cast, Robert Ryan makes an energetic and shaggy John the Baptist, Frank Thring hams it up as a sleazy Herod Antipas, Hurd Hatfield portrays a sternly reserved Pontius Pilate, and Ron Randell is good as Lucius, a fictitious Roman centurion torn between his loyalty to Rome and his sympathy for Jesus.

The Sermon on the Mount sequence is especially well done. Supposedly seven thousand extras and multiple cameras were employed to capture this key moment in Jesus's ministry, and in some ways, this lengthy oration is the highlight of the film. Instead of presenting it simply as a static speech delivered by Jesus in front of an audience, the filmmakers make the interesting choice to stage it as something of a Q&A session, during which Jesus constantly moves through the crowd while individuals shout out questions to which Jesus responds. All of Jesus's words are drawn straight from Matthew's account in the Bible, so nothing is added; for example, when a person shouts out, "How should we pray?" Jesus recites the text of the Lord's Prayer in response. This strategy appropriately emphasizes Jesus's role as a teacher, and the overall effect is quite captivating, although—as Monty Python would impishly point out a decade later—if we consider the scene from a practical standpoint, no more than a couple dozen members of the audience would actually have been able to hear anything that Jesus said.

There was controversy when distributor MGM recut Ray and Bronston's film, paring it down by forty-five minutes and adding a voice-over narration, written by Ray Bradbury and spoken by Orson Welles, to bridge the plot holes created by the editing. While some critics praised the movie, most were negative, with one even punningly labeling it "the flop of flops." The reception from the public was tepid as well, earning only $7.5 million in US box office sales against its $8 million cost. It's really not a bad movie, and it has some compelling scenes and solid performances, but any attempt to film the life of Christ in a way that is both reverential and historically accurate is bound to be a challenge.

Barabbas (1961)

Director: Richard Fleischer
Producer: Dino De Laurentiis
Production Company: Columbia
Cast: Anthony Quinn (Barabbas), Silvana Mangano (Rachel), Arthur Kennedy (Pontius Pilate), Katy Jurado (Sara), Harry Andrews (Peter), Jack Palance (Torvald), Ernest Borgnine (Lucius)

Barabbas (1961) is a curious and atypical biblical epic. In tone, it is darker and less triumphant than most depictions of early Christianity, and from beginning to end, its titular protagonist is skeptical and doubting, often even derisive, of the new religion. With the major Hollywood studios churning out a string of successful Bible movies that were typically based on best-selling books, Italian producer Dino De Laurentiis decided to make one of his own. At the suggestion of eccentric director Federico Fellini, the book he chose as the basis for his film was the 1950 novel *Barabbas*, written by Nobel Prize–winning Swedish author Pär Lagerkvist. In keeping with the highbrow aspirations of the film, poet/playwright Christopher Fry was hired to write the screenplay, and the film's cinematography would prominently and creatively employ the visual metaphor of darkness versus light. Anthony Quinn was recruited to play Barabbas, and the director was Richard Fleischer, who had a solid résumé of action movies.

The film offers an answer to the question: What happened to Barabbas, the condemned thief/rebel mentioned in the Bible who was freed by Pontius Pilate in place of Jesus? The Bible says nothing further about him, but the movie imagines an entire post-Passion history during which he has various adventures across the Roman world while struggling with survivor's guilt and being reluctantly drawn toward Christianity. Barabbas at first tries to return to his life as a bandit, but he is caught and sentenced to labor in a Roman sulfur mine in Sicily, where he toils in literally hellish conditions for twenty years. When there is an explosion at the mine, he miraculously survives, only to be shackled to a plow and used as a human ox, laboriously carving furrows in the soil. A passing Roman senator takes him to Rome and enrolls him in gladiator school, where he endures yet more physical hardship from the demanding training regime of a cruel overseer, Torvald, played as a chortling psychopath by Jack Palance. Barabbas is at last granted freedom by Emperor Nero after besting Torvald in the arena. Throughout this journey, he encounters virtuous Christians who try to convert him, yet he mulishly resists their efforts. Most meet gruesome ends, including a girl-friend who is stoned to death and a fellow mine worker turned gladiator who is executed by a firing squad of archers when he refuses to kill in the arena. When the Great Fire of 64 AD breaks out, Barabbas mistakenly believes that the Christians, with whom he has at last come to identify, are deliberately burning Rome in order to make way for a better world. Therefore, he sets fire to a warehouse, which leads to his arrest and crucifixion. Throughout this odyssey, the focus remains squarely on Anthony Quinn, who turns in a memorable performance. Quinn seems to specialize in this kind of gruff yet vigorous peasant, and here he delivers a gloomier version of his later Zorba the Greek character, mumbling and grunting inarticulately as he impassively endures an enormous amount of degradation and brutality from the Romans, and then, when he gets the chance, shoving around women and browbeating his own subordinates.

In keeping with its literary aspirations, the film is suffused with a great deal of symbolism, the most prominent examples of which are darkness versus light, and blindness versus vision; both are used to express Barabbas's mental and moral turmoil. Barabbas spends much of the film alternating between long episodes dwelling in gloomy, shadowy zones that are often literally subterranean, and galvanizing moments of exposure to bright, blinding light. There are also recurrent metaphors involving fishing and eating. When De Laurentiis learned that a total solar eclipse would take place 120 miles north of Rome, he decided to film the crucifixion of Christ using this once-in-a-lifetime opportunity as a backdrop. It was risky, since there could be no second takes, but the gamble paid off, and the eclipse imparts an eerie otherworldliness. The exciting arena fight scenes, filmed with seven thousand extras in the ruins of a real Roman amphitheater in Verona, possess a rousing grandeur.

As for the historicity of the film's episodes, there were indeed sulfur mines on Sicily, the working conditions in them were appalling and dangerous, and Roman criminals were sent to the mines as a form of punishment. The gladiator school training sequences are at least plausible, and most of their arms and armor are based on historical evidence. However, the combat scenes in the arena commit the usual fallacy of showing multiple gladiator pairs fighting simultaneously instead of one at a time. The film depicts an arena floor crowded with caves, pits teeming with lions, flaming pools, and various buildings and rocks, on and around which the gladiators fight. Such props were employed by the Romans for staged beast hunts by professional animal hunters called *venatores*, but they were not used in gladiator bouts. Still, this aspect of Roman spectacle is rarely portrayed on film, and it makes for some good drama. One minor but excellent historical detail

Figure 3.2. Soldiers of the Empire in Judea. Three film versions of Roman soldiers in Judea at the time of Christ's death from (A) *Barabbas* (1961), (B) *The Robe* (1953), and (C) *King of Kings* (1927). The last outfit was reused in *The Sign of the Cross* (1932) and *Cleopatra* (1934). Although all of these cinematic soldiers are clearly meant to be Roman legionaries, the troops stationed in Jerusalem at the time of the crucifixion were more likely auxiliaries rather than legionaries. Reconstruction (D) depicts such a Roman auxiliary of the early first century AD. *Illustrations by Graham Sumner.*

appears in a street scene when some workers erecting a large statue use a wooden crane whose lifting power is generated by men running like hamsters inside a giant wheel. This crane is directly copied from a surviving Roman sculptural relief panel from the tomb of the Haterii, now in the Vatican Museum.

Promotional material for the movie stressed the filmmakers' concern with the historical accuracy of the costumes, and Oscar-nominated designer Maria de Matteis supposedly based her designs on research done at Pompeii and Herculaneum. Unfortunately, many of the soldiers depicted in the wall-paintings at those sites were not intended as accurate representations of current Roman military practice, but rather as images of legendary figures drawn from the Hellenistic tradition. The result is that the Roman soldiers in *Barabbas* are dressed in completely erroneous outfits (Figure 3.2.A). With their large round shields, leather armor, and long thrusting spears—none of which were employed by legionaries of the first century AD—they instead resemble Greek hoplites. The Roman troops, especially the officers, also wear Attic-style helmets adorned with some of the most absurdly large and flamboyant feathered crests to appear in any film, and which were certainly never a standard part of any legionary's equipment.

The film was not a success at the box office, and the critical response was mixed, with some reviewers finding it grim and bloody, while others admired its ambition. Most agreed that Quinn brought an admirable degree of physical commitment to his performance as Barabbas. *New York Times* critic Bosley Crowther observed, "Mr. Quinn is a sensational sufferer. He grunts and sweats and strains with more credible vengeance and exertion than any actor we can name."[1] In the end, *Barabbas* contains some visually impressive moments, but the final result is a movie in which those parts are more notable and coherent than the film as a whole.

Constantine and the Cross (1961/1962 US)

Director: Lionello De Felice
Producer: Ferdinand Felicioni
Production Company: Jonia Film
Cast: Cornel Wilde (Constantine), Belinda Lee (Fausta), Christine Kaufmann (Livia), Massimo Serato (Maxentius), Fausto Tozzi (Hadrian), Tino Carraro (Maximianus), Carlo Ninchi (Constantius Chlorus), Elisa Cegani (Helena), Nando Gazzolo (Licinius)

One of the crucial turning points in Roman history, and really in all of world history, was when Constantine became the first emperor to convert to Christianity in 312 AD. After him, all emperors but one would also be Christians, the persecutions of Christians would stop, and within another one hundred years, Christianity would become the official religion of the Roman Empire. Despite the immense impact Constantine had on subsequent history, it is curious that he has rarely been represented on film. He was the subject of a 1913 silent film called *In Questo Segno Vincerai* (English title: *The Triumph of an Emperor*), and his career figures prominently in a 2014 movie, *The Decline of an Empire*. The most high-profile attempt to capture Constantine's dramatic life on film was the 1961 Italian production *Constantine and the Cross*, featuring American star Cornel Wilde in the title role. Together with *Attila* (1954/1958 US) and *Hannibal* (1959/1960 US), this film comprises an interesting subcategory of modestly budgeted, Italian-made biographies of famous ancient figures that are often classified with the exploitative peplum films of the era, but that seem to aspire to be more historically accurate in their plots. As with *Attila* and *Hannibal*, *Constantine and the Cross* awkwardly and unsuccessfully mixes together a surprising amount of actual historical details with completely invented elements and clichés drawn from other sword-and-sandal flicks.

Constantine lived during a particularly convoluted era of Roman history, during which the empire was racked by several rounds of civil war and was in the process of splitting into eastern and western halves. To complicate matters further, the dominant emperor in Constantine's youth, Diocletian, had set up a complex administrative structure in which four emperors ruled simultaneously, with the western and eastern halves each controlled by a pair consisting of a "junior" and a "senior" emperor. Constantine was the son of one of these four emperors, and a man named Maxentius was the son of another. Between AD 305 and 312, no fewer than eight men would lay claim to one or more of these titles, resulting in much political maneuvering and civil war. One by one, contenders were eliminated, with the last two, Constantine and Maxentius, fighting a decisive battle at the Milvian Bridge just outside of Rome in AD 312.

Constantine and the Cross rather gamely tries to cover all of this, which is admirable, but many viewers will likely lose track of exactly who is who among Diocletian, Maximian, Maximianus, Maxentius, Constantius Chlorus, Constantine, and Licinius. The film simplifies things a bit by portraying Maxentius as the villain who schemes from the very start to undermine Constantine. Massimo Serato imbues Maxentius with a sly smarminess that makes him a more entertaining character to watch than Cornel Wilde's Constantine, whose actions are noble, but whose personality comes off as dull and uninspiring. Constantine's love interest (played by Belinda Lee) is Fausta, the daughter of Maximian, and, this being a movie, Constantine is depicted as being deeply in love with her. In reality, the marriage was one of political convenience only made possible by Constantine divorcing his current wife, and it came to an ugly end when Constantine had Fausta executed for adultery.

Although the film generally follows the historical record, it does significantly alter some facts. Two ancient authors describe the crucial event that converted Constantine to Christianity on the eve of the Battle of the Milvian Bridge. Lactantius claims that on the night before the battle, Constantine had a dream in which God instructed him to place the Christian Chi-Rho symbol (formed by overlapping the first two letters of Christ's name in Greek) on the shields of his men. Eusebius reports a two-stage version. First, on the day before the battle, the Christian Chi-Rho symbol appeared in the sky superimposed over the sun, along with the words "In this sign, conquer." Then, later that night, Jesus visited Constantine in a dream and explained that if Constantine and his men carried the Chi-Rho symbol into battle, they would triumph over Maxentius. In the movie, Constantine does see a divine sign in the sky, but it is a simple cross, not the Chi-Rho symbol specified by both ancient authors, and God speaks the line, "In this sign, conquer," rather than it being written in the sky. Also, his men carry wooden crosses into battle, instead of painting the Chi-Rho on their shields. In the film, a major motivation for Constantine's conversion is that his mother, Helena, is represented as having been a Christian from at least the time of his birth. In reality, the sources indicate that she did not convert until after the Battle of the Milvian Bridge, when she was in her sixties.

While these examples could be viewed as the rearrangement or alteration of actual historical facts in order to fit the filmmaker's vision, the film also includes elements that are completely fictitious. Thus, the script bestows upon Constantine a best friend: a Roman officer who falls in love with a demure Christian girl, whose goodness converts him to her religion—a seemingly obligatory plot line familiar from movies such as *The Sign of the Cross* (1932), *Quo Vadis* (1951), and *The Robe* (1953). Constantine himself is given attributes of the stereotypical peplum film hero, resulting in unlikely episodes such as when he leaps down into an arena to single-handedly subdue a lion that is menacing a child. While the film has some large-scale battle scenes and the soldiers energetically splash around in the Tiber during the Battle of the Milvian Bridge, the action is undermined by a lot of fake-looking swordplay of the type found in school theater productions, with the combatants clanging their swords together while carefully avoiding hitting their opponents. The script does contain some clever bits. For instance, when Constantine's friend is offered milk by the Christian girl, he recoils in horror, calling instead for wine—an exchange that accurately captures the strong cultural prejudices that the Romans had about milk as a stereotypical drink of northern barbarians, in contrast to wine, which was what civilized Mediterranean people imbibed.

In the end, it cannot be said that *Constantine and the Cross* is a good film, but neither is it an awful one. There is still plenty of room for a definitive cinematic treatment of this important historical figure, and hopefully one day someone will make it.

Cleopatra (1963)

Director: Joseph L. Mankiewicz
Producer: Walter Wanger
Production Company: 20th Century-Fox
Cast: Elizabeth Taylor (Cleopatra), Richard Burton (Mark Antony), Rex Harrison (Julius Caesar), Roddy McDowall (Octavian), Hume Cronyn (Sosigenes), Andrew Keir (Agrippa), Martin Landau (Rufio)

The 1963 film *Cleopatra* is notorious for being excessive in almost every way, frequently in disastrous fashion. It was the most expensive film made up to that point, and, if adjusted for inflation, it may well still hold the record as the most costly film of all time. The initial attempt to film it was a catastrophe that squandered two years and $7 million, and yielded only ten minutes of usable footage. As a result, the original director was fired, most of the cast replaced, and the whole production moved from England to Italy—a shift that entailed abandoning all the vast and hideously pricey sets that had been constructed in England.

The film was eventually completed, although it continued to bleed money for 20th Century-Fox Studios at an alarming rate, ultimately costing twenty-five times its initial budget. It also established a record for the highest salary paid to an actor, with Elizabeth Taylor signing a contract for a then-unprecedented fee of $1 million and then pocketing additional millions due to overruns. Once the film relocated to Italy, more costly and gargantuan sets were built, but then barely used. For example, a highly detailed reconstruction of the Roman Forum three times the size of the actual Forum was erected at great effort and expense, but only employed in a single scene. The costumes were equally lavish, with a record-breaking sixty-five costume changes for Taylor, and some of her dresses were even fashioned out of genuine gold. In addition, the film was the center of extraordinary controversies. Although they were both married to other people, stars Elizabeth Taylor and Richard Burton embarked on a highly public affair so scandalous that it not only enraptured the popular press for several years but even provoked condemnation from the Vatican and politicians. So much money was spent on *Cleopatra* that despite being the highest-grossing film of

1963 it was still regarded as a financial disaster that drove 20th Century-Fox to the brink of bankruptcy.

All of this drama has ensured *Cleopatra*'s fame, but how is it as a historical film? It covers a pivotal period in Roman history, the final years of the Roman Republic, and features some of the most famous figures in Roman history, including Julius Caesar, Mark Antony, Octavian—who would become the first emperor, Augustus—and, of course, Cleopatra herself. *Cleopatra* is also distinctive in that it is one of the relatively few ancient epics made in Hollywood during this era that neither centers its plot around conflict between Christians and pagan Romans nor frames its story in relation to Christianity.

In its basic plot, the film is reasonably accurate. Caesar did meet Cleopatra when he came to Egypt in pursuit of his rival Pompey; the Egyptians did kill Pompey and present Caesar with his head; Caesar did take Cleopatra's side in a civil war with her brother; Caesar and Cleopatra did embark on a love affair that produced a son, Caesarion; after Caesar returned to Rome, she did follow him and make a grand entrance there; and Caesar was assassinated, after which Cleopatra went back to Egypt. Caesar's lieutenant, Mark Antony, then engaged in a struggle with Caesar's adopted son, Octavian, for control of Rome. Antony also began a passionate love affair with Cleopatra. Octavian cleverly stirred up public sentiment against the lovers and eventually, at the Battle of Actium, defeated them with the assistance of his admiral, Agrippa. After fleeing to Egypt, Antony and Cleopatra committed suicide in the manner depicted.

However, the film deviates from history in a few interesting ways. It makes a big deal out of Julius Caesar's public acknowledgment of Caesarion, his son with Cleopatra, whereas in real life he never bestowed such recognition. It completely omits the three other children that Cleopatra had with Mark Antony. It garbles a number of points concerning Caesar's ambitions; for example, incorrectly claiming that the title "dictator" that he assumed was merely a symbolic one whose power was largely curtailed by the senate, and erroneously asserting that he desired to be called "emperor," a title that did not yet exist.

On the other hand, the movie contains some impressive sequences. For instance, when Caesar is besieged in Alexandria by the forces of Cleopatra's brother, he orders a sortie to neutralize enemy catapults. His legionaries deploy into a *testudo*, or tortoise (although Caesar refers to it as a "turtle" in the film). This is a formation in which the men huddle closely together so that their rectangular shields create a solid "shell" on all four sides and overhead. In the film, the men assume this formation and then slowly march forward in step until they reach the catapults, which they set on fire. The scene illustrates the usefulness of the *testudo* when advancing under fire, as well as the rigid discipline and

Figure 3.3. Caesar at Leisure. How to portray Roman aristocrats out of armor has been a challenge for filmmakers. Rex Harrison's Julius Caesar (A) from *Cleopatra* **(1963) wears an ahistorical leather bathrobe-like garment over a long-underwear-like pants-and-shirt combo. Reconstruction (B) depicts a historically plausible outfit for Caesar featuring a linen** *subarmalis***. (C) Leather armor/***subarmalis*** of a type often used in films.** *Illustrations by Graham Sumner. Photograph and prop from The Terry Nix Collection.*

training necessary to pull it off effectively. Unfortunately, the filmmakers added inaccurate details, such as prominent hooks, spikes, and vision slits on the shields. Incidentally, these battles did indeed result in part of the Great Library of Alexandria catching fire and being destroyed, as the film depicts.

One of the most famous features of the movie is its lavish costumes and sets, on which a good deal of its massive budget was spent. During the battle in Alexandria, one Egyptian soldier can be seen wearing a suit of crocodile armor, likely based on an example found in Egypt that is now on display at the British Museum. A nice detail on the outfit worn by Antony when he meets Cleopatra aboard her fabulous barge is the leopard fur patches on his breastplate and the leopard pelt flaps that hang around his thighs. In their revels, Antony and Cleopatra liked to dress up as gods, with Antony often assuming the role of Dionysos (Roman Bacchus), the god of wine and fertility, and Cleopatra playing either Aphrodite, goddess of love and beauty, or the Egyptian deity Isis. Because Dionysos was frequently depicted in ancient art as being clad in leopard skins, Antony's armor accurately evokes his identification with the god.

The Roman military equipment is a mixture of historically plausible attire and Hollywood conventions of what they thought Roman soldiers should look like. An example of the latter is the ubiquitous leather cuirasses worn by nearly every one of the major Roman characters (Figure 3.3.C). While a staple of movies set in the ancient world, their ubiquity is not supported by ancient evidence. When on active duty, Roman officers would have donned metal breastplates rather than leather ones, or else would have been equipped like ordinary legionaries, who at this time wore chain mail. Most of the Roman officers sport an absurdly riotous plume of tall feathers atop their helmets. Actual Roman battlefield helmets would have lacked such ornamentation or, at most, would have possessed far more modest crests.

Much less historically satisfying are the costumes worn by Rex Harrison as Julius Caesar. While at first glance he seems to be dressed in the same togas and leather armor with short, fringed skirt as the other Romans, closer inspection reveals that, underneath these garments, he is clad in strange long-sleeved, tight-fitting shirts and close-fitting, ankle-length tights or pants. It looks as if he always has on long underwear beneath whatever other garb he is wearing. The color of this "long underwear" varies from white to red to purple to match whatever he has on over it, but it is present in every scene. Such garments are completely unattested as Roman apparel. The explanation for Harrison's odd attire can be found in comments by the costume designer for the film, Irene Sharaff. She said that the outfits that she originally made for Harrison were "faithful reproductions of what was worn by a man of high rank in Rome of 52 BC," but when

Figure 3.4. Caesar's Legionaries. (A) Legionary from *Caesar and Cleopatra* (1945/1946 US). Although the film is set in the first century AD, the inspiration for his equipment seems to have been the soldiers on the late second-century AD Column of Marcus Aurelius. (B) Legionary from *Cleopatra* (1963) whose equipment would be accurate for a legionary a century later, but not one of this time. (C) Reconstruction of a legionary from the actual era of Julius Caesar wearing chain mail body armor instead of the banded metal *lorica segmentata. Illustrations by Graham Sumner.*

Harrison tried them on, they emphasized his spindly legs and arms and his narrow shoulders in an unflattering way.[2] In order to create a more visually imposing Julius Caesar, they made a foam rubber cast of Harrison's torso and equipped it with broader, padded shoulders and augmented muscles. This is what was being concealed beneath the long-underwear-style shirts. Similarly, his scrawny calves and thighs were literally fleshed out with padded inserts, which were hidden inside the pants or tights. Figure 3.3 illustrates one of the outfits worn by Harrison as Caesar when at leisure (A), which includes both the odd long underwear and an equally historically inaccurate item resembling a leather kimono. While it is uncertain exactly what a high-ranking Roman would have worn in such circumstances, (B) is a more probable reconstruction, which consists of a linen garment similar to the *subarmalis* that was worn beneath armor.

The equipment of the ordinary legionaries in the film is a decent version of the banded armor known as *lorica segmentata* (Figure 3.4.B). While this would be appropriate for legionaries of a century later, it is inaccurate for Roman soldiers of the late republic. At that time, chain mail shirts would have been the most common armor they would have worn, as illustrated in the reconstructed legionary (Figure 3.4.C). This discrepancy is explained by the fact that *Cleopatra*'s propmakers were most likely basing their replicas on the most well-known depiction of Roman soldiers, those found in the reliefs carved on Trajan's Column, a monument dating to the second century AD.

Elizabeth Taylor appears in sixty-five different outfits—a new record for costume changes in a film. As one might expect, many of these are outrageously elaborate and expensive. Among the most impressive is the golden sheath dress that she wears during what is perhaps the most visually arresting scene in the movie—her spectacular arrival in Rome—when she makes her grand entrance seated atop a gigantic sphinx and accompanied by an entourage of dancers. This garment actually has a historical basis; it was inspired by a relief of Cleopatra on a temple at Dendera in Egypt. In this relief, the queen is depicted in a form-fitting gown and elaborate headdress consisting of the disk of the sun held between two horns and surmounted by two tall feathers. In the film, Taylor wears exactly this headdress, reproduced in gold. Another good historical detail appears during the coronation scene, where she is correctly shown wearing the famed double crown of Egypt, composed of the red cobra crown of the upper Nile regions and the white vulture crown of the lower Nile— although in the movie the white crown gets upgraded to one made of gold.

Some of Taylor's other costumes are less historically plausible, such as the various gauzy ensembles that look more like 1950s negligees than ancient Egyptian attire, and the rather odd headgear resembling bathing caps adorned with glued-on feathers that she wears in several scenes, which appear to have been inspired by the 1950s fad for wig-toque hats decorated with feathers or flowers. Figure 1.4 in the entry for the 1934 version of *Cleopatra* offers an example of one of the less formal outfits worn by Taylor (B), as well as a reconstruction of the significantly less stylish and form-fitting kind of Hellenistic dress (C) that the real Cleopatra was more likely to have worn.

Taylor's makeup in the film, which fully embraced the Egyptian aesthetic, is quite striking: heavy bands of black are drawn around her eyes in imitation of the kohl eyeliner used by the ancient Egyptians, augmented with broad patches of metallic green and blue eye shadow. Accompanying the film was a well-designed marketing campaign urging American women to adopt the so-called "Cleopatra Look." Makeup giant Revlon came out with a movie-inspired set of products, including a lipstick color dubbed "Sphinx Pink." Revlon print ads declared, "Revlon solves the sweetest mystery in history with The Cleopatra Look, an enchanting new kind of sorcery. 2,000 years after Cleopatra used her beauty secrets to such outrageously unfair (but oh! so feminine) advantage, Revlon distills them for you in a wonderfully wearable modern adaptation. . . . If looks can kill, this one will!"[3]

Elizabeth Taylor's memorable incarnation of the Egyptian queen is probably what most people imagine when they visualize Cleopatra, but Taylor's fans might be disappointed to hear that the surviving historical images indicate that the real Cleopatra looked nothing like her. Ancient coins and busts reveal that she had a rather lean face with a prominent jaw and a largish, hooked nose. Incidentally, Cleopatra was not a native Egyptian, but rather a direct descendant of Ptolemy I, one of Alexander the Great's generals, who had seized control of Egypt following Alexander's death. For the next three hundred years, the Greco-Macedonian Ptolemaic dynasty ruled Egypt as foreign conquerors, speaking Greek rather than Egyptian and building Greek-style temples and palaces in their capital city of Alexandria.

In terms of the film's sets, one of the most impressive is the harbor of Alexandria, constructed on a monumental scale at Cinecittà Studios near Rome. This set does an excellent job of conveying how Hellenistic Alexandria would have been a mixture of Greek and Egyptian architectural and stylistic elements. Thus, the set boasts a massive Doric-style Greek temple, but also includes uniquely Egyptian details, such as an obelisk, a sphinx, and a giant bronze scarab beetle sculpture used as a gong. Currently ongoing archaeological excavations of Hellenistic Alexandria suggest that the city did in fact feature just such a mash-up of Greek and Egyptian architectural structures and styles, but films about Egypt during this period rarely reflect this complexity.

Another amazing set, used as the backdrop for Cleopatra's entry into Rome, depicts the Roman Forum. Since a faithful reconstruction was deemed insufficiently impressive, the movie's version was built on a scale three times larger than the actual Forum. In the scene, an audience of senators and Romans is treated to successive waves of elaborately costumed and choreographed performers, including archers shooting bolts of vivid red cloth, nearly naked dancing girls, and a coterie of Black dancers whose costumes and dances look suspiciously like those of eighteenth-century Zulus rather than ancient Africans; floats bearing gold-clad, winged women representing the goddess Isis; exotic animals; and prancing horsemen. Finally, a phalanx of three hundred slaves rhythmically swaying from side to side comes into view, hauling a thirty-five-foot-high, seventy-foot-long sphinx sculpture, atop which Cleopatra and Caesarion perch. This dazzling procession enters the Forum through a full-size reconstruction of the Arch of Constantine. In addition to the oversize Forum, another historical error is that the Arch of Constantine would not be built until almost 350 years after Cleopatra's trip to Rome. While this is a visually stunning sequence, it is yet another symbol of the film's extravagance, since the vast set was only used for this single scene. So enormous was the scale of the sets erected at Cinecittà that they caused shortages of construction materials throughout Italy.

The third scene of great spectacle depicts Cleopatra traveling to the city of Tarsus in 41 BC to meet with Antony. The ancient source for this trip states that she sailed up the river Cydnus in a gilded barge powered by purple sails and silver oars, dressed as the goddess of love Aphrodite, surrounded by boys dressed as Cupids and women as sea nymphs, and accompanied by music and the burning of incense. People lined the riverbanks to witness her grand arrival. The filmmakers spared no expense in re-creating this moment. A golden ship over 250 feet long was built that replicated the original barge in every detail, down to the purple sails, the bevy of women dressed as nymphs, and the clouds of accompanying incense. It was not just a static prop, but a fully seaworthy vessel. This single item cost $250,000, equivalent to $2 million today. In the brief scene during which we see this mind-boggling vessel coming up the coast, the spectators standing on the shore can be seen dropping to their knees in astonishment, and their reactions may well have been genuine rather than feigned.

In the role of Julius Caesar, Rex Harrison received considerable critical praise, and he was the sole actor from the film to earn an Academy Award nomination. Harrison's performance does capture a sense of Caesar's intellectual sharpness and decisiveness. As Mark Antony, Richard Burton has elicited a more mixed response. Some considered his love for Cleopatra to be genuinely moving, although it may be hard to disentangle his acting from one's knowledge of their tempestuous real-life affair. Others have found his performance too self-conscious and histrionic. The real Antony and Cleopatra do seem to have had a genuine passion for one another. One problem with Burton's Antony is that he comes off as an ineffectual, moody, and indecisive figure. Although there are verbal references to his charisma and skilled generalship, we never see any of this on display. Viewers are left to wonder why anyone would have been inspired to follow this Antony or how he managed to become one of the most powerful men in the Roman world. The final film was severely shortened in editing, so perhaps the scenes establishing his heroic nature were cut.

As for Cleopatra, the real-life Egyptian queen was a highly intelligent, multilingual, resourceful woman and a shrewd and calculating political operator, but not enough of this acumen comes across in Taylor's performance. Other than a brief amusing moment when she corrects Caesar's maps, her main highlighted qualities are seductiveness and manipulativeness. Again, critical reaction was mixed, with some viewing her as an embodiment of female power, while, to quote a more negative assessment, others saw only "a suburban American housewife, alternately simpering and shrewish."[4] From a historical standpoint, one of the best bits of casting is Roddy McDowall as the young Octavian. Octavian was a complex character who was supremely gifted at political infighting, and McDowall perfectly captures his coldly rational personality as he constantly schemes and outmaneuvers those around him. The film even depicts some of Octavian's flaws; for instance, that he was not a talented general, but instead relied on the abilities of his loyal friend Agrippa, and that he had a weak, sickly constitution, humorously alluded to by a scene in which Agrippa goes belowdeck to inform him of the great victory at Actium, only to find Octavian so lost in the miseries of seasickness that he doesn't care what happened.

Ultimately, it is impossible to separate the film from its legacy and its reputation for extravagance. It had initially been budgeted at a modest $2 million—a number that steadily increased until, by the time it finally appeared in theaters, $31 million had been spent on production, a further $5 million on the abortive first attempt at filming in England, and another $13 million on postproduction, reshoots, and distribution. That total of $49 million would be equivalent to around $400 million today. The studio was driven to the edge of bankruptcy and was only saved by the phenomenal success of *The Sound of Music* two years later.

Assessing the film as history is complicated by the fact that the available versions are so truncated. The original concept had been to release two films in quick succession—the first on Cleopatra and Julius Caesar, the second on Cleopatra and Antony—each three hours long. The director's original edit matched these parameters, but the studio head wanted to take advantage of the current gossip surrounding the Taylor/Burton affair and therefore decreed that it had to be released as one film that could be no more than four hours long. This was cut down even further, to just over three hours in length, so that theaters could offer two showings per night. The four-hour version survives, but the six-hour one has been lost, so in the end we may never know if the most expensive film of all time might have lived up to its full potential.

The Fall of the Roman Empire (1964)

Director: Anthony Mann
Producer: Samuel Bronston
Production Company: Bronston-Roma
Cast: Alec Guinness (Marcus Aurelius), Sophia Loren (Lucilla), Stephen Boyd (Livius), Christopher Plummer (Commodus), James Mason (Timonides), John Ireland (Ballomar)

A Roman priest who has just sacrificed a bird turns to the emperor Marcus Aurelius and somberly declares, "The omens are bad. I could not find a heart." This is the opening line of dialogue in the 1964 epic *The Fall of the Roman Empire*, and this chilling prophecy sets the mood for what will unfold over the next three hours. It will not be a feel-good film. It will not have a happy ending. This is confirmed when the emperor's reaction to this unpromising portent is to muse, "When I was a child . . . I had a secret fear that night would come, and would never end." The subject matter of the movie will be the doomed effort to hold back the metaphorical night from engulfing and snuffing out the light that is Roman civilization.

The omens were equally bad for the film itself. Like *Cleopatra*, which had been released one year earlier, it was one of the most expensive films ever made, and it, too, featured massive sets built on an unprecedented scale. While *Cleopatra* had trouble recouping its oversize budget, it was nevertheless the top-grossing movie of its year, and eventually did turn a profit. *The Fall of the Roman Empire*, however, was an unmitigated financial disaster, costing $19 million and earning a paltry $4.75 million in return. While the studio that made *Cleopatra* survived to flourish again, *The Fall of the Roman Empire* drove its studio to bankruptcy, killing it forever. Together, the failure of these two films brought the classic Hollywood era of ancient epics to a crashing halt and so thoroughly poisoned the genre that no major epics would be made for three decades. Nevertheless, a number of critics and classical scholars regard *The Fall of the Roman Empire* as one of the most thoughtful takes on the classical world from the Golden Age of Hollywood ancient epics.

The film and its messages were very much shaped by the visions of two men: Anthony Mann, the director, and Samuel Bronston, the head of the studio. Bronston had established his own independent studio in Spain that specialized in entertaining yet fact-based historical films such as *El Cid* and *55 Days at Peking*. Many of his movies, including these two, featured the theme of individuals or groups from different cultures or nations uniting in order to achieve a common goal—a premise that would figure prominently in *The Fall of the Roman Empire*. The director, Anthony Mann, was no stranger to ancient epics, having directed the Great Fire of Rome sequence in *Quo Vadis* and also, as the initial director of *Spartacus*, having filmed all of the opening scenes before being replaced by Stanley Kubrick. Both men shared a keen interest in creating historical films that made statements about the contemporary world. As Mann explained, "The reason for making *The Fall of the Roman Empire* is that . . . the past is like a mirror; it reflects what actually happened, and in the reflection of the fall of Rome are the same elements in what is happening today, the very things that are making our empires fall."[5]

With the United States then at the pinnacle of its economic and political power and influence, the question, "How does a great civilization unravel?" held obvious interest for Americans of the mid-1960s. This focus also shifted the role of the Romans in the film. In most earlier ancient epics, the Romans were the villains, portrayed as imperialistic oppressors of some group, usually either slaves or Christians. In this movie, however, the viewer is asked to identify with the Romans and to see them as the benevolent defenders of civilization against the forces of anarchy and destruction. Mann was quite explicit about his desire to deviate from the usual ancient formula, asserting, "I did not want to make another *Quo Vadis* . . . or any of the others. . . . Those films gave the impression that the Christian movement was the only thing the Roman Empire was about, but it was a minor incident in the greatness of the Roman Empire."[6]

Like almost every other ancient epic, this film begins with a voice-over by a solemn narrator, but whereas the prologue in previous films had usually set up a simplistic dichotomy between good and evil, *The Fall of the Roman Empire* instead poses complex and open-ended questions: "Two of the greatest problems in history are how to account for the rise of Rome and how to account for her fall. We may come nearer to understanding the truth if we remember that the fall of Rome, like her rise, had not one cause but many. And it was not an event, but a process spread over three hundred years. Some nations have not lasted as long as Rome fell." This is an unusual beginning that places the focus squarely on the process of historical interpretation rather than on the events themselves. The phraseology "we may come nearer to understanding the truth" also acknowledges that such an investigation will always remain inconclusive and that we can never fully comprehend the causes of Rome's fall. The best we can hope for is to asymptotically approach such an understanding. This kind of nuanced and sophisticated analysis will delight professional historians, but it may not be as suited to entertaining a mass audience of moviegoers seeking sensationalism and spectacle. Mann admitted as much, commenting that the film "has a defeatist theme. I was very conscious that I might be stepping into a hole in doing this, because I just don't think people are interested in defeat."[7] Despite the lofty aspirations expressed in the prologue, in the end much of the film served up the traditional toga epic diet of chariot races and battles and replaced a good deal of the complicated analysis of causation with a simple story of the personal rivalry between a good man and his evil antagonist.

The moment that the filmmakers selected to encapsulate Rome's decline is borrowed from the famous eighteenth-century historian Edward Gibbon, who posited that the period between AD 98 and 180—a time when Rome was ruled by the so-called "five good emperors"—was a Golden Age "during which the condition of the human race was most happy and prosperous." This era came to an end when the last of the five, Marcus Aurelius, was succeeded by his son Commodus, who proved to be a mentally unstable tyrant. In both Gibbon's and the filmmakers' assessment, although the empire would last for several more centuries, it was all downhill from here. While a bit of an oversimplification, this is a plausible interpretation. Although Aurelius has otherwise been praised for his wisdom, selecting Commodus as his heir is viewed as an atypically horrible decision.

The film deviates from the historical record in a significant way by having Aurelius disinherit Commodus and instead elevate a general named Livius as his successor. Livius is completely fictitious, and it is very clear that, in reality, Commodus was Aurelius's enthusiastic choice. In the movie, before the change can be made official, Aurelius is poisoned and dies, Commodus becomes emperor, and Livius remains just a general. Commodus revokes Aurelius's enlightened policies of rulership and embarks on a career of personal debauchery and public mismanagement. Eventually, this behavior provokes rebellions and tests Livius's loyalty, culminating in a gladiator-style duel between the two men during which Livius kills Commodus. Disgusted by the corruption and sycophancy displayed by Rome's senators and citizens during Commodus's reign, Livius refuses the throne and goes into self-imposed exile, abandoning the degenerate empire to what seems an inevitable path toward decline and fall.

The nuanced exploration of historical causation promised by the prologue is thus mostly transformed into a more conventional story of hero versus villain. Still, traces of that greater ambition can be found throughout the film. One example is the very first large-scale spectacular sequence. Where other movies might open with combat or a race, the viewer is instead treated to what is, essentially, a conference, at which the emperor Marcus Aurelius, played by British actor Alec Guinness, summons representatives of all the nations, ethnic groups, and provinces that are part of the Roman Empire. It is a visually exciting scene as each group, wearing their distinctive costumes, rides up in front of Aurelius, is formally greeted, and then joins the assembled throng. Aurelius delivers a speech in which he urges unity and proposes bestowing universal Roman citizenship upon them. Furthermore, he explicitly equates the glory and strength of the empire with the diversity of those who compose it.

Here is the key section of Aurelius's oration: "You do not resemble each other, nor do you wear the same clothes, nor sing the same songs, nor worship the same gods. . . . Yet, you are the unity which is Rome. Look about you and look at yourselves and see the greatness of Rome. Here, within our reach, golden centuries of peace. A true Pax Romana. Wherever you live, whatever the color of your skin, when peace is achieved it will bring to all the supreme rights of Roman citizenship." He memorably concludes with the line: "No longer provinces or colonies, but Rome. Rome everywhere. A family of equal nations." For mid-1960s audiences, such a "family of equal nations" would unavoidably have brought to mind the United Nations, and the United States as the driving force behind it. The actual Marcus Aurelius, known as "the philosopher-emperor," was a devoted adherent of the Stoic school of philosophy. He also wrote a book of Stoic ruminations called the *Meditations*, which outlines a benevolent, humanistic set of values. Thus, ascribing to Aurelius an enlightened vision of a grand union of humanity, as laid out in this speech, is not an implausible idea on the filmmakers' part. One passage in the *Meditations* (4.4) that seems to reflect this theme of universal brotherhood states: "There is a world-law; which in turn means that we are all fellow-citizens and share a common citizenship, and that the world is a single city."

Another issue with contemporary resonance was immigration. The first half of the film takes place in and around a grimly imposing legionary fortress located along Rome's northern frontier. Aurelius is portrayed as having been battling barbarians here for decades, but he now wishes to shift imperial policy more toward accommodation and cooperation than conquest and exploitation. The real Aurelius did both, spending much of his career fighting in the north as depicted, but also engaging in diplomacy and even settling some barbarians on vacant farm land in Italy. One of the strengths of the Roman Empire, and one of the secrets underlying both its success and its longevity, was that the Romans were quite open to incorporating conquered peoples, and they actively co-opted the most dynamic provincials into working for Rome rather than against it. Roman imperialism was certainly accompanied by instances of cruelty and exploitation, but through institutions such as the army *auxilia*, it also offered routes for upward mobility. In modern terms, Rome was a thoroughly multicultural empire.

A surprising amount of the film deals with this key historical issue of how best to treat provincials, the conquered, and those barbarians not yet vanquished. At one point, there is a debate in the Roman senate during which Commodus and his minions urge a policy of shameless exploitation backed up by military force, while Livius and others try to preserve Aurelius's dream of inclusivity. An elderly Roman senator, clearly meant to be a figure of great dignity and wisdom, declaims: "There are millions waiting at our gates. If we do not open these gates, they will break them down and destroy us. But instead let us grow ever bigger, ever greater: let us take them [in] among us." As scholars have noted, this scene presents rival conceptions of the Roman Empire that reflect Cold War ideology. In one, the empire is based on equality, participatory citizenship, peace, and an open-door immigration policy, creating, in the words of one critic, "an idealized form of the United States." In the other, it is a "cruel, militarist, totalitarian tyranny" that recalls stereotyped images of the Soviet Union.[8] While obviously inspired at the time by the Cold War, this sixty-year-old scene still possesses contemporary resonance, given the current impassioned debate about immigration and what policies countries should adopt toward those seeking entry. In the film, the adherents to Aurelius's position win the debate, and a group of Germanic barbarians is allowed to settle on unused land in Italy. There, the once-savage barbarians create an idyllic farming community and, somewhat improbably, produce so much surplus food that these new immigrants to the empire are shown jubilantly bestowing their agricultural bounty upon the starving citizens of the city of Rome. It is an appealing vision, but unfortunately, the reality was less heartwarming. Aurelius's actual attempt to settle Germans on empty land in Italy ended in dismal failure when the barbarians revolted and sacked a Roman city.

Alec Guinness is fantastic in the role of Marcus Aurelius. Sporting a full beard, he bears a very close resemblance to surviving portrait busts of Aurelius. In purely visual terms, Guinness as Aurelius is one of the best casting jobs in any Roman movie. He also radiates a convincing blend of benevolence, wisdom, and authority that conforms to descriptions of the historical Aurelius. Finally, likely drawing upon his experience as an actor in the theater, he knows how to project his voice to a large audience, and his speech to the assembly of nations is one of the most convincing exhibitions of genuine oratory to be found in an ancient epic. Far too often in such scenes, actors mumble or speak

Figure 3.5. Legionaries of the Decline and Fall. Legionaries from two films set around 180 AD: (A) *The Fall of the Roman Empire* (1964) and (B) *Gladiator* (2000). (C) is a reconstruction of a Roman legionary of that era. His helmet is based on one found at Heddernheim, Germany (see Figure 3.6.E), while his armor and shield are derived from soldiers on the Column of Marcus Aurelius. *Illustrations by Graham Sumner.*

in a tone that would barely be audible to listeners in a small room, let alone a large outdoor audience. Christopher Plummer, who plays Commodus, does an excellent job as well. His performance effectively conveys a mix of boastfulness and insecurity consistent with the historical Commodus. He also makes Commodus's degeneration from pleasure-loving ne'er-do-well to mentally unbalanced megalomaniac seem credible. While he makes a fine Commodus, the real Commodus was in his late teens when elevated to the emperorship, whereas Plummer is in his mid-thirties.

The unedited version of the film includes a scene in which it is revealed that, rather than being Aurelius's natural son, Commodus was the result of his wife's affair with a gladiator. This becomes a convenient way to explain how the apparently wise Aurelius could have had such a wastrel son, and perhaps also why, as the movie emphasizes, Commodus so admires gladiators and even aspires to fight as one in the arena. It is well documented that the real Commodus shared this obsession with gladiators, and one ancient source even records the rumor about Aurelius's wife, so neither of these details were inventions of the filmmakers. However, as this source is a particularly unreliable one, it is likely that Commodus really was Aurelius's progeny.

Perhaps the most famous fact regarding *The Fall of the Roman Empire* is that it boasted the most elaborate reconstruction of the Roman Forum in any film before or since. The promotional materials produced by the studio delight in listing the impressive statistics concerning the size of this set and its alleged historical accuracy. Erected on the studio's lots outside of Madrid, it consisted of 27 full-scale three-dimensional structures, many containing elaborate interiors. Here are a few more statistics: it included 350 individual statues, 8 victory columns, 610 columns in buildings, and 1,000 hand-sculpted relief panels. Manufacturing the set consumed 12 tons of nails, 170,000 pavement blocks, 22,000 feet of concrete steps and stairs, 230,000 roofing tiles, and 320 miles of tubular steel framework. The entire Forum set was 1,300 feet long by 750 feet wide and required the labor of 1,100 workmen for 7 months.

On the whole, the filmmakers did a fine job. Probably the most notable discrepancy from the real Forum is that the statues and buildings are almost all white or natural stone in color. In reality, the Romans often painted them, sometimes in rather garish colors. In defense of the filmmakers, however, an understanding of just how extensively the Romans painted their stonework arose from scholarship done after the movie's completion. Another flaw is the prominent line of commemorative columns that runs down one side of the Forum. These were installed over a hundred years after the events of the film. Similarly, the gate to the city that appears in one scene, while a good

Figure 3.6. Inspirations. Drawings depicting ancient evidence that heavily influenced movie versions of Roman helmets and armor. (A) is an oft-copied "Attic-style" helmet from a relief now in the Palazzo Ducale, Mantua. (B) and (C) are reliefs featuring the banded armor known as *lorica segmentata*, a staple of Roman movies. (D) and (E) are helmets found at Heddernheim, Germany, that were copied in *The Fall of the Roman Empire* and other films. *Illustrations by Graham Sumner.*

copy of one of Rome's gates, was not built until a century later. One of the highlights of the Forum set is its rendition of the great Temple of Jupiter Optimus Maximus on the Capitoline Hill overlooking the Forum. The interior of this important temple, which accurately features an imposing sixty-foot-high gold-and-ivory statue of the god Jupiter, appears in several scenes. The interior of the senate house is superior to the version in most films, since it correctly makes the room rectangular rather than semicircular, as is usually depicted; however, where there should be a statue of the goddess Victory, the film substitutes a reproduction of the famous statue of the she-wolf that raised the city's legendary founders, Romulus and Remus. The huge, brooding legionary fortress at the beginning of the film is also impressive, but while superficially recalling structures carved on Trajan's Column, it does not resemble any known legionary outpost.

The range of equipment on display in the film is truly staggering. The northern legionaries wear either leather *lorica segmentata* or *musculata* with "Italic" type helmets. The equipment was so well made that a few items still appear to have been in use in more recent epics, such as *Ben-Hur* (2016). In contrast, the eastern legionaries wear noticeably different equipment, with "Attic" helmets, previously seen in *King of Kings*, and jerkins with metal fittings, as pictured in Figure 3.5.A. Among the many warriors who show up in various scenes are Britons, Thracians, Armenians, Parthians, and Praetorians. The costume designers gave each group distinctive arms and armor, often based on actual finds or ancient descriptions; for instance, the eastern cataphract cavalry are covered in heavy scale armor. The film popularized two trends that still persist in modern epics. Roman generals wear heavy cloaks trimmed with fur, even in hot climates, and while it was not the first film to do so, every legionary is equipped with leather arm bracers, now a standard part of the Hollywood Roman uniform, even though there is no evidence to support their use. It's a shame that the wonderful sets and costumes produced by the design team of Veniero Colasanti and John Moore were not nominated for Academy Awards, but perhaps indicative of the declining popularity of the ancient epic, the awards that year went to the musicals *My Fair Lady* and *Mary Poppins*.

Classics scholar Martin Winkler has written extensively about *The Fall of the Roman Empire*, and, as he has pointed out, the ending of the film is uniquely bleak. Every other ancient historical epic concludes on some kind of positive note, usually to the accompaniment of an angelic chorus. *The Fall of the Roman Empire*, by contrast, delivers exactly what its title describes. At first, the film seems to be treading a familiar path, with the hero vanquishing the villain in a dramatic one-on-one duel. But then, when Livius is offered the throne by men representing the irredeemably corrupt army and senate, he rejects it, and quite literally walks away from them and out of the film. Seen in a wide shot, he strides off at a corner of the screen while the camera stays centered on the Forum, where the army is now holding an auction, selling the Roman Empire to the highest bidder. The film's conclusion proposes a doubly pessimistic thesis: not only is there no hope for the survival of civilization, as embodied in the form of the Roman Empire, but it has become so degenerate that it is not even worth saving. As this degrading auction—which, by the way, is based on a real event—continues, the voice of the omniscient narrator that began the movie returns to intone its final words: "This was the beginning of the fall of the Roman Empire. A great civilization is not conquered from without until it has destroyed itself from within." With this line, the film circles back to the agenda set out in the prologue: to explore reasons for the collapse of the Roman Empire.

While potentially offering useful historical insights, the movie did not prove to be a satisfying experience for viewers. First, the rather open-ended conclusion does not actually show the collapse and fall of the empire but rather just the onset of that process. Second, there is absolutely nothing uplifting or rousing about it. And finally, Livius is not a particularly appealing or inspirational protagonist, since he repeatedly makes rather bone-headed blunders and, in the end, basically gives up and quits his job, abdicating his responsibilities. Given its depressing plot, the predictable result was that the film was a colossal failure at the box office, driving Samuel Bronston's once-flourishing studio into bankruptcy.

The Greatest Story Ever Told (1965)

Director: George Stevens
Producer: George Stevens
Production Company: United Artists
Cast: Max von Sydow (Jesus), David McCallum (Judas), Charlton Heston (John the Baptist), Claude Rains (Herod the Great), Telly Savalas (Pilate), Carroll Baker (Veronica), Van Heflin (Bar Amand), Dorothy McGuire (Mary), José Ferrer (Herod Antipas), Sidney Poitier (Simon), John Wayne (Centurion)

Rounding out the trio of disastrous and costly flops of the 1960s credited with killing the ancient epic genre, along with *Cleopatra* (1963) and *The Fall of the Roman Empire* (1964), was 1965's *The Greatest Story Ever Told*, a well-intentioned biography of Jesus. Although development of this film began back in the mid-1950s at 20th Century-Fox Studios, it moved so slowly that rival MGM's own Jesus bio, *King of Kings* (1961), handily beat it to theaters. The movie was a labor of love by producer-director George Stevens, who was, at the time, a hot commodity, fresh off a string of critical and commercial successes. It was based on a popular 1949 book of the same title by Fulton Oursler. The film had a troubled evolution: Stevens labored over the script for years and employed a series of half a dozen writers to fiddle with it, including poet Carl Sandburg. At one point, MGM unsuccessfully tried to buy out the project in order to cancel it and prevent competition with *King of Kings*, but Stevens doggedly persevered, eventually moving the production from Fox to United Artists.

In a quest for authenticity, the filmmakers planned to shoot in the actual locations where Jesus's life had played out, and accordingly, Stevens spent six weeks scouting in Israel and Lebanon. However, he found the actual terrain of the Holy Land visually uninspiring and made what would prove to be a controversial decision to instead film everything in the far more dramatic American desert landscapes of Utah and Arizona, famous as the setting of innumerable westerns. Stevens claimed that these "looked more authentic" to him, and they did certainly provide imposing backdrops for Christ's ministry, but they also led some critics to comment that, when watching the film, they constantly expected a swarm of cowboys and Indians to emerge from behind the nearest majestic butte.

Filming finally began in 1962, and while it was supposed to take three months, this expanded to nine due to Stevens's insistence on shooting multiple takes of every scene. The production continued to eat up both money and time. Forty-seven major sets were built, including nine that cost more than $100,000 each. Six months were expended searching for just the right white donkeys for Christ to ride during his entrance into Jerusalem. After filming finally ended, Stevens then spent several years meticulously editing the eight hundred thousand feet of footage that he had shot. The studio patiently waited, believing that Stevens was crafting a masterpiece. United Artists executive Arthur Krim assured worried stockholders that "the film would be seen by more people over a longer period of time than has been true of any other motion picture in the history of motion pictures."[9] The original budget had been $7 million, but by the time it was completed $20 million had been spent, making it the second most expensive film up to that point, after *Cleopatra*. It was also exceptionally long, clocking in at three hours and forty-five minutes.

Finally released to coincide with Easter 1965, the long-awaited movie had a high-profile premiere, with Lady Bird Johnson, the wife of President Lyndon Johnson, in attendance. Unlike *King of Kings*, which added material concerning the political struggles between Romans and Jews in Judea and even managed to work in some action scenes, *The Greatest Story Ever Told* maintains a very tight focus solely on the events of Jesus's life as described in the Gospels.

It covers these episodes in a reverential way and at a slow pace. In the role of Christ, Stevens cast Max von Sydow, an actor relatively unknown to American audiences, and he portrays the Savior as an introspective, rather otherworldly figure. It is a pious but not particularly warm characterization, and viewers were further emotionally distanced from the story by the decision to film many scenes with very wide-angle framing, which reduced the characters to tiny figures against vast, imposing landscapes. Also, a number of the miracles that Jesus performs actually happen offscreen, so that instead of the viewer directly observing them, the camera focuses on reaction shots of the spectators witnessing them or even just talking about them afterward. For audiences accustomed to being served up biblical miracles with plenty of spectacle and special effects, as in the recent and hugely popular *The Ten Commandments* (1956), this indirect approach was unsatisfying. From a technical perspective, there is much to admire in the panoramic landscapes, the moody lighting, and the soundtrack, which makes effective use of pieces such as Handel's "Hallelujah Chorus." A patient and pious viewer can find it rewarding as a depiction of the life of Jesus, but the film is not well suited to provide thrills for moviegoers seeking escapist entertainment.

Critical response was mixed, but generally negative. The dominant reaction is summed up in a *Time* magazine review in 1965 written by Shana Alexander, which characterized the film as "three hours and 41 minutes' worth of impeccable boredom." Another aspect of the film that provoked derision was the inclusion of a myriad of cameos, with very famous actors constantly popping up throughout the film for brief, sometimes even nonverbal appearances. Some viewers felt that this detracted from the film's high-minded seriousness by turning it into a game of "spot the celebrity" ("Look, that leper is Shelley Winters!"). The most maligned of these cameos was John Wayne as the Roman centurion at the crucifixion, who undercuts the solemnity of an otherwise effective and moving moment when, just after Jesus dies, Wayne flatly delivers his only line in his unmistakable slurred cowboy drawl: "Surely, this man was the son of God."

Despite UA's efforts, audiences did not flock to the theater to see it, and against its enormous $20 million cost, the film took in less than $7 million in its initial domestic release. Coming on the heels of the box office flops of *Cleopatra* and *The Fall of the Roman Empire*, its failure at the box office cemented the idea that the day of the grand ancient epic was over. Unlike those other two films, which drove their respective studios into either dissolution or near bankruptcy, UA survived this one because they were able to offset its losses against the healthy profits turned by several other movies around the same time. However, it did effectively end George Stevens's filmmaking career. He would only make one more movie, and that not until a full decade later.

~

CHAPTER FOUR

The Late 1960s through the 1980s

Searching for a New Direction—
Parody, Porn, Plays, and TV

After the mid-1960s, with audience tastes changing and burned by a series of high-profile financial disasters, studios shied away from making big-budget ancient epics for the next three decades. Nevertheless, from the late 1960s through the 1980s, the ancient world would still appear onscreen in a variety of creative new forms. Two of the most successful types were parodies, such as *Carry On Cleo* (1964), *A Funny Thing Happened on the Way to the Forum* (1966), and *Monty Python's Life of Brian* (1979), and TV miniseries, exemplified by *I, Claudius* (1976), *Jesus of Nazareth* (1977), and *Masada* (1981). Finally, the 1970s and 1980s witnessed a number of hard-to-categorize cinematic projects that reflected the very personal visions of their makers, including Federico Fellini's bizarre experimental film *Fellini Satyricon* (1969), pornography entrepreneur Bob Guccione's X-rated *Caligula* (1979), and legendary director Martin Scorsese's controversial Bible movie, *The Last Temptation of Christ* (1988).

Carry On Cleo (1964/1965 US)

Director: Gerald Thomas
Producer: Peter Rogers
Production Company: Peter Rogers Productions/Adder
Cast: Sidney James (Mark Antony), Amanda Barrie (Cleopatra), Kenneth Williams (Julius Caesar), Joan Sims (Calpurnia), Kenneth Connor (Hengist), Charles Hawtrey (Seneca), Jim Dale (Horsa)

As the Golden Era of the historical epic came to an end in the early 1960s, one of the first films to parody the genre was *Carry On Cleo* (1964/1965 US). It was part of the "*Carry On* . . ." series of comic films that began in 1958 with *Carry On Sergeant* and eventually numbered thirty-one films. Made cheaply at Britain's Pinewood Studios with an ensemble cast of regulars, the *Carry On* franchise was the brainchild of producer Peter Rogers and director Gerald Thomas. Drawing upon the campy comedy of the British music hall tradition, the films were enormously popular in the United Kingdom, although their distinctive sense of humor and culturally specific references often failed to translate successfully to American audiences. According to Rogers, the *Carry On Cleo* installment had its origins in a bet that he made in the bar of Pinewood Studios. *Cleopatra*, starring Richard Burton and Elizabeth Taylor, was then undergoing its doomed initial attempt to be filmed at Pinewood, and Rogers wagered that he could create an entire movie in the time that it took the Hollywood production to construct just one of its elaborate sets.

Carry On Cleo was indeed completed very quickly, coming out in theaters barely a year after *Cleopatra* (1963) and ruthlessly mocking many of that film's most iconic scenes. For example, *Carry On Cleo* naturally includes a version of the famous meet-cute between Cleopatra and Julius Caesar in which she is secretly carried into his presence concealed in a rug, which is then unrolled to reveal her lying in a carefully composed, seductive posture. In *Carry On Cleo*'s version, the carpet is unrolled with too much vigor, so that Cleopatra tumbles clumsily into a table laden with food, then dazedly emerges from the wreckage festooned with appetizers. Despite a carpet unrolling scene being a highlight of almost every film involving Cleopatra, including those with Claudette Colbert in 1934, Vivien Leigh in 1946, and Elizabeth Taylor in 1963, all the cinematic depictions of this episode contain a minor historical error. The ancient source describing this dramatic event is the biographer Plutarch, who specifically notes that Cleopatra was carried to Caesar concealed, not in a fine carpet, but in a rather more mundane item—a type of sack that was used to store household bedding and linens (*Life of Caesar*, 49.1)

Carry On Cleo also pokes fun at the hoary cinematic tradition of ancient temptresses bathing in asses' milk, going back to films such as *The Sign of the Cross* (1932) with Claudette Colbert as Empress Poppaea and continuing through Elizabeth Taylor's baths as Cleopatra. In *Carry On Cleo*, almost every scene featuring Cleopatra (played by a big-eyed Amanda Barrie) either starts or ends with her lounging or frolicking in a milk bath, suggesting that (at least in the movies) this is pretty much what female ancient rulers spent all their time doing. While filming these scenes, the milk supposedly turned sour from long exposure to the hot lights, making it rather unpleasant for the actors.

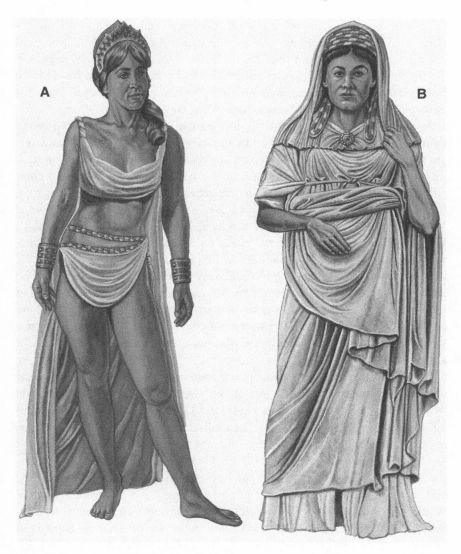

Figure 4.1. Vestal Virgins. From the silent era onward, filmmakers loved to portray Vestal Virgins in rather skimpy ahistorical attire. A typical example is (A) this Vestal from *Carry on Cleo* (1964/1965 US). Real Vestals (B) wore considerably more modest outfits befitting their role as revered priestesses charged with tending the sacred flame of Rome. *Illustrations by Graham Sumner.*

A particular target of the film (as in many British comedies) is authority figures—in this case, almost every important Roman of that era. The movie's portrait of Julius Caesar is particularly unflattering, with the decisive and able commander and statesman depicted here as an ineffectual ditherer. Another clichéd type of scene that gets played for laughs occurs when two captured

Britons-turne-slaves have to do a stint as oarsmen on a Roman warship à la *Ben-Hur*. The convention of a solemn-voiced narrator describing the historical context or commenting on the action also receives sharp parodic treatment. To fill this role, the filmmakers enlisted E. V. H. Emmett, who would have been a familiar voice to moviegoers since he had provided voice-overs for newsreels and had narrated other films of the time.

In many ways, the movie simply follows the tradition of ancient Roman comic plays, such as those written by Plautus, in which all of the characters are familiar stereotypes and audiences are bombarded with a mix of slapstick physical buffoonery and bawdy humor. A standard character in ancient comedies is the scheming slave who is much smarter or far more competent than his or her master. Thus, in *Carry On Cleo*, a movie chock-full of renowned Roman warriors, by far the most deadly fighter turns out to be the slave Horsa. For extra comic effect, the credit for his impressive rampages, during which he single-handedly slaughters entire platoons of soldiers, is repeatedly mistakenly ascribed to his hapless and very unmartial friend Hengist, who gets to swagger around flaunting his undeserved laurels. Censors limited how explicit the unrelenting stream of double entendres could be, but there are still plenty of lines like the narrator's comment on Cleopatra: "What a woman she was . . . immortalized in Macaulay's famous poem . . . the lay of ancient Rome."

While the *Carry On* series productions were usually low-budget affairs, some of the sets and costumes in this one are surprisingly elaborate. This is because when the first attempt to film the big-budget Hollywood *Cleopatra* in England fell apart and production shifted to the United States, the *Carry On Cleo* crew opportunistically took advantage by utilizing some of the abandoned *Cleopatra* sets and costumes in their own film. Thus, *Carry On Cleo*'s Mark Antony wears the same armor with leopard skin patches seen on Richard Burton's Antony, and many of the legionaries sport armor that had been made for *Cleopatra*. While there is a long tradition of filmmakers putting Vestal Virgins in ahistorically revealing outfits, *Carry On Cleo* features one of the most outrageous examples, with the priestess's costume resembling a bikini (Figure 4.1.A). Actual Vestals were heavily and modestly swathed in layers of fabric (Figure 4.1.B).

While there are clever bits, the movie is uneven and contains some odd elements. For example, apparently to emphasize their primitiveness, the Britons are depicted as prehistoric cavemen—dressed in furs, wielding clubs, dragging women around by their hair, and being eaten by dinosaurs. A lot of the humor also depends on a knowledge of British culture, such as the slave auctioneers' names referencing British retailer Marks and Spencer. How amusing you find the film probably hinges on your tolerance for unrelenting puns and slapstick antics.

A Funny Thing Happened on the Way to the Forum (1966)

Director: Richard Lester
Producer: Melvin Frank
Production Company: United Artists
Cast: Zero Mostel (Pseudolus), Phil Silvers (Lycus), Michael Crawford (Hero), Annette Andre (Philia), Jack Gilford (Hysterium), Leon Greene (Miles Gloriosus), Patricia Jessel (Domina), Michael Hordern (Senex), Buster Keaton (Erronius)

While there have been numerous cinematic adaptations of ancient Greek plays, the theater of ancient Rome has proved considerably less inspirational to filmmakers. A notable exception is *A Funny Thing Happened on the Way to the Forum* (1966), which, though not based on any single ancient play, instead wittily distills and combines elements drawn from the entire genre of Roman comic plays, as exemplified in the surviving works of Plautus and Terence. The comedies written by these playwrights in turn closely imitated earlier Greek theatrical forms, especially the plays of Hellenistic New Comedy authors such as Menander.

What all these ancient plays had in common was that they were intended as escapist entertainment, filled with jokes, slapstick, and buffoonery. The plots were formulaic and predictable, usually centering around frustrated love affairs and improbable coincidences. The characters in Plautus's plays were easily recognizable stereotypes. Among the most common were the *adulescens* (youth), a good-looking but often vapid and naive young man seeking love; the *servus callidus* (tricky slave), a clever and scheming slave, often the servant of the *adulescens*, who seeks personal gain while assisting the youth's quest for love; the *virgo* (maiden), a beautiful and virtuous young woman who serves as the love interest of the *adulescens*; the *senex* (old man), a traditionally minded but lascivious old man, often the father of the *adulescens*, who attempts to thwart his romance and is sometimes a rival for the *virgo*; the *matrona* (matron), an older woman, usually the mother of the *adulescens*, who henpecks her husband and also generates impediments to the *adulescens*'s romance; the *leno* (pimp or slave dealer), a greedy, selfish, and immoral character from whose clutches the *virgo* often has to be rescued; and the *miles gloriosus* (braggart soldier), an egotistical and cowardly soldier who is the main rival of the *adulescens* for the *virgo*'s affections. Chance, disguises, and mistaken identities occupy prominent roles in Plautus's plays, and there are an inordinate number of abductions of children by pirates, serving as a plot device to establish an obstacle that the protagonists must overcome.

A *Funny Thing Happened on the Way to the Forum* contains every one of these elements and characters, and deftly weaves them together to create a manic modern version of a Plautine comedy. The film has its origins in a popular 1962 Broadway play written by Stephen Sondheim, which enjoyed a long theatrical run and won numerous Tony Awards. The star of the stage production was Zero Mostel, who played Pseudolus, the *servus callidus* or "tricky slave" character, and he reprised this role for the film adaptation. Jack Gilford, another veteran of the stage production, appeared in the film as a second scheming slave, while Phil Silvers was recruited as the sleazy *leno*, and a young Michael Crawford, later to achieve fame as the Phantom of the Opera, was the clueless *adulescens*. Rounding out the stock roles, Annette Andre was the literally virginal *virgo*, Michael Hordern the leering but ineffectual *senex*, Patricia Jessel the shrewish *matrona*, and Leon Greene a hilariously self-adoring *miles gloriosus*.

There are some differences between the stage and screen versions, including the addition to the film of an episode set in a gladiator school and a prolonged chariot chase at the end. These were clearly intended as parodies of famous scenes in recent ancient epic films, such as *Spartacus* and *Ben-Hur*. The theatrical show was a musical, and although some of the songs were omitted in adapting it for the big screen, several were retained. While these musical numbers might appear modern in sensibility, they faithfully recall ancient Roman comic plays, which featured musical interludes as a part of the performance. One prominent aspect of both play and movie that is not a significant component of Plautus's ancient plays, but reflects contemporary sensibilities, is Pseudolus's determination to attain his freedom.

The movie contains a number of minor elements that reveal a surprisingly deep knowledge of Roman culture. For example, one of the prostitutes in the *leno*'s brothel is named Tintinabula, which literally means "bells" in Latin and is appropriate because she wears clothing adorned with bells that jingle when she performs an erotic dance. There is an additional layer of allusion, however, because Roman homes were often decorated with good luck charms called *tintinnabula*, cast in the shape of bells suspended from an erect phallus—certainly an appropriate symbol for a prostitute. In another scene, Pseudolus is reprimanded for "parading like a citizen" instead of "walking humbly like a slave." As scholars have argued, ancient Rome was a society much obsessed with gait and posture as indicators of status, so this exchange neatly illustrates this facet of their culture.

In contrast to the glorious city of shining marble and monuments on display in films such as *Cleopatra*, director Richard Lester wanted to offer a vision of ancient Rome that emphasized the grubby underbelly of the city and highlighted the injustices endured by exploited members of society such as slaves. The film wastes no time in establishing its perspective, beginning with a montage of daily life scenes in which the streets are covered in mud and strewn with rotting vegetables, and we witness Rome's lower-class inhabitants engaging in graft and scams, like the man industriously painting stripes on a donkey in order to make it look like a zebra, presumably so that he can make a profit by selling it as an exotic beast for a public spectacle. The first words spoken by Mostel in his opening monologue are: "Our principal characters live on this street—in a less fashionable suburb of Rome." These characters are all shameless social climbers, and, as Lester stated in a *New York Times* interview on November 7, 1965, "We tried as hard as we could to create bad taste—bad Roman taste of the first century AD. It's about the back streets, the suburbia of Rome, and it has a very nouveau riche quality." The filmmakers' pursuit of shabby realism was so dedicated that the rotten vegetables on set attracted hordes of flies, which in many scenes are conspicuously visible perching on and flitting around the actors. The flies' onscreen prominence resulted in a joke in the film's credits, where animated flies repeatedly land on the text as it scrolls by. The movie was shot in Spain and was able to reuse sets and costumes that had been made at Bronston Studios for the lavishly budgeted epic *The Fall of the Roman Empire*.

A *Funny Thing Happened on the Way to the Forum* was a solid if unspectacular commercial and critical success, but it perhaps deserves more credit for the clever way in which it seamlessly combines all the historically accurate characteristics of the genre of Roman Comedy and presents them to modern viewers in the form of a frantic, no-holds-barred farce.

Fellini Satyricon (1969/1970 US)

Director: Federico Fellini
Producer: Alberto Grimaldi
Production Company: Produzioni Europee Associati
Cast: Martin Potter (Encolpius), Hiram Keller (Ascyltus), Max Born (Giton), Salvo Randone (Eumolpus), Mario Romagnoli (Trimalchio)

Fellini Satyricon (1969/1970 US) is a bizarre, subversive film by acclaimed Italian director Federico Fellini that surreally mixes ancient and modern imagery. Made at the height of the social and sexual revolutions of the 1960s during an era of experimental avant-garde filmmaking, the movie was indelibly marked by both of these movements. It is based on an ancient novel, the *Satyricon*, written by the Roman author Petronius, who lived during the reign of Emperor Nero in the first century AD. The *Satyricon* is a racy picaresque novel that traces the amorous, serio-comic adventures of Encolpius, a pleasure-seeking young Roman man. There is a three-way love triangle involving another decadent young man, his some-time friend and sometime rival Ascyltus, and Encolpius's pretty sixteen-year-old slave boy, Giton, who is an object of lust for both. The novel has not survived intact; what remains consists of several fragments from the middle of what was originally a significantly longer work. Nevertheless, the surviving pieces are substantial, amounting to over one hundred pages in a standard modern paperback.

The film that Italian director Federico Fellini based on this source material is a controversial one. Critics and audiences were (and still are) sharply divided in their reactions, with some hailing it as a sophisticated work of genius that is a brilliant commentary on the process of interpreting the past and our inability to truly understand ancient civilizations, while others were left confused and alienated by its off-putting narrative structure and style and repulsed by what they viewed as its excessive, even deviant, sexuality. Some sense of this can be gained by considering the review written in 1970 by famous film critic Roger Ebert, who stated: "We're cast adrift in a universe of grotesques and dwarfs and cripples, lesbians and homosexuals and hermaphrodites, gluttons and murderers and the robbers of graves. And it is a masterpiece. Some will say it is a bloody, depraved, disgusting film; indeed, people by the dozens were escaping from the sneak preview I attended. But *Fellini Satyricon* is a masterpiece all the same."[1] Thirty years later, in 2001, Ebert felt compelled to post a second review, in which he was less enthusiastic, confessing, "Today I'm not so sure it's a masterpiece, except as an expression of the let-it-all-hang-out spirit of the 1970s world. A film that deals in visual excess like no other, showing a world of amorality, cruelty, self-loathing, and passion."[2]

The incomplete nature of the novel is clearly one of the aspects of the project that excited Fellini. He wanted his film to have a similarly fragmented quality. Additionally, rather than attempting a veristic reconstruction of the Roman world, it would instead offer an imaginative vision inspired by certain elements of it. His stated goal was "to evoke an unknown world of two-thousand years ago, a world that is no more. To work as an archaeologist does, when he assembles a few potsherds, or pieces of masonry, and reconstructs not an amphora, or a temple, but an artifact, in which the object is implied."[3] A number of critics, especially classical scholars, have admired this quality of the film, praising it as a sophisticated exploration of how our interpretations of antiquity are really modern constructs, and how we can never know what the past was really like.

Fellini was energized by how much remains unknown about Roman civilization, stating, "I realize that we don't know one damn thing for sure about Rome thousands of years ago. It is one big *nebuloso*, full of myth, fairy tale, Cecil B. DeMille information. Now I am excited because I know that the picture will be a trip in the dark, a descent by submarine, a science-fiction, a psychedelic picture. . . . An unknown planet for me to populate."[4] The finished film certainly reflects this philosophy. Like Petronius's text, it is fragmentary, with long digressions and gaps in the story; and, like the novel, the film begins abruptly and then literally ends in the middle of a random sentence. Fellini deliberately keeps viewers distanced and confused through sudden, inexplicable jumps to new locations and situations, and characters who seem to die in earthquakes or be murdered, then show up later, unharmed, without explanation. The audience is not meant to empathize with these characters, who are petty, self-absorbed, and unreflectingly engage in numerous acts of criminality and debauchery, but rather just to observe their actions.

Visually, the film is overwhelming, packed with Fellini's trademark collection of misfits, freaks, and grotesques. It is a feverish odyssey through a garish Roman netherworld—a surreal and nightmarish carnival of lurid and disturbing images and people—staged on sets that at times resemble an Escher drawing, with disorientingly jumbled networks of staircases, ramps, passages, and levels. Every sense is assaulted and bewildered, including hearing. The film's music is intentionally discordant and bizarre, incorporating everything from spacey synthesized bleeps, to jarring sound effects, to contemporary ethnic music. The characters speak a perplexing and illogical mixture of languages, including Italian, Latin, Greek, German, English, Turkish, and, in some cases, pure gibberish. In an interview, Fellini stated that "the atmosphere is not historical, but that of a dream world. . . . *Satyricon* should have the enigmatic transparency, the indecipherable clarity, of dreams."[5] To further distance the characters and their actions from the viewer and impart the sense of an alien world, Fellini has the actors frequently make enigmatic gestures. As he explains, "The customs of these characters must appear to us totally incomprehensible, some of their extravagant gestures as indecipherable; grimaces, winks and other codes whose meanings we have lost. We no longer know the allusions behind them . . . as if we were watching a documentary on some Amazon Basin tribe."[6] As one critic has commented, the only consistent principles in the movie are ambiguity and incomprehension.[7]

Nevertheless, many scenes, and even large chunks of dialogue, come straight from Petronius's text. The longest and most famous section of both the novel and the movie is an extravagant dinner hosted by a former slave-turned-millionaire-businessman named Trimalchio. In a vulgarly ostentatious display of his wealth, Trimalchio serves up a succession of over-the-top dishes and entertainments to his guests. Fellini vividly brings to life even the most outrageous elements of this meal and then adds his own embellishments. Certain episodes are derived from or inspired by other ancient authors. Thus, a scene in which Encolpius has to fight a gladiator-style combat against an opponent dressed as a minotaur and then have sex with a woman in front of the audience is obviously modeled after a similar incident in Apuleius's novel *The Metamorphoses*. A sequence in which an aristocratic Roman couple free their slaves and commit suicide after a political regime change mirrors any number of similar actual suicides in Roman history, including Petronius's own. None of this is explained to the viewer in any way, so unless you have an extensive knowledge of Roman history and literature, you will probably just be left puzzled by what appears to be a seemingly random assortment of disturbing images.

The film mingles modern elements with details that reflect a deep knowledge of ancient Roman daily life. For example, a scene of a marriage ceremony accurately includes a "bride" with an orange veil, the guests' congratulatory shouts of "*feliciter*," and the ritual of throwing nuts at the couple. In an extended sequence near the movie's beginning that follows Encolpius as he strides through a Roman bath, then a brothel, and, finally, the cavernous, multilevel interior of a high-rise apartment building in a slum of ancient Rome, we are treated to a rapid series of vignettes of life in each location. Although not realistic in a literal sense, the sequence captures something wonderfully true to life about the city of Rome as a bustling, crowded, vibrant, diverse, and alternately magnificent and sordid urban space.

The final shot of the film is a close-up of Encolpius, on whom the camera freezes, and then the actor's image gradually morphs into a painting on a wall. The camera pulls back to reveal all of the other characters, also in wall painting form—but significantly, on a crumbling section of wall that is part of a ruined building, and the images are cracked and faded. This serves as a final distancing mechanism and reminder of the inscrutability of a world long gone. Watching the movie is like looking at a two-thousand-year-old fragment of a painting on a Greek vase and trying to envision the whole, not with the intent to fashion a plausible historical reconstruction, but rather as a personal act of imagination. Whether or not one enjoys watching this film is very much a function of one's taste. Even for those who admire its intellectual content, it can be a hard slog to get through. The movie contains images that some might find disturbing, but it raises interesting questions about the nature of historical reconstruction and the limits of knowledge. In the end, as Ebert noted in his second review, Fellini's stream-of-consciousness, let-it-all-hang-out outburst of creativity and lurid overindulgence is perhaps best considered as a product of the era when it was made.

Julius Caesar (1970/1971 US)

Director: Stuart Burge
Producer: Peter Snell
Production Company: Commonwealth United/American International
Cast: Charlton Heston (Mark Antony), Jason Robards (Brutus), John Gielgud (Julius Caesar), Richard Chamberlain (Octavius), Diana Rigg (Portia)

Despite its star power, this version of Shakespeare's play was not a success. When assessing it from a historical perspective, it is hard to get past the issue that it has the unfortunate distinction of featuring arguably the most unhistorical costuming of any film in this book, worse even than is typically encountered in exploitative, low-budget peplum flicks. In terms of the casting, Heston and Gielgud are solid as Antony and Caesar, although both are about a decade too old for the parts, and Heston's sonorous voice works quite well for Antony's famous funeral oration. In the crucial role of Brutus, however, Jason Robards—who is a good actor in other films—flubs this one very badly, uttering his lines in a monotone that manages to be both abrasive and wooden. He conveys absolutely none of the inner conflict and depth of character necessary for Brutus that James Mason so wonderfully captured in the superior 1953 film version of the play directed by Joseph Mankiewicz.

The costumes here are a truly bizarre mix, drawn from a range of wildly different historical eras and cultures. Quite a few of the ordinary women of Rome wear what appear to be eighteenth-century European bonnets and dresses that make them look like extras who wandered in from a production of Les Misérables. Meanwhile, many of Rome's male citizens apparently stepped into the picture from a movie taking place during the Middle Ages, since they are wearing the distinctive peasant hoods, pants, and boots of that period. At times, characters sport Renaissance or early modern outfits that would be appropriate for someone like Machiavelli or Sir Thomas More. The "togas" of the senatorial characters, rather than being the historical plain white woolen garments bearing a purple stripe, instead seem to be fabricated from women's silk dresses of wholly unsuitable colors, such as pale lavender and baby blue, and adorned with decorative pleats and embroidered panels. When Charlton Heston's Antony goes off to war, he is clad in a thoroughly Renaissance-looking outfit that consists of high leather boots, a poufy pleated and embroidered swashbuckler-type shirt, and tights—none of which were worn in ancient Rome. The armor on the film's soldiers is equally strange. The ordinary legionaries' body armor is unlike anything historically attested, but perhaps most resembles a blacksmith's leather apron, and perched on their heads are odd helmets with high metal crests. The upper-class characters' armor is seemingly based on the fanciful and elaborate armor depicted in Renaissance art, as in the drawings of Leonardo da Vinci, rather than that of ancient soldiers. Finally, many of the aristocratic Roman characters have thick, full beards and mustaches when, in reality, upper-class Romans of the late republic were always clean-shaven.

The film was both critically panned and a commercial failure. Despite this, producer Peter Snell and Heston would immediately team up again to make a second Shakespeare play, again featuring Heston as Mark Antony (see next entry). Of all the anachronisms that mar this film, perhaps the most amusing is that Caesar somehow seems to have gotten his hands on a llama from South America, which marches among the wild animals being exhibited in his triumphal parade.

Antony and Cleopatra (1972/1973 US)

Director: Charlton Heston
Producer: Peter Snell
Production Company: The Rank Organisation/Peter Snell Production
Cast: Charlton Heston (Mark Antony), Hildegard Neil (Cleopatra), John Castle (Octavian), Jane Lapotaire (Charmian), Fernando Rey (Lepidus), Freddie Jones (Sextus Pompey)

Fresh from playing Mark Antony in the 1970 film version of Shakespeare's *Julius Caesar*, Heston returned to the same character is this 1972 adaptation of Shakespeare's *Antony and Cleopatra*. It seems to have been something of a vanity project for Heston, and he not only starred in the film, but also directed and coauthored the adaptation. It was shot on a modest budget in Spain, and Heston had to creatively string together financing from multiple sources to get it made. To further economize yet still impart a big-budget feel, he cut a deal with MGM that allowed him to use footage shot for the naval battle in *Ben-Hur* to augment this film's scenes of the Battle of Actium. Also, some costumes, notably armor for the legionaries, were reused from *The Fall of the Roman Empire*, which, like this movie, was shot in Spain.

In *Julius Caesar*, where Antony's main purpose is to deliver inspirational oratory, Heston made a respectable Antony, but in this film, in which the character is more nuanced and complex, he is less convincing. Heston seems to play every role the same way. All the characteristic Hestonisms are on full display here: lots of groaning and jaw clenching to convey strong emotions intermingled with outbursts of stentorian declamation. The distinctive Heston persona was very effective in roles such as Moses and Ben-Hur, but when depicting a character like Antony, whose personality is historically attested, it becomes more problematic. Here, Heston fails to convey either Antony's soldierly charisma or his tendency toward self-indulgence. A relative unknown, Hildegard Neil, was cast as Cleopatra, and while she is beautiful and can handle Shakespearean diction, her characterization does not suggest any of the historical Cleopatra's intelligence or considerable political savvy.

The filmmakers' selective editing of Shakespeare's text does Cleopatra no favors either, as it plays up her catty jealousy of Antony's wife, Octavia, rather than focusing on any of her positive qualities. Film versions of Shakespeare often shorten the plays by cutting out entire scenes or speeches, but for this adaptation, the unfortunate decision was made to cut and paste individual words and clauses and then string them together. Thus, Heston, who cowrote the screenplay, might take seven words from the first line of a speech, connect them with five more from the middle, and then nine others from the end. While the end product is technically all Shakespeare, this process completely destroys the rhythm of the original, obscuring Shakespeare's frequent use of alliteration and rhyme.

Despite its flaws, the film is visually creative in the many ways it finds to insert episodes of physical action into Shakespeare's text. Thus, it has lengthy battle scenes both on land and at sea, and multiple dynamic sequences of messengers on horseback galloping frantically to and fro. Most inventive is the manner in which it spices up a summit between Antony and Octavian by intercutting their conversation with a gritty and violent bout between two gladiators that the generals watch as they conduct their negotiations.

I, Claudius (1976/1977 US)

Director: Herbert Wise
Producer: Martin Lisemore
Production Company: BBC Films
Cast: Derek Jacobi (Claudius), Siân Phillips (Livia), Brian Blessed (Augustus), George Baker (Tiberius), John Hurt (Caligula), Patrick Stewart (Sejanus)

During the 1970s, a time when big-screen ancient epics were out of favor, antiquity found a new path to success on television, particularly in the form of the miniseries. One of the earliest and most acclaimed of these was *I, Claudius*. It brazenly flouted the earlier conventions of the ancient epic by providing no stirring large-scale battles or gladiator fights, no gigantic sets or lavish costumes, no cast of thousands, no visual spectacles of any kind. Instead, it offered up thirteen hours of seasoned actors from the British theater sitting around a handful of fairly crude indoor sets and holding lengthy conversations. With such an approach, it could even be labeled an "anti-epic." Yet, it proved to be a resounding critical and popular success and resulted in one of the most influential and memorable envisionings of the ancient world to ever appear onscreen.

The *I, Claudius* miniseries, produced by the BBC, was based on two novels written by Robert Graves and published in the 1930s. It premiered on BBC2 from September through December of 1976 and then, the following year, was shown in the United States on PBS as episodes of the show *Masterpiece Theatre*. Both novel and miniseries are told from the perspective of the elderly emperor Claudius. The action is set between 24 BC and AD 54, an eventful period in Roman history covering the reigns of the first four emperors, Augustus, Tiberius, Caligula, and Claudius. All belonged to the Julio-Claudian dynasty, and these familial connections are the key to understanding the show's approach to Roman history, for above all, it is the story of a family, and the rivalries, jealousies, and infighting among its members. That this particular family just happens to control a vast political empire takes second place to their interpersonal relationships. Rather than showing the great events of history as shaping their personal lives, *I, Claudius* inverts this formula, giving us a group of people whose personal lives shape history. The promotional material put out by *Masterpiece Theatre* made this quite clear: "Based on the best-selling novels about dirty work in ancient Rome, the . . . series lavishly depicts the orgiastic society of the all-powerful Claudians, the family whose business was ruling the world."

The miniseries thus has much in common with the format of a soap opera, which typically focuses on an extended family and its often lurid tribulations. The enormous popularity of soap operas is a testament to how effective and appealing such an approach can be. Furthermore, the family in the spotlight here is not just rich, but also the hereditary ruling family of an empire—the Roman equivalent of England's royal family. This enabled *I, Claudius* to tap into a whole second group of people: those obsessed with royalty. The show created a feeling of intimacy, as if you were eavesdropping on the private interactions of famous people and privy to secret knowledge. *I, Claudius* served up a clever stew of sensational soap opera, royalty watching, and *Lifestyles of the Rich and Famous*, spiced with enough convincing period detail to lend it the wholesome aura of a history lesson. The director, Herbert Wise, stated, "We agreed right at the beginning that we weren't going to make a period piece. We wanted to make it contemporary. We wanted to make the point that human psychology hasn't changed much in the last 2,000 years."[8]

The writers made the dialogue match the approach, giving the characters a chatty, colloquial style of speech that was markedly different from the stiff "pseudo-classical dialogue" of earlier classical epics. The head writer of the miniseries, Jack Pulman, initially struggled with the tone, but finally found his groove when he had the insight of envisioning the Julio-Claudians as the equivalent of a mafioso family, like the one featured in the *Godfather* films. Pulman noted, "I couldn't write it, until I thought of the mafia." Despite its dramatic and sometimes violent subject matter, the dialogue also includes humorous bits, and in writing these, Pulman found another comparison helpful, saying that for such moments, he imagined the show as "a Jewish family comedy."[9]

The tight focus on the imperial family kept production costs down, which amounted to only about $2 million for all thirteen hours. Almost all filming was confined to interiors, primarily rooms in the imperial household, with very few exterior scenes. Crews fabricated only enough of a set to allude to the whole; for instance, a few interior sections of the senate house subbed for the whole thing. This was the complete opposite tack from that taken by films such as *The Fall of the Roman Empire*, with its colossal, detailed reconstruction of the Forum. In place of the "cast of thousands," *I, Claudius* made do with only about fifteen extras. Take, for example, its depiction of a gladiator game. Only the imperial viewing box was built, and the camera stays tightly focused on the members of the imperial family. Sound effects such as the roar of the crowd and the clashing of swords are employed to conjure the illusion of a large audience and as a stand-in for the violence taking place. Instead of visual spectacle, we get character exposition as we observe their reactions: the young Claudius, at his first gladiator game, swoons and faints at the kill, while his sister Livilla's intense enjoyment of the violence intimates her immoral tendencies. Similarly, viewers experience the disastrous Roman defeat at the Battle of the Teutoburg Forest not through a giant set-piece battle scene, but instead solely through a courier's verbal description to Emperor Augustus and his anguished reaction.

These scenes exemplify the great importance of the camerawork in *I, Claudius*. Shot with multiple cameras, the miniseries has been compared to live theater, and indeed many involved came from a theater background. The classic epics of the 1950s and 1960s were filmed using systems with names like Cinerama, CinemaScope, Panavision, and VistaVision that stressed the size of the screen and the panoramic nature of the cinematography. The small TV screen couldn't achieve that kind of grandeur, but it could create a greater sense of intimacy, which *I, Claudius* cannily exploits. Many of the takes are extremely long—four to five minutes without a cut, which again resembles theater—and the viewer is constantly given very tight close-ups of the actors' faces. A good example is the famous death scene of Emperor Augustus. In it, he lies on a bed, unmoving and unspeaking, while his wife, Livia, delivers a long monologue. Rather than showing Livia speaking, however, the camera stays riveted on Augustus's face for almost five full minutes. Left to our own impulses, we would probably watch the speaker, but the camera tells us where to look—at the silent man's facial expression, especially his eyes. Director Herbert Wise said he wished to show "the light going out in Augustus' eyes. . . . We're going to see Rome die. We're going to see the Empire die on [his] face."[10] Big-screen movies almost never use such prolonged, tight close-ups. With its in-depth exploration of the characters' personalities, its literate and often witty dialogue, its multigenerational saga of a family, and its clever staging and camerawork, *I, Claudius* found a way to inject high drama back into the ancient epic without resorting to expensive sets, costumes, or visual spectacles.

To be successful, a story needs compelling characters as well as skilled actors, and *I, Claudius* had a plethora of both. The historical Claudius was the step-grandson of the first emperor, Augustus, but most members of his family viewed him with contempt. This was because Claudius had been born with a variety of physical disabilities, including tremors, a limp, and a speech impediment. Since Roman society placed a high value on looking dignified, these infirmities made him an object of cruel scorn. His body, however, harbored a sharp, if somewhat eccentric, mind, and Claudius found solace in intellectual pursuits. He lived through the reigns of Augustus and Tiberius, and probably only survived the tenure of the mad emperor Caligula by playing the fool. Then, in an unlikely twist, after the Praetorian Guard had murdered Caligula, they elevated Claudius to the emperorship apparently on a whim. This challenging role is superbly performed by Derek Jacobi, who makes him a sympathetic narrator for the tale. It is a tour-de-force acting job, especially considering that he had to play Claudius from the time he was a young man all the way through old age, requiring heavy use of old-age makeup. *I, Claudius* was one of the first productions to take advantage of new advances in facial prosthetics. Because the techniques were still being developed, prosthetics frequently fell off during filming or else stuck to the actors too well, rendering their removal extremely painful. Jacobi hit upon a procedure for removing his old-age makeup relatively painlessly by wearing a snorkel and submerging himself in a bathtub to gradually soak it off.

Perhaps the most memorable character, and the most controversial in terms of the accuracy of her depiction, is Augustus's wife, Livia, played in the series by Siân Phillips. The show presents her as scheming, manipulative, coldly intelligent, and amoral, and the true power behind the throne. The significance of the first emperor, Augustus, is thus diminished, as the credit for many of his strategies and achievements is shifted to her. While the primary sources and historical evidence could be read to suggest that Livia was an active partner to Augustus, nowhere is it implied that she was basically the brains behind the entire operation.

Brian Blessed portrays Augustus as a bluff, hearty fellow who, although prone to flashes of temper and violence, basically means well. He's also kind of clueless—blissfully unaware of Livia's machinations until nearly the end of his life, and also seemingly the only one ignorant of his daughter Julia's many affairs. Director Herbert Wise advised Blessed that, rather than acting like an emperor, he should just "be an ordinary guy." The show's Augustus does possess more force, agency, and decisiveness than in Graves's novel, because Blessed, with his brawny physique, booming voice, and confident manner, can't help but project energy and authority. Others defer to him, even Livia, and his occasional eruptions of anger give him a certain unpredictability and underlying menace. The historical sources suggest that the real Augustus was clearly far more of an active agent and that he possessed the cunning, manipulativeness, and ruthlessness here attributed to Livia. In physical appearance, Blessed is also pretty much the opposite of the historical Augustus, who is described as slight of build, on the short side, and often sickly.

The series' and books' conception of Livia goes much further than just showing her as a behind-the-scenes puppet master pulling the strings of her husband, however; they turn her into a mass murderer who kills multiple members of her own family in order to advance her agenda. She wants Tiberius, her son by a previous husband, to become the next emperor, but Augustus dislikes Tiberius and prefers various other relatives as his successor. Thus, Livia sets out to eliminate these rivals one by one. She poisons the first presumptive heir, Augustus's nephew, Marcellus. Then, when Augustus's old friend Agrippa is designated as his successor, Livia poisons him. Next, Agrippa's sons are adopted by Augustus and primed as successors, so Livia poisons one of them herself, persuades someone else to drown a second, and gets the third falsely accused of rape and exiled. She also connives to have Augustus's daughter by a previous wife exiled. It is implied that, in order to pave the way for Tiberius, she intended to kill another of her sons and a grandson, but they expired first without her intervention. Finally, she tricks the head Vestal Virgin into giving her access to Augustus's will so that she can substitute a fake one, and ultimately murders Augustus with a poisoned fig.

This is quite a laundry list of crimes. Was Livia really such an amoral villain? One of the most appealing aspects of both books and the miniseries is that, in general, they adhere more closely to actual ancient sources than many cinematic depictions of the ancient world. Robert Graves drew heavily on the Roman historian Tacitus and the biographer Suetonius, who wrote about the lives of the first dozen emperors. Many incidents, details, and even bits of dialogue are taken directly from these sources. For example, the show's Augustus likes to use the distinctive phrase "as quick as boiled asparagus" to indicate something done rapidly. Suetonius relates that this was one of Augustus's favorite sayings. Similarly, Suetonius describes Augustus as habitually wearing a broad-brimmed hat, enjoying gambling, and eating sparingly—all of which are faithfully reproduced onscreen. Regarding Livia, however, the majority of the ancient sources were actually relatively neutral in tone or even positive. Suetonius, for instance, who normally delights in recounting lurid details about sex and violence among the Julio-Claudians, has little negative to say about Livia.

The notion that Livia was systematically eliminating all possible successors to Augustus in order to clear the way for her son Tiberius can be traced to the ancient Roman historian Cassius Dio. He mentions the rumor that Livia smeared poison on figs in order to kill Augustus, but he's wishy-washy about it, adding that Augustus sickened "from this or from some other cause" (*History of Rome* 56.30.3). Of the deaths of Agrippa's sons, Gaius and Lucius, he inconclusively comments that "suspicion attached to Livia" (*History of Rome* 55.10a). Dio thus records rumors about Livia without endorsing them. Tacitus seems to have had a strong dislike for Livia, but also tends to make insinuations rather than outright accusations. He never plainly states that she killed Tiberius's rivals, but instead hints at it, saying that he is simply relating rumors that he has heard, or slipping in unfounded alternative explanations without any actual evidence. About the deaths of Agrippa's sons, he says, "Untimely fate, or the treachery of their stepmother Livia, cut off both Lucius and Gaius Caesar" (*Annals* 1.3). On the death of Augustus, he blandly comments, "there were some who suspected foul play on the part of his wife" (*Annals* 1.5). Actress Siân Phillips has stated that she initially tried to find some justification for Livia's actions and to make her sympathetic, but director Herbert Wise advised her, "Just be evil. The more evil you are, the funnier it is, and the more terrifying it is."[11]

Whether true from a historical perspective or not, Siân Phillips's characterization of Livia is an indelible one that affected how several generations viewed Livia and initiated a vogue for scheming upper-class female characters. HBO's *Rome* miniseries created its own scheming Livia-like figure in the character of Atia, whom the show keeps artificially alive for seven years after her actual death so that she could be part of the series through its end. The enduring influence of *I, Claudius*'s Livia is found even in nonhistorical shows. Consider, for example, the hugely popular mobster series *The Sopranos*, where the name of Tony Soprano's manipulative, abusive mother is Livia, clearly intended as a nod to the first empress.

Phillips, Jacobi, and Blessed all gave wonderful performances in their roles as Livia, Claudius, and Augustus, and *I, Claudius* can attribute much of its success to the fact that its entire cast was an extraordinarily talented group of British thespians, many of whom went on to become quite famous. A young John Hurt delivers a delightfully wicked performance as a nutty, flamboyant, mad emperor Caligula. George Baker gives us a gruff, long-suffering Tiberius chafing under his overbearing mother's abuse—a performance that allegedly inspired the character of Stannis Baratheon in George R. R. Martin's *Song of Fire and Ice* novels. And long before gaining TV fame as Captain Picard on *Star Trek: The Next Generation*, a young and hirsute Patrick Stewart plays Tiberius's suavely ambitious Prefect of the Praetorian Guard, Sejanus.

Critical reaction to the series in the UK was initially negative. This might be attributable to several causes: the levels of sex, nudity, and violence were, at that time, unprecedented and shocking in a television show, and in contrast to the publicly funded BBC's traditional mission of presenting "morally wholesome" adaptations of classic literature and educating its audience, *I, Claudius* was more akin to a contemporary soap opera. From the start, however, the response of television audiences in both the UK and the US was enthusiastic. After their initial shock, critics also soon came around. *I, Claudius* garnered three British Academy of Film and Television Arts awards, including Best Actress for Siân Phillips and Best Actor for Derek Jacobi. In 2000, the British Film Institute placed *I, Claudius* twelfth in the list of 100 Greatest British Television Programmes of all time. For many, the show's portraits of Livia and Claudius are the definitive ones and have permanently influenced how their historical counterparts are viewed.

In more recent times, some have asserted that the show had a misogynistic tone. This criticism is not without basis, since many of the female characters—most prominently, of course, Livia—are portrayed as immoral schemers, while their male counterparts are often good-natured but ineffectual, or else constantly being manipulated by the women. On the other hand, for the time when it was made, simply showing female characters as powerful, determined, smarter, and more competent than the male ones was a relatively rare step. Regardless of such issues, *I, Claudius*, the anti-epic, definitively proved that it was possible to make a show set in the ancient world, without a huge budget or lavish spectacle, that could still be highly entertaining, have contemporary relevance, and be intellectually sophisticated and stimulating.

Jesus of Nazareth (1977)

Director: Franco Zeffirelli
Producer: Vincenzo Labella
Production Company: ITC/RAI Co-Production
Cast: Robert Powell (Jesus), Olivia Hussey (Mary), Michael York (John the Baptist), Anne Bancroft (Mary Magdalene), James Farentino (Peter), Ian McShane (Judas), James Mason (Joseph of Arimathea), Peter Ustinov (Herod the Great), Christopher Plummer (Herod Antipas), Valentina Cortese (Herodias), Yorgo Voyagis (Joseph), James Earl Jones (Balthazar), Donald Pleasence (Melchior), Fernando Rey (Gaspar), Laurence Olivier (Nicodemus), Ralph Richardson (Simeon), Ian Holm (Zerah), Stacy Keach (Barabbas), Ernest Borgnine (Centurion), Anthony Quinn (Caiaphas), Rod Steiger (Pontius Pilate)

The television miniseries *Jesus of Nazareth* (1977) was an ambitious British-Italian coproduction directed by Franco Zeffirelli. Shot at locations in Tunisia and Morocco, it was the most expensive miniseries made up to that time. Despite its more than six-hour length, this miniseries is among the best of the various Jesus biographies. It succeeds as a pious expression of faith for the religious viewer, and as a movie that can be enjoyable for nonbelievers as simply a well-made and engaging narrative.

A common tactic of Jesus biographies is to have all the characters constantly adopting attitudes of extreme reverential piety, and while this perhaps helps the filmmakers to signpost the significance of the events being portrayed, this approach also strips the characters of much of their credibility as actual human beings. In contrast, while Jesus in this miniseries is indeed given an otherworldly holiness—primarily through the camera's emphasis on Robert Powell's preternaturally light blue eyes and the fact that he never blinks—crucially, the characters surrounding him have an ordinary down-to-earth quality. For example, the early scenes depicting the daily life and rituals of the little Jewish community of which Mary and Joseph are members have a prosaic, matter-of-fact vitality that anchors the later supernatural occurrences. When first confronted by prophecies or even miracles, the characters are often initially and realistically suspicious before coming to acknowledge the divine nature of the occurrences that they are witnessing. Also, the costumes and the Tunisian and Moroccan sets have a dusty, impoverished-looking authenticity. Collectively, all of this realistic background renders Jesus's teachings and miracles all the more miraculous and convincing when they do finally happen.

The script, cowritten by director Zeffirelli, experienced screenwriter Suso Cecchi d'Amico, and renowned author Anthony Burgess, seems particularly attuned to the power of language. This is appropriate since, after all, the Jesus of the Bible leaned heavily on parables and storytelling as a teaching method. This word-centered approach is captured in a number of scenes where Jesus says, to various audiences, "Let me tell you a story," such as when he relates the parable of the prodigal son at a banquet at the house of Matthew. There are several surprisingly lengthy but nonetheless engrossing debate scenes, such as the ones featuring the Jewish elders, which create the opportunity to offer a more complex and nuanced portrait of how Jesus and his ministry both built upon and sometimes challenged existing social, religious, and political ideas and structures.

The film is full of cameos by famous actors. In *King of Kings*, which similarly cast a plethora of celebrities in minor roles, this practice was at times distracting or even grating. Here, they are more successful. For example, as the trio of Magi, James Earl Jones, Donald Pleasence, and Fernando Rey effortlessly impart gravitas without stealing the spotlight from Mary, Joseph, and Jesus. Michael York is a dynamic and, for once, appropriately youthful John the Baptist. As a self-centered Herod the Great fearing the rise of a messiah to challenge his rule, Peter Ustinov brings his usual wit to the role, lamenting to a visiting Roman that "literacy has had a disastrous effect on this country." James Farentino delivers a forceful performance as Peter, bringing a humanizing element to the familiar Bible stories with his portrait of Peter as a reluctant disciple who comes to understand that joining Jesus's ministry will entail forever abandoning everything that he had previously valued, including his job, home, and family. Ralph Richardson, Laurence Olivier, Ian Holm, Christopher Plummer, James Mason, and Ian McShane are all effective in minor roles without being intrusive. Even Ernest Borgnine is surprisingly touching as a gruff Roman centurion sympathetic to Jesus's movement.

There are a few places where the script invents characters who are not attested in the Bible, and switches around where and when events take place, but these divergences are relatively minor, and the majority of Jesus's words are taken from the four Gospels that describe his life. While the costumes of the Jews and other ordinary people are unusually convincing, those of the Roman legionaries commit many of the usual historical inaccuracies, such as leather armor and ubiquitous pants. Making a cinematic depiction of Jesus's life and death is by its nature an inherently challenging and problematic endeavor, but this has not stopped filmmakers from attempting it, and *Jesus of Nazareth* succeeds at offering a solid middle ground between reverential and entertaining.

Caligula (1979/1980 US)

Directors: Tinto Brass, Bob Guccione
Producer: Bob Guccione
Production Company: Penthouse Films International
Cast: Malcolm McDowell (Caligula), Peter O'Toole (Tiberius), Teresa Ann Savoy (Drusilla), Helen Mirren (Caesonia), John Gielgud (Nerva), Guido Mannari (Macro)

Caligula (1979/1980 US) is one of the strangest films that has been made about ancient Rome. It was a pet project of Bob Guccione, the publisher of *Penthouse* magazine, and, as you might expect of a film made by a professional pornographer, it contains explicit unsimulated sex, as well as scenes involving the rape of both women and men, incest, necrophilia, and a great deal of very graphic violence. It is an extremely unpleasant film to watch. Famous film critic Roger Ebert was so repulsed by it that it was one of the very few movies that he ever walked out of, and he characterized it as "sickening, utterly worthless, shameful trash." He ends his review by approvingly quoting a fellow theatergoer who exclaimed, "This movie is the worst piece of shit I have ever seen."[12] One might well ask, "If it is so terrible, why even discuss it?" In addition to completeness, there are two other reasons the film is of interest. First, astonishingly, it features four eminent and talented British actors: John Gielgud, Peter O'Toole, Helen Mirren, and, in the title role, Malcolm McDowell. Second, although large sections of its script and plot are invented, other portions reveal one of the closest readings of, and incorporation of, material from an ancient primary text of any film set in the Roman world.

The text in question is a collection of biographies of the early Roman emperors, including Caligula, written by a man named Suetonius. He was a bureaucrat in the Roman administration at the end of the first century AD, and due to his position, he probably had access to official state archives and documents. This should make Suetonius one of the most reliable sources we have for this era, but he was not interested in writing serious history, instead delighting in dwelling on salacious tales about the misbehavior of the emperors. A sense of his tastes can be inferred from the titles of some of his other works, such as *Biographies of Famous Prostitutes* and *Obscene Greek Terms of Abuse*.

The makers of *Caligula* plainly read Suetonius very attentively, and quite a few of the most distasteful episodes in the film are drawn directly from his pages. McDowell's dialogue also incorporates numerous quotations that Suetonius reports, probably accurately, as having been spoken by Caligula, for instance, "I can do anything I like to anyone," "Let them hate me so long as they fear me," and "If only all the Roman people had one neck." Specific details from Suetonius depicted in the movie include Caligula's infatuation with his favorite horse, Incitatus, and his desire to appoint this animal to the highest magistracy in the government; his opening of a brothel in the palace unwillingly staffed by upper-class married women; his incestuous relationship with his sister Drusilla; his predilection for outrageously gaudy outfits; his farcical "invasion" of Britain; his chronic insomnia; his fear of going bald; the specifics of how he had various unfortunate senators and attendants sadistically murdered; the oath of personal loyalty to himself and his sister that he instituted; and the perversities practiced by the previous emperor, Tiberius, at his villa on the island of Capri. All these things are vividly described by Suetonius, are possibly true, and are enthusiastically and luridly re-created by the filmmakers.

The convoluted production history of the project perhaps explains why such distinguished actors as Gielgud and O'Toole chose to associate themselves with it. Its origins lay in a play by renowned author Gore Vidal, who also wrote several other works based on ancient figures. Vidal was fascinated by Suetonius's biographies as cautionary tales that held a valuable lesson for a modern American empire regarding the allure of decadence that, if indulged, could bring it crashing down. He believed that all human beings contain elements of both good and evil and are "half-tamed creatures whose great moral task is to hold in balance the angel and the monster within—for we are both—and to ignore this duality is to invite disaster."[13] This led to his writing a screenplay titled *Gore Vidal's Caligula*. Meanwhile, Guccione had decided to try to expand his porn empire into the mainstream market by producing a film that would contain explicit sex but still be seen as a legitimate movie. Therefore, he enlisted director Tinto Brass to film Vidal's screenplay, and provided the financing. Brass was lured to the project because he harbored dreams of making an arty spectacular along the lines of *Fellini Satyricon*. The involvement of both Vidal and Brass and the movie's seemingly highbrow ambitions were enough to persuade Gielgud, O'Toole, Mirren, and McDowell to sign on. After the principal photography had been completed and it became apparent what sort of picture it would be, both Vidal and Brass withdrew their participation and demanded that their names be removed from the credits. Guccione re-edited Brass's cut of the film, shot new scenes of Penthouse "pets" engaging in X-rated sex, and intercut these with the existing sequences featuring the famous actors.

During the 1970s, there was a fad among a segment of mainstream moviegoers for films that skirted or even crossed the line between porn and "legitimate" cinema. Movies such as *Midnight Cowboy*, *Last Tango in Paris*, and *Deep Throat* were able to attain critical or commercial success, and sometimes both. *Caligula* tried to position itself so as to take advantage of this trend, and although it was abused by critics such as Ebert, it nonetheless succeeded in hauling in almost $24 million at the box office—more than was earned by the critically adored Martin Scorsese masterpiece *Raging Bull*, released the same year. *Caligula* is a genuine curiosity: a hard-core trainwreck of a movie that also stars top-notch actors and draws upon considerable amounts of actual history. Recently, some scholars have argued for its recognition as a cult classic, and there are even ongoing attempts to restore versions that resurrect both Vidal's and Brass's original visions. However, as it currently stands, it is unquestionably a film that is not only badly made but also a thoroughly unpleasant viewing experience.

Monty Python's Life of Brian (1979)

Director: Terry Jones
Producer: John Goldstone
Production Company: HandMade Films/Python Pictures/Orion
Cast: Graham Chapman (Brian, Biggus Dickus), John Cleese (Reg, High Priest), Eric Idle (Cheeky, Stan/Loretta), Terry Jones (Mandy Cohen, Colin, Simon the Holy Man), Michael Palin (Big-Nose, Francis, Pontius Pilate), Terry Gilliam (Prophet, Gaoler)

Monty Python's Life of Brian (1979) followed in the footsteps of *Carry On Cleo* (1964) and *A Funny Thing Happened on the Way to the Forum* (1966), which set out to lampoon the hoary clichés of the ancient epic genre. Drawing upon both the Python troupe's comic genius and their deep knowledge of history, the film elevated such parodies to new heights. Monty Python was an irreverent group of six highly educated men, mostly from Britain, who had achieved a cult following in the United Kingdom and the United States as a result of their groundbreaking BBC sketch comedy television show, *Monty Python's Flying Circus*. After this ended, they made the feature film *Monty Python and the Holy Grail*. Released in 1975, it was a clever spoof of both the legends surrounding King Arthur and films set in the Middle Ages generally. The movie was an unexpected success, and so, by the mid-1970s, the Pythons were at the peak of their popularity and seeking inspiration for a follow-up project. While doing publicity for the *Holy Grail*, when Python Eric Idle was asked what their next movie would be, he flippantly replied, "Jesus Christ: Lust for Glory."[14] They all ended up liking the idea, and from this origin was born their unique take on biblical and Roman epics, *Monty Python's Life of Brian* (1979).

Their first notion was to do a film on the life of Jesus, but they soon realized that this wouldn't work, because they didn't see much to mock in Jesus's core teachings of love, peace, and tolerance. However, in their eyes, the historical setting for Jesus's life, and aspects of organized religion in general—such as humanity's tendency to conformity, factionalism, and blind adherence to dogma—seemed riper targets for comedic criticism. They eventually came up with the idea of presenting a biography of a character named Brian of Nazareth, a fictional nobody who lived at exactly the same time as Jesus and whose life paralleled that of the Christian savior. While intended as a comedy, the film would also have a more serious purpose by, in the words of Python John Cleese, offering a critique of "closed systems of thought, whether they are political or theological or religious or whatever."[15] The film was shot in Tunisia, whose dusty landscapes lend it a nice authenticity, and the Pythons were even able to reuse some of the sets that had been built there a few years earlier for *Jesus of Nazareth* (1977).

Monty Python's Life of Brian methodically moves through a number of the most well-known clichés of the ancient epic, which had previously been presented in a solemn or reverential manner, and uses humor to deflate their pretentiousness. We already see this in the opening shot, which, at first, seems like a standard depiction of the birth of Christ, complete with angelic choir, shepherds, the Star of Bethlehem, and the three wise men coming to worship the messiah. However, they mistakenly enter the wrong manger, encounter the newborn Brian and his mother, and bestow upon the puzzled woman their gifts of gold, frankincense, and myrrh. Soon realizing their error, they unceremoniously rip the gifts out of her hands and proceed next door to where Jesus has just been born. Minus the mistaken identity, this is how *Ben-Hur*, arguably the most famous of the 1950s biblical epics, had begun, and the parallels continue during the credits that follow. The movie's title is spelled out in colossal, imposing stone blocks, just as the posters for *Ben-Hur* had presented that film's title; but in Python's version, the massive stones ignominiously crumble and collapse, dissolving into one of Terry Gilliam's trademark zany animated sequences with bits of famous classical statuary zooming around.

The movie then jumps ahead three decades to Jesus delivering the Sermon on the Mount, with Brian and his mother among those in attendance. In previous Bible epics, including *King of Kings* (1961), *The Greatest Story Ever Told* (1965), and *Jesus of Nazareth* (1977), the Sermon on the Mount had been a centerpiece of the film, and public speechmaking was a staple of almost every historical epic. A particularly common scenario involved the hero giving a rousing speech before a battle in order to inspire his troops. Historical films of every era love this particular cliché; think, for example, of Mel Gibson's "freedom" speech in *Braveheart*. Python brilliantly subverts this trope through the simple expedient of pointing out the practical problems with delivering an outdoor oration before the invention of microphones and loudspeakers. As recent scholarship has demonstrated, the words of anyone attempting to communicate in such a fashion would in reality have been inaudible to anyone beyond the handful of people within a couple dozen yards of the speaker. However implausible they are in practical terms, Hollywood keeps serving up these scenes because they make for such good drama.

The Pythons begin their version of the Sermon on the Mount with the camera tightly focused on Jesus, and we hear his words clearly. Then it steadily pulls back, and our perspective recedes away from him, out over the heads of the gathered crowd, until Jesus has been reduced to a small figure in the distance. As the camera withdraws, the volume of Jesus's voice steadily decreases and the ambient noise increases, until we arrive at the back of the crowd, where, instead of Jesus's sublime words, all we can clearly hear are the voices of several of the spectators who are inanely bickering with one another. Nor can the crowd members themselves hear, so that when Jesus declaims, "Blessed are the peacemakers," and one of them asks what he said, another replies, "I think it was, 'Blessed are the cheese-makers,'" prompting the puzzled rejoinder, "What's so special about the cheese-makers?" Shortly thereafter, Jesus's statement, "Blessed are the meek," is misheard as, "Blessed are the Greek." Here, Python presents a much more realistic rendition of what attending an ancient public oration would actually have been like than appears in any earnest historical epic.

The Pythons provide their uniquely insightful take on another staple of ancient epics: extravagant entertainments in the arena. Gladiator battles or chariot races are usually the dramatic highlights of films set in the Roman world, and these are invariably staged as exciting, if violent, spectacles. The Pythons' version of an amphitheater scene deflates this cliché and astutely emphasizes how the practical details of such an event might undercut its glory. Hollywood epics, especially those of the 1950s, loved to present gladiator fights, but usually shied away from showing just how gruesome such entertainments would actually have been. Python immediately shoves this aspect of the games in our faces by opening their amphitheater scene with a bored slave shuffling around the blood-soaked sand of the arena in the aftermath of a gladiator fight, picking up sundry dismembered limbs and organs, and dumping them into a basket. Meanwhile, in the stands above, instead of the usual densely packed mob of enthusiastically shouting spectators, we see a sparse audience listlessly looking on with bored expressions.

Once the body parts have been cleared away, a deep-voiced herald dramatically announces the next bout, featuring a gladiator with the menacing name of "Frank Goliath the Macedonian Baby-Crusher." Two gladiators emerge, one a tall, muscular, imposing figure in armor with his face concealed by a helmet, and the other a scrawny man equipped in the standard gear of a *retiarius*-style gladiator, with a net in one hand and a trident in the other. Rather than attacking one another in a furious and dramatic display of skilled swordplay, as previous films have accustomed us to expect, the scrawny *retiarius* emits a frightened squawk, drops all his weapons, and runs away from his opponent. His more heavily armored foe laboriously chases him and the two repeatedly circle the arena until the pursuer suffers a heart attack and drops dead. The unexpectedly successful, if faint-hearted, *retiarius* then capers about in a ludicrous victory dance. Thus, in their amphitheater scene, the Pythons subvert the conventions of gladiator movies, presenting us with realistic gore, but not the accompanying glorious spectacle, and with cowardice triumphing over martial skill.

The amphitheater scene satirizes another modern stereotype of Roman culture: their reputation for dining on exotic delicacies. The banquet scene in which decadent aristocrats stuff themselves with an endless array of elaborate dishes is a staple of ancient films. Admittedly, this idea has some basis in reality, since it is true that the very wealthiest class of Romans did sometimes enjoy lavish feasts at which the fare might be composed of expensive and even bizarre ingredients, such as flamingo tongues. While such recipes were extremely atypical exceptions rather than reflecting the diet of ordinary Romans, the sumptuous and exotic Roman feast has become a standard cinematic cliché. The Pythons naturally jump on the comic possibilities of this stereotype by making Brian a snack vendor at the amphitheater, who wanders up and down the stands, hawking his trayful of absurd Roman delicacies to the apathetic audience. Among the treats on offer are wrens' livers, chaffinch brains, jaguars' ear lobes, ocelots' spleens, dromedary pretzels, Tuscany fried bats, and even wolf's nipple chips, of which Brian cheerfully comments, "Get them while they're hot, they're lovely!" One of the spectators plaintively asks, "Don't you just have any nuts?" When Brian suggests badgers' spleens instead, the spectator complains that he doesn't want "any of that Roman rubbish," which he characterizes as "rich imperialists' tidbits." But he ends up settling for a bag of otters' noses.

How does Python represent the Romans themselves? It had become a convention to cast British actors with posh upper-class accents in the roles of Roman authority figures, such as generals and politicians—a trend perhaps best exemplified by Sir Laurence Olivier's aristocratic turn as Crassus in the film *Spartacus*. This casting decision lent an undeniable air of seriousness, authority, and all-around gravitas to such figures. The Pythons naturally cannot resist poking fun at this hoary cliché. Thus, they saddle the two highest-ranking Romans in the movie with outrageously exaggerated speech impediments. The result is that the solemn authority these men hope to project is undercut, literally, with every word that they speak. The joke is intensified by the fact that they are completely unaware of their verbal mannerisms. They repeatedly make portentous declarations, such as, "Vewy well, I shall welease Wodewick," and, "Thitizens! We have Thampthon the Thadduthee Thwangler," but are then puzzled by the crowd's laughter and the snickering of their own guards produced by such utterances. Mocking pretentiousness and authority figures is a staple of the Pythons' repertoire, and in this film, the well-established trope of the aristocratically accented upper-class Roman offers them a ripe target for one of their favorite types of comic social criticism.

Another aspect of Roman civilization that has less to do with ancient history than with the English educational system of the twentieth century gets highlighted when Brian, who wants to join the anti-Roman revolutionary group, the People's Front of Judea, is given the mission of painting anti-Roman graffiti in the public square. In the middle of the night, Brian scrawls a phrase in Latin that he believes means "Romans Go Home," but is caught in the act by a Roman centurion. Rather than killing or imprisoning him, however, the centurion sternly berates Brian for his Latin grammar, and, twisting Brian's ear like a schoolmaster punishing an ill-prepared schoolboy, pedantically forces him to conjugate verbs and decline nouns until he hits upon the correct form—"Romani ite domum"—then orders him to write it out one hundred times on the wall. The scene playfully recalls what would have been a familiar experience for generations of British schoolboys forced to study Latin. A more serious scene involving the Romans occurs at a meeting of the People's Front of Judea, when their leader, Reg, delivers a fiery screed denouncing Roman imperialism and their cruel exploitation of the provinces. In the course of his invective, Reg dramatically exclaims, "They've taken everything we had. . . . And what have they ever given us in return?" This is meant as a rhetorical question, but one of his men pipes up and says, "The aqueduct." Others chime in, listing additional benefits of Roman civilization, which results in Reg modifying his statement to: "Apart from the sanitation, medicine, education, wine, public order, irrigation, roads, the fresh water system, and public health, what have the Romans ever done for us?" When someone answers, "Brought peace," the enraged Reg responds with an exasperated, "Oh, peace! . . . Shut up!"

It's a funny moment, but in this brief scene, the Pythons quite effectively give a nutshell summary of one of the most complex and interesting debates about the Roman Empire. The Roman conquest of the Mediterranean was accompanied by a great deal of violence and exploitation of the provincials, but for many regions, the arrival of Rome also brought order, prosperity, opportunity, and culture. It is an age-old argument that touches on questions of colonialism, imperialism, the merits of spreading so-called "civilization," and whether or not the attendant loss and assimilation of indigenous cultures is ultimately offset by whatever supposed benefits the conquering civilization brings. Roman writers such as Tacitus raised these issues two thousand years ago, and they remain hotly debated and relevant topics today. It is rare for even serious historical films to tackle such complicated and contentious subjects, yet Python manages to do so in a way that is both concise and amusing. It is one of the best moments in any film dealing with the ancient world.

Although actually quite respectful of Jesus, the film is fiercely critical of organized religion and, really, any sort of bureaucracy. Many of the movie's sharpest jabs are directed at the human tendency toward factionalism and tribalism. Accordingly, Judea is depicted as rife with rival Jewish rebel groups who are more passionate about their hatred of each other than of their Roman overlords. Thus, the People's Front of Judea is deeply offended at being mistaken for the Judean People's Front, and both organizations despise the Judean Popular People's Front. All the factions are portrayed as being more prone to talking and passing resolutions than taking action. The one time that the People's Front of Judea does try to do something, by kidnapping Pontius Pilate's wife, the plan goes awry when they run into The Campaign for Free Galilee, which is attempting the same scheme. The two gangs start fighting, prompting Brian to plead, "Brothers! We should unite against the common enemy," whereupon the members of both groups exclaim, "You mean the Judean People's Front!" to which the exasperated Brian replies, "No, no—the Romans!" In the end, as Roman soldiers bemusedly look on, shaking their heads, the two groups slaughter one another.

Ancient Judea was indeed a hotbed of religious factionalism and what the Pythons aptly refer to as "messiah mania." In one memorable scene,

Brian walks down a street on which, every dozen or so feet, there is a different self-proclaimed "prophet" loudly proselytizing for some new religion. Forced to imitate one while fleeing from the Romans, Brian inadvertently attracts a throng of ardent followers, who obsequiously address him as "master" and interpret his every platitudinous comment as revealed divine wisdom. Attempting to instill some actually useful advice, he tells them: "You don't need a leader. . . . You've got to think for yourselves. . . . You're all individuals"—to which his horde of adherents ironically chants back, in unthinking unison, "Yes, we're all individuals." Brian's fawning disciples are eager to interpret anything he says or does as evidence of his holiness, so that when one complains about being hungry and he helpfully points out a nearby juniper bush, they all excitedly declare it a miracle and beg him to perform another. When he claims not to be the messiah, they simply respond with: "It is a sign! . . . Only the true messiah denies his divinity!" When Brian persists in saying, "I am not the messiah," one dismissively replies, "I say you are, Lord, and I should know. I've followed a few."

Fleeing from his adoring supporters, Brian loses one of his sandals and gives away a gourd that he had been carrying. The mob instantly seizes upon these mundane items as holy relics of their messiah and carry them about triumphantly as objects of veneration. Almost immediately, however, disagreement arises between followers of the gourd and followers of the sandal, and furthermore, the sandal adherents begin squabbling among themselves over the symbolic meaning of the relic and whether they should express their adoration for it by holding aloft one sandal or by collecting a huge pile of sandals. Again, in an amazingly brief scene, the Pythons effectively present in microcosm how almost every religion has developed, including a founder figure, the evolution of theology and doctrine, the establishment of symbols, and the seemingly inevitable schism into an ever-increasing number of rival sects, each rabidly espousing some relatively trivial variant on the core system of beliefs.

Although they had harbored some concerns about religious groups responding negatively to the film, the Pythons seem to have been surprised by the vehemence of the hostility that it provoked. It was banned in Ireland, Italy, and Norway, and elicited formal charges of blasphemy in Britain. In the United States, some theaters showing the film were targeted by picketing and even bomb threats. Jewish, Catholic, and Protestant groups all issued denunciations. Each of the Pythons made statements in defense of the film. For example, John Cleese argued, "What is absurd is not the teachings of the founders of religion, it's what followers subsequently make of it. And I was astonished that people didn't get that."[16] Terry Jones pointed out, "You've got Christ preaching a gospel of peace and love and charity to all, and for the next 2,000 years, people are killing each other and torturing each other because they can't agree about quite how he said it."[17] And Graham Chapman summarized their stance thus: "That movie, if it said anything at all, said, 'Think for yourselves, don't blindly follow,' which I think isn't a bad message."[18]

Much of the animosity came from people who had not actually seen the film, and who insisted on believing that the Pythons intended Brian to be Jesus, and thus that anything comic involving Brian constituted mockery directed against Jesus. This is a reading that the Pythons adamantly denied, since the entire reason why they had based the movie around Brian and not Jesus in the first place was to prevent such an interpretation. In the end, the controversy probably did more to help the film than harm it by drawing more attention to it and increasing its box office take. Today, it is considered a comedy classic, and is even ranked as the greatest comedy of all time in several polls. The film concludes with a well-known scene that recalls previous ancient epics, although in a way that is more of an homage than a critique. Brian, along with a large number of other condemned prisoners, is sentenced to be crucified, but, at the last minute, a centurion shows up, announcing that Pilate has issued a reprieve for Brian and asking which of them he is. Cleverly inverting the famous "I am Spartacus" scene, in which Spartacus's followers all claim to be Spartacus in order to prevent his being singled out for punishment, all of Brian's fellow prisoners shout out, "I am Brian," in an attempt to avoid punishment. It doesn't work, they are all crucified, and the film closes with the prisoners hanging on their crosses and, in a rather literal display of gallows humor, cheerfully singing the ditty, "Always look on the bright side of life."

History of the World Part I (1981)

Director: Mel Brooks
Producer: Mel Brooks
Production Company: Brooksfilms
Cast: Mel Brooks (Comicus), Dom DeLuise (Nero), Madeline Kahn (Empress Nympho), Gregory Hines (Josephus), Ron Carey (Swiftus)

Although parodic treatments of ancient Rome might be considered to have reached an apogee with *Monty Python's Life of Brian* in 1979, they continued into the early 1980s with *History of the World Part I* (1981). This film was written, produced, and directed by Mel Brooks, who made an entire cinematic career out of crafting satires of various film genres in a distinctive style combining broad slapstick and bawdy humor with a sprinkling of clever, pointed, and sometimes surprisingly topical social commentary in movies such as *The Producers* (1968), *Blazing Saddles* (1974), and *High Anxiety* (1977). He next turned his attention to the historical and biblical epic with *History of the World Part I*, which consists of a series of unrelated sketches ranging from the Stone Age through the French Revolution. By far the longest of these, taking up just over half the film's running length, takes place during the early Roman Empire, with Brooks appearing as Comicus, a "stand-up philosopher"; Dom DeLuise as Emperor Nero; Madeline Kahn as his wife, Empress Nympho (in a performance clearly inspired by cinematic portrayals of Poppaea); and Gregory Hines as a slave named Josephus.

The Rome sequence immediately launches into its parody of the ancient epic by opening with a deep-voiced narrator (Orson Welles) solemnly delivering an absurdly hyperbolic succession of lines: "Rome! Vortex of modern civilization. Rome! Fountainhead of culture. Rome! Blazing pronouncement of mankind's most glorious achievements!" The first scene, set in the bustling Roman Forum, promptly undercuts these grand pronouncements by showing a more tawdry version of antiquity, thus establishing the episode's satiric style. As pedestrians hurry to and fro, we see shifty salesmen aggressively hawking their wares: "Columns, columns, get your columns here, Ionic, Doric, Corinthian. Put a few columns out front, turn any hovel into a showplace!" Background signs bear advertisements such as, "Temple of Eros. Annual Orgy and Buffet. First Served, First Come." A motley line of people waits for government handouts at the "Unemployment Office," where a bored official berates a despondent gladiator: "Did you kill last week? Did you try to kill last week? Listen here, this is your last week of unemployment insurance— either you kill someone this week or we're gonna have to change your status." Maintaining this snarky tone, the film briskly runs through the usual array of obligatory ancient Roman scenes: a slave auction, a palace orgy, an over-the-top erotic dance, a gladiator fight, a senate meeting, and a chariot race.

The movie gleefully juxtaposes ancient and modern, with a man strolling through the Forum carrying a boombox blasting "Funkytown," Caesar's Palace in Las Vegas standing in for Caesar's palace, references to Trojan brand condoms, and Comicus and friends using papyrus paper to roll a massive marijuana joint. Comicus's agent gets him a gig performing at "the main room" in Caesar's palace, where he encounters Nero, broadly played by DeLuise as a crude, belching, farting, spitting, gluttonous, jaded tyrant. Here, the film is riffing on Peter Ustinov's memorable performance as Nero in *Quo Vadis*, particularly when DeLuise foppishly proclaims, "The muse is upon me," preparatory to reciting a poem. As scholar Monica Cyrino points out, another scene that seems to directly allude to earlier epics has Empress Nympho lasciviously inspecting a row of bottomless legionaries in order to select men for that night's orgy—a bit that recalls when, in *Spartacus*, a pair of spoiled aristocratic women ogle muscular near-naked gladiators and pick the handsomest ones to fight to the death for their pleasure. At the palace, Comicus's routine offends the emperor, who sentences him to death. In response, Comicus laments, "When you die at the Palace, you really die at the Palace"—a line that is perhaps more apt than Brooks realized, as it accurately reflects the historical Nero's penchant for staging "fatal charades," or theatrical entertainments that incorporated real violence and death.

Perhaps due to its episodic nature, *History of the World Part I* is an uneven film, and much of the humor is admittedly sophomoric, but it still manages to effectively parody some of the most clichéd elements of the ancient epic while providing some laughs.

Masada (1981)

Director: Boris Sagal
Producer: George Eckstein
Production Company: Universal
Cast: Peter O'Toole (Flavius Silva), Peter Strauss (Eleazar ben Yair), Barbara Carrera (Sheva), Giulia Pagano (Miriam), Anthony Quayle (Rubrius Gallus), David Warner (Falco), Timothy West (Vespasian)

In the late 1970s and early 1980s, the history-themed TV miniseries was enjoying a moment of great popularity, and the ancient world was a natural topic for producers seeking to replicate the success of series such as *Roots* (1977). Made by Universal and broadcast on ABC, *Masada* (1981) was an ambitious and expensive offering that told a dramatic story set during the First Jewish Revolt (AD 64–74) when a Roman legion besieged a group of Jewish rebels who had taken refuge in the seemingly unconquerable fortress of Masada, situated atop a mesa in Judea. Made at a then-record cost of $25 million, the six-and-a-half-hour miniseries was based on the novel *The Antagonists* by Ernest K. Gann, which was adapted for television by Joel Oliansky.

The miniseries dusted off Hollywood's long-standing tradition of ancient epic accent coding in order to signal who the good and bad guys were; thus, the main Romans are played by British actors, whereas the principal Jews are all Americans. Peter O'Toole turns in an excellent performance as Lucius Flavius Silva, the commander of the besieging Roman legion who, although he is an able and dutiful soldier, is weary of fighting and wants peace so that he can go home. Anthony Quayle is memorable as Silva's highly competent chief military engineer who designs the colossal ramp that must be constructed so that the Roman siege engines can reach the walls of

Masada, while David Warner makes an oily but charismatic Roman politician. On the Jewish side, Peter Strauss is an appropriately fiery and energetic Eleazar ben Yair, the leader of the Sicarii, the Jewish rebels. To provide a love interest for O'Toole, the script gives Silva a Jewish slave/mistress played by Barbara Carrera.

The actual story of the Jewish Revolt and the siege of Masada is known primarily through the writings of Flavius Josephus, a Jew who initially fought against Rome, was captured, became an intimate of the emperor Vespasian and his family, and wrote several lengthy histories of the Jews and their struggles against Rome. Silva and Eleazar were real figures who appear in his history, but Josephus says almost nothing about their personalities. The siege itself is only treated by Josephus quite briefly, so again, many of the episodes that occupy the six-hour miniseries are the products of the filmmakers' imaginations. Nevertheless, *Masada* contains some excellent generic scenes of a sometimes underappreciated aspect of the Roman war machine: its proficiency at military engineering.

The miniseries opens with the capture and destruction of Jerusalem by the Romans in AD 70. During the sack of the city, thousands of Jews were slain, the Great Temple was looted, and its sacred objects were carried off to be displayed in the triumph of the Roman general Titus. One of the most famous Roman sculptural reliefs, which appears on the Triumphal Arch of Titus erected in Rome to celebrate this event, depicts a group of legionaries bearing an enormous seven-branched menorah—presumably the very one stolen from the Great Temple. The miniseries cleverly alludes to this relief when, during a montage of scenes showing the chaotic sack of the city, we see a squad of Romans running down a street carrying the huge golden menorah.

Eleazar ben Yair, the leader of a Jewish faction that favors continued violent opposition to the Romans at any cost, escapes the burning city with his family and a small band of followers and takes refuge in the fortress of Masada. His raids on neighboring settlements provoke the Romans to dispatch the Tenth Legion, under the command of Flavius Silva, to seize Masada and capture or kill the last Jewish rebels. The holdouts atop Masada were estimated to number 960, including some women and children, while the Roman legion, plus its auxiliary troops and various support elements, was probably around 10,000 strong. Silva and his engineers determine that the only way to take the fortress is to erect a huge earthen ramp up one side of the mountain and, despite the blistering desert heat, they begin its construction.

Thus far, the miniseries and history align fairly closely. However, Josephus provides almost no further details until the actual moment when the Romans complete the ramp and launch their attack on the walls of Masada. Therefore, to flesh out the story, the miniseries stretches the building process out over six months (archaeologists estimate it would have required only one) and introduces sundry episodes that almost certainly never happened, including several face-to-face meetings between Silva and Eleazar, a peace agreement between Silva and Eleazar that is ruined by politics at Rome, raids by the Jews to disrupt construction, a subplot involving spies representing both Emperor Vespasian and one of his political rivals, a psychological warfare campaign waged by the Jews to discourage the Romans, and the love story of Silva and his Jewish mistress.

The sets and costumes are a mixed bag, with some excellent details drawn directly from ancient sources, and others that are erroneous or invented. Among the better examples are a scene of grain being ground using a stone hourglass-shaped mill that is exactly like those found at sites such as Pompeii, and several portrayals of the Romans performing animal sacrifices in which the priests are assisted by attendants who do the actual killing and butchering of the animals. These were known as *cultrarii* and *victimarii*, and the miniseries depicts them precisely as they appear on ancient reliefs: bare-chested, wearing a leather apron, and with a triangular pouch of knives at their waists. Among the instruments carried by the legion's musicians are the distinctive Roman G-shaped horn known as a *cornu* as well as the trumpet-like *lituus*, both of which are shown correctly. On the other hand, they also employ drums, which is not attested.

The costume designer was Vittorio Novarese, who also worked on *Cleopatra* (1963). The auxiliary archers dressed in flowing robes and conical helmets closely resemble ones sculpted on Trajan's Column. However, as portrayed in Figure 4.2, the legionaries (B) erroneously wear leather rather than metal body armor and their shields are too small; both items are likely recycled from *The Fall of the Roman Empire* (1964). Many soldiers and officers wear pants—a rarity among Romans and an especially unlikely choice in such a hot climate. Comparison with a reconstruction of a historically accurate mid-first-century AD legionary (Figure 4.2.C) reveals clear differences in equipment. The film's centurions (Figure 4.3.B) also wear similar leather armor and sport unusual helmets (apparently made for the film) that feature little triangular tufts on each side, almost like furry animal ears, rather than the large transverse crest worn by actual centurions (see Figure 4.3.C for a reconstructed centurion of this era).

In terms of the siege's conclusion, the miniseries adheres to Josephus's account reasonably closely. The Romans did move a siege tower equipped with a battering ram up the completed ramp; the Jews did temporarily thwart it by constructing a second wall of timbers packed with shock-absorbing

Figure 4.2.   Legionaries of the Early Empire. First century AD legionaries from (A) *Quo Vadis* **(1951) and (B)** *Masada* **(1981). Both soldiers wear body armor of a type used at this time, but (A) is missing the chest and back plates, while (B) is of leather rather than metal. Both their shields are too small and of the wrong shape. (C) Reconstruction of a first-century AD legionary showing the correct form of this armor and proper shield.** *Illustrations by Graham Sumner.*

Figure 4.3. Centurions of the Early Empire. First century AD centurions from (A) *Ben-Hur* (1959) and (B) *Masada* (1981). Neither has the distinctive transverse helmet crest that was one of the identifying hallmarks of centurions, as shown in the (C) reconstruction of a first-century AD centurion. Compare his accurate *phalerae* with those in Figure 1.5.A. *Illustrations by Graham Sumner.*

earth behind the outer stone wall; the Romans then set the timber wall on fire; and finally, realizing that they could not prevent the Romans from breaking in, the Jews decided to commit suicide. As shown in the miniseries, only one woman and a few children survived by hiding, but Eleazar and over nine hundred of the Jews did indeed kill themselves.

Masada was a modest hit with viewers and was nominated for twelve Emmys, winning two. Apparently in a bid to give it more contemporary relevance or interest, the ancient story was rather awkwardly bookended by a prologue and epilogue of modern Israeli soldiers taking their military oaths at Masada. The miniseries was edited down and released as a two-hour film called *The Antagonists*, but with most of its narrative coherence lost, this version was not a success.

The Last Temptation of Christ (1988)

Director: Martin Scorsese
Producer: Barbara De Fina
Production Company: Universal/Cineplex/Odeon Films
Cast: Willem Dafoe (Jesus), Harvey Keitel (Judas), Barbara Hershey (Mary Magdalene), David Bowie (Pontius Pilate), Harry Dean Stanton (Paul)

Acclaimed director Martin Scorsese had long wished to make a movie about Jesus, an ambition that was finally realized with *The Last Temptation of Christ* (1988). The film is based on the novel of the same name published in 1955 by Greek author Nikos Kazantzakis. Scorsese acquired film rights to the novel in the 1970s and commissioned Paul Schrader to write a screenplay. By the early 1980s, he had obtained financing from Paramount to make the film, lined up a cast of talented actors, arranged to film on location in Israel, and even obtained a large budget of $14 million. Just when everything seemed in place, growing criticism from religious groups caused the controversy-averse studio to cancel the project. Scorsese was determined to make the movie and, several years later, managed to convince Universal Studios to back a version with the budget slashed in half to $7 million and filmed in the more inexpensive location of Morocco. This time around, production proceeded relatively smoothly; the film was shot in 1987 and appeared in 1988. Both before and after its release, however, the movie was the target of substantial vitriol from a wide range of Christian groups, and still remains one of the more controversial Jesus films today.

What is it about the film that provoked such animosity? Its source material, Kazantzakis's book, had also been vigorously denounced, even being officially condemned as heretical by both the Catholic Church and the Greek

Orthodox Church. Many of the objections to both book and film centered around their portrayals of Jesus feeling human emotions such as doubt, anger, and even lust. Standard Christian doctrine asserts that Jesus was both "fully human and fully divine," and it is this potential paradox that Kazantzakis and Scorsese investigate by inventing incidents not attested in the Bible during which Jesus experiences various human emotions and temptations. Most controversial is an episode in which Jesus is tempted by Satan with a vision of an alternative life as a "normal" man rather than as the messiah, during which he marries Mary Magdalene, has children, and grows old. Although Jesus ultimately rejects this hypothetical life, choosing instead to be crucified to ensure the salvation of humanity, and despite Scorsese being careful in the film to explicitly state that it is a totally fictional creation not intended to depict the biblically attested life of Jesus, critics were still outraged at this allegedly blasphemous sequence of scenes. To attempt to forestall such attacks, Scorsese begins the movie with two text passages, the first quoting Kazantzakis about his fascination with the dual nature of Jesus, followed by the statement, "This film is not based upon the Gospels but upon this fictional exploration of the eternal spiritual conflict."

Leaving aside its religious aspects, in terms of the film's historical accuracy, the Moroccan sets possess a dusty, grubby authenticity that allows them to fill in nicely for ancient Judea. The costumes of Jesus and his disciples are plausible, and the tools, utensils, and other props, as in an early scene of Jesus practicing his trade as a carpenter, are effectively re-created. On the other hand, the armor and clothing of the Roman soldiers are atrocious, with not a single element correctly reflecting anything actually worn by either legionaries or auxiliaries. They do, however, carry short swords which bear at least a superficial resemblance to a Roman *gladius*. Many of the background extras look more medieval than ancient, and some of the details of their costumes appear to have been inspired by later Islamic and Arabic cultures. However, Scorsese has stated that one of his goals was to capture a sense of the multicultural nature of the place and time in which Jesus's ministry took place, and the movie does convey this idea fairly well. It is worth noting that the soundtrack for the film, composed by Peter Gabriel (formerly a member of the rock group, Genesis), is particularly effective in this regard and contributed to the popularization of "world music."

Upon its release, the film was positively reviewed by movie critics, but also prompted boycotts,· protests, death threats against Scorsese, and the firebombing of a theater in Paris that was screening it. Scorsese (who is a devout Catholic) clearly intended the movie as a sincere exploration of faith, but likely also realized that the manner in which this was done would offend some people. Ultimately, whether or not one finds the film theologically or morally objectionable is a personal reaction contingent upon how open one is to envisioning Jesus as a human being subject to human weaknesses, and whether or not one regards any sort of speculation about his life that is not explicitly mentioned in the Bible as inherently distasteful or blasphemous.

~

CHAPTER FIVE

The Twenty-First Century

The Ancient Epic Gets Revived and Updated for a New Millennium

A new era was sparked by the commercial and critical triumph of director Ridley Scott's *Gladiator* (2000), which single-handedly revived the popularity of the big-budget ancient history epic. While no subsequent movie was quite able to match *Gladiator*'s success, the next two decades have seen a steady stream of projects that have taken Roman movies in a number of directions. One of these is the popularity of Roman Britain as a setting. A quartet of films (*King Arthur*, 2004; *The Last Legion*, 2007; *Centurion*, 2010; and *The Eagle*, 2011) all explored facets of Roman imperialism on the fringes of the empire. On the new medium of premium television, HBO and STARZ each created expensive and well-received series about famous figures from Roman history: *Rome* (2005–2007), depicting Julius Caesar, Octavian, Mark Antony, and Cleopatra; and *Spartacus* (2010–2013), about the rebel gladiator. Finally, as in the previous era, there were also more idiosyncratic projects, including Mel Gibson's *The Passion of the Christ* (2004); *Agora* (2009/2010 US), a biography of the female philosopher Hypatia; and *The First King* (2019), about the legendary founders of Rome, Romulus and Remus.

Gladiator (2000)

Director: Ridley Scott
Producer: Douglas Wick
Production Company: DreamWorks/Universal

Cast: Russell Crowe (Maximus), Joaquin Phoenix (Commodus), Connie Nielsen (Lucilla), Oliver Reed (Proximo), Richard Harris (Marcus Aurelius), Djimon Hounsou (Juba), Derek Jacobi (Gracchus)

Gladiator single-handedly resuscitated the genre of the big budget sword-and-sandal epic that had lain dormant for almost four decades. A mainstay of the 1950s and 1960s, these films had fallen out of favor after the financial excesses of *Cleopatra* and *The Fall of the Roman Empire*. In 2000, director Ridley Scott returned to the genre with *Gladiator*, a loose remake of 1964's *The Fall of the Roman Empire*, sharing the same second-century AD setting, main characters, and initial plot as the earlier movie. However, Scott's film had the benefit of the very latest computer technology, with CGI (computer-generated imagery) taking the place of the lavish sets and thousands of extras of earlier epics. By any measure, *Gladiator* was a smashing success. It raked in $458 million at the box office worldwide, and also managed to garner the highest critical accolades, snagging no fewer than five Oscars, including Best Actor and Best Picture. It even spawned a host of memorable catchphrases: "Strength and honor!" "What we do in life echoes in eternity!" "Are you not entertained?" and "It vexes me. I'm terribly vexed." Finally, it inspired a slew of new sword-and-sandal epics during the next decade, including *Alexander*, *Troy*, and *300*.

Gladiator begins in AD 180 during the campaigns of the emperor Marcus Aurelius (Richard Harris) against Germanic tribes. After a victorious battle, Aurelius informs his leading general, Maximus (Russell Crowe), that he wants Maximus as his successor rather than his own son Commodus (Joaquin Phoenix), whom he regards as unfit to rule and "not a moral man." Commodus responds by strangling his father and sending assassins to kill Maximus, his wife, and their child. While Commodus is acclaimed emperor, Maximus, fleeing the assassins, is captured by slave traders, who sell him to Proximo (Oliver Reed), the owner of a provincial gladiator school in North Africa. Proximo takes his gladiatorial troupe to Rome, where they fight in the Colosseum, and Maximus unexpectedly triumphs, earning both popular adulation and the hatred of Commodus, who recognizes his old enemy. Eventually, Commodus faces Maximus in single combat in the arena, and although the contest is rigged against him, Maximus kills Commodus. He then orders the restoration of the republic before nobly expiring from his wounds.

How accurate is *Gladiator* as history? The film opens with the familiar trope of an onscreen written prologue, which solemnly informs us that "in 180 AD, Emperor Marcus Aurelius's twelve-year campaign against the barbarian tribes of Germania was drawing to an end. Just one final stronghold stands in the way of victory and the promise of peace throughout the empire." In 180, the emperor was indeed Marcus Aurelius, and he had in fact been battling

Germanic barbarians for over a decade. However, this war was nowhere near reaching a decisive military conclusion, and Rome was not close to winning. Nor was there any "final stronghold" in Germania whose conquest would bring peace.

Just as in the earlier film on which *Gladiator* was based, while Emperor Marcus Aurelius and his son Commodus were real people, the main character is a complete invention of the filmmakers, with the minor twist that *Gladiator* changes the name of the protagonist from Livius to Maximus and makes him a far more dynamic, charismatic, and sympathetic figure that the audience can actively root for. Although Maximus is fictitious, he is an accurate representation of a type that played an important role in the empire, since Rome was particularly adept at identifying promising provincial elites and harnessing their energies on behalf of the empire.

A second major unhistorical element is that the plot turns on Marcus Aurelius's decision to pick Maximus over Commodus as his successor. In reality, Aurelius vigorously promoted Commodus as his heir, bestowed a plethora of imperial honors and titles upon him, and had him elected as consul—the chief magistrate of Rome—at the tender age of fifteen. Far from trying to disinherit him, Aurelius did everything in his power to ensure that Commodus would be his successor. A third significant deviation from history is the ending. In the movie, Maximus kills Commodus soon after he has taken the throne. In reality, Commodus enjoyed a long reign as emperor of the Roman world, ruling for twelve years after Aurelius's death. Also, as the movie ends, it is strongly implied that the Roman Republic will be restored. In reality, by AD 180, the institution of the emperorship was firmly established, and no one—neither emperor, senate, army, nor people—was looking to revive the old Republican form of government.

What about the main characters? Maximus is invented, so little can be said about him, but Aurelius and Commodus are well-attested figures about whom much is known. Marcus Aurelius, famously an adherent of the Stoic school of philosophy, wrote a work called the *Meditations* expressing Stoic sentiments. In keeping with this persona, Aurelius departed from the Roman tradition of being clean-shaven by affecting a beard in emulation of Greek philosophers. The movie accurately portrays him with such a beard and emphasizes his philosophical inclinations. Several lines of dialogue even seem to have been inspired by passages in the *Meditations*, such as when the screen version of Aurelius declaims, "Death smiles at us all. All a man can do is smile back," a line that almost certainly deliberately paraphrases a passage in the *Meditations* that urges: "Do not fear death, but smile at its coming for it is among the things that Nature wills to all" (9.3). While his beard is accurate, the cinematic Aurelius is a frail old man, but at the time of his death, he was only fifty-eight years old and, despite some health issues, still very active.

Commodus, the villain of the film, is depicted as a mentally unstable, vain, vindictive, and cruel man who is preoccupied with public entertainments and fancies himself a great warrior. This is not so far from the mark. One ancient source describes Commodus as "immoral, shameless, cruel, lecherous, and depraved."[1] The real Commodus was obsessed with spectacles and staged elaborate gladiator shows and beast hunts. He also participated in them himself, slaughtering hundreds of animals and supposedly fighting as a gladiator, although these contests were almost certainly rigged. He terrorized the senate, had a number of senators put to death, renamed one of the months after himself, and wanted to change the name of Rome to Commodiania. Most disturbingly, he seems to have aspired to be thought of as a god. He associated himself with the demi-god Hercules, going so far as to dress up in a lion skin and carry around a club, just like his mythological hero. There are even surviving portrait busts that show him in this ridiculous costume. Although Joaquin Phoenix does a nice job of capturing the personality of Commodus, he does not look much like him. At the time of his accession, the real Commodus was just eighteen years old, had light blonde hair, and is known to have fought left-handed. Phoenix is in his late twenties, has black hair, and fights right-handed.

The producers' stated intention was to avoid the stereotypical clichés of the older epics and go for a more "authentic look." Ridley Scott claimed that he wanted the costumes to be "real, correct and lived in." Furthermore, according to visual effects supervisor John Nelson, Scott wished the audience to feel "as if they had seen a documentary on Rome."[2] However, when historical reality clashed with Hollywood drama, it would be history that lost out.

The makers of Gladiator did have access to expert knowledge regarding ancient Rome. Early in the production process, they hired Professor Kathleen Coleman of Harvard University as a historical consultant. She is one of the foremost experts on gladiators and thus was an excellent choice. However, she soon became disillusioned with her role and frustrated that the filmmakers seemed less interested in hearing what she had to say than in trying to get her to confirm their own erroneous ideas. For example, at one point, she received a message from the filmmakers stating that they wanted to depict female gladiators with razor blades on their nipples and requested that Prof. Coleman provide historical evidence to support this. Needless to say, she could not validate this notion. She ultimately grew so exasperated that she asked to have her name removed from the film's credits. Thus, she is not listed as the historical consultant, although she does appear among the people who are thanked by the filmmakers.

To be fair, when discussing the historicity of his film, Ridley Scott admitted, "I felt the priority was to stay true to the spirit of the period, but not necessarily to adhere to facts. We were, after all, creating fiction, not practicing archaeology."[3] While this is a reasonable position, one complication is that the film often seems less concerned with being true to the spirit of real history than with aligning with the general public's often stereotyped and inaccurate preexisting ideas about it. For example, in palace scenes, most of the costumes and sets are inspired less by archaeological evidence than by much, much later artists' and writers' creative reimaginings of antiquity. Arthur Max, the production designer, freely admitted as much: "We tried to bring to *Gladiator* a sense of the Roman empire in decline—its greatness and at the same time its corruption and decay. And to do that, we found ourselves looking not so much to the scholarly historical realm as to interpretations of Rome by certain 19th-century painters."[4] The main artist that he is talking about here is painter Lawrence Alma-Tadema, who specialized in fanciful depictions of antiquity for his Victorian audience. Alma-Tadema's paintings create compelling images of decadence and wealth, but they are not the most realistic portrayals of Roman clothing and settings. His Romans do, however, represent what the general public expects to see in a Roman movie, and the makers of *Gladiator*, well aware of these expectations, delivered what the audience wanted. Alma-Tadema's evocative and titillating paintings had also been an influential visual inspiration for many earlier productions during the Golden Era of Hollywood. The result is a film in which many familiar (but inaccurate) Roman stereotypes show up, such as the fact that the emperor seems to wear armor at all times.

The dramatic highlights of the film are its gladiator contests and military battles. How accurate are these? Let's begin with an aspect of Roman gladiatorial entertainments rarely depicted onscreen—the re-creation of Promixo's gladiator school in the backwater provincial town of Zuccabar in North Africa. Zuccabar was an actual Roman city located in what is today Algeria, and, as portrayed in the film, every Roman city of any size would have had its own miniature amphitheater, which hosted small-town versions of the great games staged in the capital. Proximo also presents beast hunts. In one scene, he upbraids a supplier for having sold him unsuitable giraffes. Roman audiences' insatiable appetite for watching exotic beasts being slaughtered resulted in a sizable infrastructure of dealers who captured and transported the unfortunate creatures. This scene is a colorful but accurate representation of this trade.

Less authentic is the first gladiatorial combat that we witness in Zuccabar. Maximus and other recently acquired gladiators are flung, with only minimal training, into the arena, where they are collectively pitted against a group of more experienced warriors. A chaotic bloodbath ensues, with gladiators fighting all over the arena until the majority of them are slain. In reality, gladiators, although slaves, were highly trained professionals who received extensive weapons instruction before entering the arena. They were valuable commodities to their owners and would not have been wasted in such a cavalier fashion. Also, gladiators almost never fought as groups. Gladiator combats were one-on-one matches in which the Romans tried to pit two fighters of similar skill levels against each other. A good modern analogy would be professional boxing. At a boxing event, you wouldn't see a dozen boxers of different weight classes and abilities thrown into the ring at the same time, beating on one another in a confused melee. Instead, you watch a succession of one-on-one fights between boxers of similar skill and weight, with matches between the less famous fighters coming first, leading up to the main event between two well-known champions. Gladiator games worked exactly the same way.

When the action moves to Rome, *Gladiator* makes extensive use of computer-generated imagery (CGI) to re-create the buildings of ancient Rome—in particular, the Colosseum, more correctly known as the Flavian Amphitheater. When Maximus and his companions first step out onto the floor of this amphitheater, there is an impressive 360-degree pan around the interior of the building, as seen from their perspective. Overall, the filmmakers did a respectable job with the Flavian Amphitheater. They correctly show such details as the multiple levels of the exterior and the interior, reserved seating for high status groups such as senators and Vestal Virgins, and the imperial box where the emperor and his entourage sit. They highlight the technologically sophisticated features of the building, giving prominence to the retractable awnings called the *velarium* that were employed to shade the spectators, as well as to the elevators and trap-doors in the floor of the amphitheater that enabled fighters and wild beasts to spring up into the arena. One conspicuous element in the movie that absolutely did not exist in the real Flavian Amphitheater is the sixteen large, conical pillars that dot the floor of the arena. While these objects are indeed found in a Roman entertainment structure, that building is actually the Circus Maximus, where chariot races were held. Called *metae*, these pillars were the turning posts around which the chariots circled. In *Gladiator*, the filmmakers apparently decided to transpose them from the Circus to the Amphitheater.

The first combat sequence in the Flavian Amphitheater is another pitched battle involving several dozen gladiators; in this case, Maximus and his fellow gladiators from Proximo's school versus a swarm of chariots occupied by female gladiators dressed in golden armor and wielding bows and spears. This fight is presented as a reenactment of a historical event: the battle at which the Romans defeated the Carthaginian military genius Hannibal, ending the second Punic War. The herald introducing the spectacle refers to it as the "Battle of Carthage," although strictly speaking, it is known as the Battle of Zama, and it took place in the desert outside Carthage. This scene correctly captures another aspect of Roman games that has often been ignored in gladiator films—the fact that the Romans were quite fond of staging elaborate spectacles that re-created famous historical or mythological episodes. However, the combatants in such large-scale reenactments would have been prisoners of war rather than valuable, trained gladiators.

Where this sequence in the film fails badly as history is in the details. The outfits are horribly wrong—the equipment of Maximus and his band, who are supposedly playing the Carthaginians, is much closer to that used by Roman legionaries, while the alleged "Romans" are kitted out in some sort of fantasy gold breastplate-and-helmet ensemble that would be more appropriate in a Conan the Barbarian movie. Furthermore, Roman soldiers of Scipio's time (or of any era, for that matter) did not fight from chariots,

Figure 5.1. Maximus versus Tigris from *Gladiator* (2000). Although it is a thrilling sequence, there is little that is historically accurate in this combat between champion gladiators. The equipment, the presence of tigers, and the conical pillars on the amphitheater floor are all unhistorical additions of the filmmakers. *Lifestyle Pictures/Alamy Stock Photo.*

Figure 5.2. Roman Gladiator Combat. Reconstruction of a bout between two histori-cal types of Roman gladiators, a Thracian and a hoplomachus. Romans enjoyed watch-ing combats pitting different types of gladiators against one another. The man with the stick is the bout's referee. *Illustration by Graham Sumner.*

nor were there ever any Amazon-like female warriors in the Roman military. There are equipment problems with the other gladiator sequences as well. In reality, each individual Roman gladiator was trained to fight as one very specific type of gladiator, each of which had a distinctive and well-defined set of armor and weapons. Over a dozen of these different gladiator types are known. In the movie, neither Maximus nor the other gladiators are depicted as training or fighting as any of the historically attested types. Many of the weapons and armor that they employ are not merely inappropriate, but some are not Roman at all. Gladiators in the film do battle wearing armor from entirely different cultures and time periods, including helmets that appear to be from the seventeenth-century Mughal Empire in India and seventh-century Anglo-Saxon Britain. There are a number of anachronistic weapons from medieval Europe, while others are simply fantasy weapons invented by the propmakers.

Figure 5.1 shows another spectacular fight in the amphitheater, this time between Maximus and a champion gladiator named Tigris of Gaul. One of the transposed Circus *metae* is clearly visible in the background. Tigris's tiger-themed outfit is pure fantasy, and while Maximus carries a legionary-style *gladius* sword, his set of equipment does not match any known gladiator type. While the Romans certainly staged wild animal hunts and spectacles involving tigers, such animals would not have been intermingled with professional gladiator bouts. Figure 5.2 illustrates a reconstruction of a more realistic combat between two gladiators. The lightly armed figure with the smallish round shield and curved dagger represents the style called a *Thraex*, or Thracian, while his more heavily armored opponent is of the type known as a *hoplomachus*, whose equipment is based on the arms of a Greek hoplite warrior. The other man, carrying a stick, is a figure rarely depicted in film— the bout's referee. Ancient mosaics show such referees intervening during gladiatorial combats, though the exact nature of the rules they were enforcing is not fully understood.

The other major set-piece action sequence is the battle between the Roman army and Germanic barbarians that begins the film. The Roman marching camp looks good but is inaccurate, since it has been constructed within a forest with neither visible perimeter defenses nor any recognizable layout. According to writer David Franzoni, the opening battle scene was intended to be "*All Quiet on the Western Front*, realistic, brutal, not glorious."[5] Perhaps it is no coincidence, then, that the tracking shot of Maximus walking along the lines and greeting his troops recalls Kirk Douglas doing the same as Colonel Dax in Stanley Kubrick's First World War drama, *Paths of Glory*.

Most of the legionaries wear a generic version of the *lorica segmentata*, an armor composed of metal plates bound together with leather straps, resembling the segments of a lobster. (See Figure 3.5.B for a painting of a typical legionary from *Gladiator*.) While some details are off, this was a legitimate variety of Roman military armor, and it is complemented by approximations of legionary helmets of the so-called Gallic type. They wield the distinctive Roman *gladius*, or short sword, and bear large, slightly curved, rectangular shields, both of which are accurate. Two errors are that the Romans are equipped with leather or metal forearm guards, which are not attested, and that the Roman cavalry have stirrups, which were not yet in common use. The propmakers wanted the military equipment to appear worn and well used, and, according to costume designer Janty Yates, it was intended to have a Vietnam soldier look. The film's Praetorians (see Figure 2.2.C) wear similar armor, although painted a menacing black, with purple cloaks, black helmets, and black shields. There is no evidence for Praetorians wearing black, but this reflects a long-standing cinematic convention of visually likening Praetorians to Nazi Waffen SS soldiers. Figure 5.3.C shows a variety of Roman prop shields used in *Gladiator*, including a black Praetorian one. All the designs painted on these are based on historical evidence. The legionaries' German opponents are outfitted in a variety of often implausible costumes, including some attire that makes them look more like Stone Age cavemen than second-century AD Germans.

In Figure 5.3, (A) depicts the costume worn by Maximus in battle, while (B) illustrates how a historically accurate Roman general might have looked at the time of Marcus Aurelius. The "corrected" reconstruction is based on surviving images of Roman officers in Roman art, such as stone and bronze statues and reliefs. The film's Maximus wears a metal breastplate, which is accurate, although it would certainly not have had the large metal shoulder plates shown in the film. The breastplate would probably have featured relief decorations on the chest, but instead of the wolf motif of the film, an apotropaic Medusa head would be more likely. The griffins on Maximus's chest were perhaps inspired by similar designs on the armor of the famous statue of Emperor Augustus from Prima Porta, now in the Vatican. As a member of the senatorial class, a real Roman general would have worn a tunic with two broad purple stripes under his breastplate. Roman soldiers of this era posted to northern climes wore leather pants that reached down to the calf, as seen in the right-hand figure. Maximus's prominent "skirt" of leather straps, known as *pteruges*, would more probably have been cloth, as shown in the corrected version. The film Maximus sports large metal greaves, but such shin guards were worn neither by generals nor ordinary legionaries, nor did either utilize the forearm guards worn by Crowe. The footgear on the movie Maximus seems to be an invention of the propmakers, whereas the corrected Maximus is shod in a type of officer's boot frequently seen in

Figure 5.3.   Roman General. (A) Costume worn by Roman general Maximus in *Gladiator* (2000). (B) Reconstruction of a typical second-century AD Roman general's attire. (C) Three shields carried by Roman soldiers in *Gladiator* (2000). The shield types and their painted designs are all based on historically attested ones. *Illustrations by Graham Sumner. Photograph and props from The Terry Nix Collection.*

sculptures. Finally, it is certain that a high-ranking officer such as Maximus would have followed the prevailing fashion of the day for a curlier hairstyle and a longer beard—a trend that began in Hadrian's reign and continued through that of Marcus Aurelius. Therefore, our historical general has such a coiffure instead of the rather modern-looking scruffy beard and spiky hair of Crowe's Maximus.

Gladiator's battle sequence begins promisingly enough, with the Romans marching back and forth and assembling into orderly ranks and formations. The primary characteristics of the Roman army were discipline and organization, and the pre-battle scenes capture this well. In contrast, the Germans are simply massed into a loose mob, which accurately reflects their combat tactics. When the legionary troops advance into battle, they still have their distinctive throwing spears, known as *pila*. However, when the German tribesmen charge, the *pila* have mysteriously disappeared without having been thrown—a shame, since a *pila* volley would have been something worth seeing. The Roman archers then unleash a barrage of flaming arrows, and the catapults hurl dozens of clay pots, which explode upon contact into huge napalm-like fireballs that set the forest, as well as a large number of Germans, ablaze. While all of this looks visually dramatic, it bears little resemblance to actual Roman military practice. The large artillery pieces shown in the film would normally only have been used in siege warfare and would have been constructed on site, as they were too cumbersome to move. There is no evidence that the Romans ever hurled large amphorae filled with oil that exploded on impact. There were archer contingents in the Roman army, but they most certainly would not have used flaming arrows in this situation. In fact, wrapping incendiary material around an arrow would have rendered it less accurate, greatly decreased its range and penetrative power, and made it much easier for your opponents to dodge. The anachronistic and ahistorical use of various flaming and exploding weapons is one of the most common flaws of movies set in the ancient and medieval worlds, but this convention persists for the obvious reason that it looks impressive on film.

The two sides then crash together. This scene is initially good, with the Romans realistically maintaining their formations while the Germans surge forward in a disorganized mob. Maximus charges in at the head of the Roman cavalry, and the battle then unfortunately degenerates into a confused melee. This allows Maximus and others to engage in heroic-looking one-on-one duels, but it is a violation of every Roman tactical rule. The whole point of the Roman army's style of combat, and the reason for its success, was to fight as a group, not as individuals. The legionaries should be arrayed in organized lines, collectively making precise stabbing and thrusting motions from behind the unified wall of their shields—not engaging in individual leaping, whirling, kung-fu-like combat. No senior Roman general would be on the front lines either, as Maximus is in this scene. The use of cavalry to charge through heavy forest to outflank the Germans was not a standard Roman tactic, but a similar stratagem had appeared in *The Fall of the Roman Empire*.

Gladiator marked a significant moment in the history of cinema, and particularly of films set in ancient Rome. Despite its shortcomings as a realistic depiction of history, it was a high-profile and influential commercial and critical success. Additionally, it sparked renewed interest in historical epics, presented never-before-seen high-tech CGI reconstructions of ancient Rome, and engaged a new generation of audiences with the topic of ancient history, all of which are positive developments for anyone who cares about history and its continuing importance.

Attila (2001)

Director: Dick Lowry
Producers: Michael Joyce, Sean Daniel, James Jacks, Caldecot Chubb
Production Company: Alphaville/Michael Joyce
Cast: Gerard Butler (Attila), Powers Boothe (Flavius Aetius), Alice Krige (Galla Placidia), Tim Curry (Theodosius), Simmone Jade Mackinnon (N'Kara/Ildico), Reg Rogers (Valentinian)

Certain ancient figures seem to be perennially popular with filmmakers, and *Attila* (2001) joins *Sign of the Pagan* (1954) and *Attila* (1954/1958 US) as attempts to craft cinematic biographies of the notorious king of the Huns who menaced both the Eastern and Western Roman Empires during the fifth century AD. This time around, action-movie stud Gerard Butler takes on the title role previously played by Jack Palance and Anthony Quinn, while Powers Boothe portrays Attila's nemesis, the Roman general Flavius Aetius. This production, filmed with a sizable budget in Lithuania, was first shown as a three-hour miniseries on the USA Network.

The miniseries offers a rather sympathetic portrait of Attila, painting him as a heroic warrior and charismatic leader who is honest and straightforward, even a bit naive. Despite a few requisite scenes of Huns rampaging, murdering, and pillaging, Butler's Attila is oddly (and rather unbelievably) chivalrous, seducing female captives solely through his irresistible manliness and gruff charm rather than by coercion or force. It is an entertaining and likeable characterization that is well suited to appeal to a TV audience, but it owes more to twenty-first-century notions of the appropriate qualities for a leading man than it does to late antique Hunnic cultural norms. To be fair, almost nothing is known of Attila's personality other than that he was a strong leader, so the filmmakers do have some leeway for invention. The film depicts Flavius Aetius as very much a foil to Attila: cold, calculating, and manipulative where Attila is warm, impulsive, and open. The historical Aetius managed to survive and thrive for a long time at a court that was a hotbed of intrigue and backstabbing, so this is not an improbable characterization, and Powers Boothe does a good job of conveying his cunning and intelligence.

Several characters who play major roles in the miniseries are completely fictitious: Galen, the Hunnish witch who predicts and guides Attila's rise; N'Kara, Attila's beloved first wife, whose romance with Attila occupies considerable screen time; and Lydia, Aetius's adopted daughter, who is the child of Aetius's late wife and her ex-husband, the king of the Visigoths—a rather bizarre and completely unattested union. Other characters are based on actual historical figures, although the filmmakers frequently deviate from what is known about them in order to further their plot points. An example is Bleda, Attila's brother, who is presented as a rather villainous individual and a longtime rival to Attila. In the miniseries, immediately upon the death of the previous king of the Huns, Attila and Bleda fight a dramatic duel on horseback during which Attila slays his brother in order to determine who will take the throne. In reality, Attila and Bleda ruled the Huns jointly with apparent amicability for over a decade until Bleda died in a hunting accident (which admittedly may have been engineered by Attila).

Valentinian III, the emperor of the Western Roman Empire, was indeed a relatively young and rather weak and ineffectual leader, though perhaps not quite as utterly gormless as he is depicted here. Like her onscreen counterpart, his mother, Galla Placidia, was an ambitious, scheming, and capable woman who was likely the real power behind the throne, but she would have been considerably older than the actress portraying her, and, in fact, she died before some of the occurrences that the film shows her taking part in. The film's portrait of the Eastern Roman emperor Theodosius II, played amusingly if somewhat hammily by Tim Curry, conforms to his historical identity as a clever diplomat ready to make or break alliances with anyone depending upon what was expedient at the moment.

The film roughly follows historical events, although, as might be expected, with a good deal of simplification and omission; for example, Attila's campaigns against the Eastern Empire are completely left out. Attila's attack on Orleans is presented as having captured the city, whereas, in reality, his siege was unsuccessful. The miniseries builds toward a showdown at the Battle of the Catalaunian Plains (also called the Battle of Chalons), where, as depicted, the combined armies of the Western Roman Empire (under Aetius) and the Visigoths (under their king, Theodoric I) fought Attila to a standstill and effectively stopped him from advancing further. Perhaps the greatest historical omission of the miniseries is that it then skips ahead a year to his marriage to the barbarian girl Ildico, entirely leaving out Attila's invasion of Italy, during which he mysteriously turned back after a famous meeting with Pope Leo I. The film ends with Attila being murdered by his new wife, Ildico, who poisons him on their wedding night. While Attila did die on his wedding night and there are rumors that Ildico was responsible, the true cause of his death remains unknown. With the threat of Attila removed, Aetius was murdered by Valentinian, as is shown.

The movie makes much of Attila's supernaturally assisted and melodramatically staged discovery of the alleged "Sword of the War God"—an occurrence that he interprets as a divine omen promising that he will conquer the world. This is actually based on a short passage in the *History of the Goths* by the Roman historian Jordanes, although in his account the sword is found not by Attila himself, but rather less dramatically by a herdsman whose cow steps on the blade and hurts its foot, after which he presents the sword to Attila. There is no evidence that Attila ever visited Rome, as the film portrays. While there, he attends a PG-13-rated orgy at the palace, and although an orgy seems to be required in any movie set in ancient Rome, such revels would have been extremely unlikely in the late antique and completely Christian imperial court of Valentinian (or any other Roman emperor of that period).

The costumes and sets are serviceable. Some of the Huns' outfits bear a closer resemblance to the clothes of medieval western Europeans rather than Eurasian nomads. Similarly, the walled city of Orleans and the other besieged towns look more like late medieval castles than Roman fortifications. The trebuchets used by Attila to batter down the walls of Orleans are a medieval form of catapult that probably didn't yet exist. The Roman legionaries wear the usual inaccurate leather armor and bracers stereotypically found in most Roman movies, and in the big battle scene, their equipment seems to be based on that used by the Roman army in the first and second centuries AD rather than the fifth. The palace in Constantinople contains a replica of the mosaic of Empress Theodora from the Basilica of San Vitale in Ravenna, and while this mosaic was not created until about a century later, it at least provides an apt reference to an actual Byzantine imperial decoration.

Attila is very much a romanticized version of the life of this famous king of the Huns, and although it takes many liberties with the events being covered, the miniseries does manage to introduce the major figures of the era and conform to the general course of history.

King Arthur (2004)

Director: Antoine Fuqua
Producer: Jerry Bruckheimer
Production Company: Touchstone Pictures
Cast: Clive Owen (Arthur), Ioan Gruffudd (Lancelot), Keira Knightley (Guinevere), Mads Mikkelsen (Tristan), Ray Winstone (Bors), Stellan Skarsgård (Cerdic)

Director Antoine Fuqua, writer David Franzoni (who also wrote *Gladiator*), and producer Jerry Bruckheimer have stated that their intention was to make a movie about King Arthur that was a gritty, realistic look at the possible historical origins of the tale. Furthermore, they wanted to completely eschew all of the magical and romanticized elements that became associated with his story during the Renaissance, which had featured prominently in earlier Hollywood versions of Arthur's life. While it might seem odd to include a film about the legendary British ruler in a book on cinematic Romans, many have speculated that he might have a historical basis in the period of Roman Britain. This is an intriguing idea that may even contain a kernel of truth, and the notion of an unsentimental Arthurian origin story has promise. Unfortunately, the filmmakers present a number of highly speculative theories as established fact, claiming in the text scroll that begins the movie that "historians agree" about them—which they most certainly do not. They further assert that the film is based on "recently discovered archaeological evidence," by which they seem to mean the "Artognou stone" discovered at Tintagel Castle in 1998, which was put forward as proof of a historical Arthur—an interpretation that most scholars do not agree with.

Rather than relying on the popular medieval romances about the origins of Arthur and his knights, the movie is based on theories proposed some years ago by anthropologist C. Scott Littleton, Ann C. Thomas, and folklorist Linda A. Malcor that the Arthurian myths had Scythian origins, combined with a tenuous scrap of evidence that there may have been an actual late second- to early third-century Roman officer serving in Britain called Lucius Artorius Castus, from whom the name "Arthur" may have been derived. In the film, Arthur/Artorius (played by Clive Owen) is depicted as a half-British, half-Roman officer who is the hereditary commander of an elite unit of cavalry recruited from the Sarmatians (a successor culture to the Scythians), who lived near the Black Sea. The Sarmatians were famously adept at mounted warfare, and the Romans did indeed routinely recruit soldiers from martially inclined conquered peoples, so a unit of Sarmatian cavalry serving in Britain is not only possible but also supported by some evidence. The film, however, anachronistically refers to these troops as "knights" and lets them keep the French and English names bestowed on the knights of the Round Table by late medieval writers, with the result that these alleged Sarmatians from the eastern steppes bear the extraordinarily improbable names of Lancelot, Tristan, Gawain, Galahad, Bors, and Dagonet.

Merlin appears in the guise of a leader of the indigenous Britons. The film labels these people "Woads," which is not the name of any tribal group, but rather is the term for the bluish pigment that the Celts and Picts smeared on their bodies as decoration. Why the filmmakers did not simply call them Picts is a mystery. Regardless, the movie's Merlin does not possess any supernatural abilities, but is instead portrayed as a skilled master of guerrilla warfare tactics. Guinevere (another thoroughly French name) here is a bow-wielding warrior woman of the Woads who is rescued by Arthur from the bizarre underground torture chamber of some sadistic Christian monks, and she allies with him and his "knights" to fend off an invasion of marauding Saxons.

Other than a brief prologue, the film is set in AD 467, but it plays fast and loose with history, taking a number of actual characters and events from late antiquity and ahistorically mingling them together at the same moment. Among the elements tossed into this melting pot are Bishop Germanus of Auxerre, who visited Britain twice circa AD 429 and AD 447; the Saxon leaders Cerdic and Cynric, who arrived in Britain around AD 495; the Roman withdrawal from Britain, which happened around AD 410; and the Battle of Badon Hill, which probably occurred around AD 500. The film shifts all of these to the same year of AD 467. It also features a flashback appearance, set during the 450s, by the heretical theologian Pelagius, who actually died around AD 420.

In addition to flawed chronology, some of the other historical inaccuracies in the film include the invading Saxons' land in what is now eastern Scotland rather than southeastern England; the theologian Pelagius's teachings on free will are misrepresented, and he was not executed as a heretic; the pope was not the political authority in charge at Rome, did not command "papal armies," and would not have issued orders to Roman military units; trebuchet-type catapults were not used in Europe until several centuries later; and the Saxons would not have had crossbows, which similarly are later medieval weapons. In what have become seemingly obligatory clichés for ancient epic films, the battle scenes also prominently feature flaming arrows, whose use is nonsensical in military terms, but which are visually spectacular, as well as catapults hurling napalm-like explosives of a potency wholly unattested in ancient warfare.

An interesting aspect of the movie is its depiction of Hadrian's Wall, a large section of which was elaborately reconstructed for the film, and which serves as the backdrop for many of its scenes and battles. The set includes a fort, a gateway, and a section of wall almost a kilometer long. These seem to have been based on the fort at Housesteads and the nearby Knag Burn gateway. While the film's wall and fort look brand new and more like they would have when first built rather than several centuries later, the film does show the soldiers' families living within the fort, which is historically correct for the late Roman period. A dramatic battle pitting Arthur and his knights against a Saxon army takes place on a frozen lake, culminating with many of the Saxons plunging through the ice. For this scene, the filmmakers were plainly copying the famous "battle on the ice" episode in Sergei Eisenstein's acclaimed cinematic classic *Alexander Nevsky* (1938). The frozen lake battle took almost nine months to shoot and, together with the extensive wall set and the 2,500 costumes made for the movie, accounts for its hefty $120 million budget.

The plot seems heavily influenced by events at the time of its filming. In this instance, as critics such as Chris Davies have pointed out, it can be read as an allegory of the US's invasions of Iraq and Afghanistan, with echoes of the earlier conflict in Vietnam.[6] Arthur and his men are portrayed as weary of fighting a seemingly endless, morally questionable, and ultimately doomed war in a distant foreign land on behalf of an imperialistic nation that does not appreciate their sacrifices and begrudges them the rewards that they have earned in its service. At the beginning of the film, their only desire is to fulfill the terms of their enlistment and return home to Sarmatia. However, in a standard movie trope, they are coerced into undertaking one last (likely suicidal) mission. An additional ideological anachronism that has become an absolute staple of ancient epics is that the characters are all obsessed with the ideas of freedom and equality. Arthur and others constantly and grandly speechify about gaining freedom (at least twenty-four times!) in a manner that reflects modern sensibilities but would have been extraordinarily unlikely coming from a fifth-century Roman officer.

King Arthur is a big-budget epic with an intriguing concept made by a skilled production team, but the many elements that it tries to juggle never gel in a coherent way, and it falls prey to many clichés. Its uneven tone partly stems from disagreements between the director, Antoine Fuqua, who wanted a darker, more realistic R-rated film, and the producer and studio, who re-edited the movie, adding comic scenes and cutting out gore in order to produce a more accessible and less violent PG-13-rated film. In a reversal of the usual procedure, blood was actually digitally erased from the print during postproduction.

The Passion of the Christ (2004)

Director: Mel Gibson
Producers: Bruce Davey, Mel Gibson, Stephen McEveety
Production Company: Newmarket
Cast: Jim Caviezel (Jesus), Maia Morgenstern (Mary), Hristo Shopov (Pontius Pilate), Monica Bellucci (Mary Magdalen), Mattia Sbragia (Caiaphas), Luca Lionello (Judas), Francesco De Vito (Peter)

The Passion of the Christ (2004) was an enormous financial success, raking in over $300 million in the United States and over $600 million worldwide. It set a number of records domestically, including highest box office for an R-rated film and highest for a subtitled film. Nevertheless, it remains a controversial movie that seems to provoke intense "love it" or "hate it" reactions among viewers, with some hailing it as the best film ever made about Jesus, and others condemning it as being anti-Semitic or an exercise in "torture porn" akin to the *Saw* or *Hostel* horror-movie franchises. It also forms an interesting companion piece to Martin Scorsese's similarly praised and loathed Jesus movie, *The Last Temptation of Christ* (1988). As with that earlier film, the motivation for making *The Passion of the Christ* stems from a famous director's compulsion to explore his own relationship with his faith, in this case, Mel Gibson. While both Scorsese and Gibson are devout Catholics, it is fascinating to observe how the films they created concentrate on completely different aspects of Jesus's life and its interpretation.

The Passion of the Christ was very much a personal project for Gibson, whose production company provided $30 million of financing for it. Unlike most previous films about Jesus, which typically depict his entire ministry, Gibson focuses very narrowly on the last few hours of Jesus's life, beginning with his capture in the garden of Gethsemane, through his trials by both the Jewish priests of the Temple and the Roman administrator Pontius Pilate, and ending with his crucifixion. Gibson has asserted that his goal was to produce the most accurate portrait of these events: "I think that my first duty is to be as faithful as possible in telling the story so that it doesn't contradict the Scriptures."[7] Gibson's desire for realism led to the unusual decision of having all the characters speak in the ancient languages that would have been in use at that time and place. Initially, Gibson opposed the inclusion of subtitles to provide translations, since he wanted viewers to experience the film in exclusively visual terms, but he eventually gave in on this point.

The resulting movie is unrelenting in its violence. Most of the film's running time consists of one brutally graphic scene after another of Jesus being beaten, whipped, punched, kicked, mocked, and spat upon. He is wrapped in chains and flung off a wall, pummeled with heavy wooden rods, and flagellated with a multi-thonged whip tipped with barbs that literally rips out chunks of his flesh. We witness each gruesome detail of his crucifixion, including every nail pounded into his flesh, his body being crushed beneath the cross, and his bones being dislocated and shattered. Mark 15:15 simply states, "Pilate took Jesus and had him flogged," but here we get twenty minutes' worth of savagery performed by a bestial crowd of gleefully leering Romans who beat Jesus to a pulp and partially flay the skin from his body employing a tableful of sadistic (and historically unattested) torture implements. The centurion counts out over seventy blows, and we observe nearly all of these landing on Jesus's mutilated flesh in lovingly detailed close-ups. Famous film reviewer Roger Ebert wrote that The Passion of the Christ was the most violent film he had ever viewed, and critic David Edelstein labeled it "a two-hour-and-six-minute snuff movie—the Jesus Chainsaw Massacre."[8]

It is clear that the ferocity of the violence depicted was Gibson's intent. He has said that he wanted to shock the viewer with it in order to stress the enormity of Jesus's sacrifice on behalf of humanity. All filmmakers have the freedom to select which elements of a story they wish to emphasize, and Gibson chose to single-mindedly concentrate on Jesus's suffering. The film contains virtually nothing about Jesus's words, teachings, actions, and ministry. In this movie, Jesus is a passive recipient of abuse, and that's pretty much it. Gibson strips away all of the usual messages associated with Jesus, advocating love, forgiveness, faith, and tolerance, in favor of an unrelenting focus on the core tenet that "Jesus died for our sins," with a heavy emphasis on the dying part. It is up to individual believers (and viewers) to decide for themselves whether or not they agree, or are comfortable, with Gibson's directorial decision, and how one answers this question will likely determine one's general response to the film.

While one's stance on this matter is a personal judgment, it is possible to assess other issues relating to the film's historical accuracy with a greater degree of objectivity. In regard to how closely it adheres to the accounts in the Bible, Gibson's assertion that it is completely accurate is somewhat deceptive. While the movie follows the general narrative laid out in the Gospels, it adds a huge number of details, events, and characters that are not actually in the Bible. Some of these incidents come from later medieval writings, while others appear to have been derived from later depictions of Jesus's life in painting and sculpture. One major source that Gibson seems to have leaned especially heavily on is the writings of a nineteenth-century German nun named Anne Catherine Emmerich, who described a series of visions of Jesus's passion that she had experienced.[9] The traditional "Stations of the Cross," developed during the Middle Ages, also seem to have inspired elements of the film. From a purely historical standpoint, there are problems with the film's use of ancient languages. The actors speak Aramaic and Latin, but the language most likely to have been employed in exchanges between the Romans and the locals at this time would have been Greek. Also, when speaking Latin, the Roman characters adopt a later medieval ecclesiastical pronunciation rather than the classical form thought to have been used by the Romans.[10]

As for the accusations of anti-Semitism, while one could argue that there is nothing explicitly anti-Semitic in the film, it is possible for a viewer to interpret it in that way. The Jewish priests are characterized as one-dimensional villains who aggressively demand Jesus's death, while Pilate is treated sympathetically as a reluctant oppressor. Some lines in the Bible that might complicate or help to explain the priests' animosity are omitted. The film's single-minded focus on Jesus's final hours inevitably opens it up to this kind of criticism because the viewer gets none of the complicated historical, religious, and social context for what is happening onscreen. Without this context, the Jewish priests (and, for that matter, everyone else in the movie) are reduced to superficial figures who seem to lack motivations or explanations for their actions.

It is interesting that the two most recent Jesus biopics are the most controversial, and also that they most overtly reflect the personal visions of their directors. Gibson found the ultimate meaning of Jesus's life in his suffering, while Scorsese perceived it as Jesus's shared humanity. Which you prefer is up to you.

Empire (2005)

Directors: John Gray, Kim Manners, Greg Yaitanes
Producers: Carrie Henderson, Jacobus Rose, Nick Gillott
Production Company: Storyline/Touchstone
Cast: Jonathan Cake (Tyrannus), Santiago Cabrera (Octavius), Vincent Regan (Marc Antony), Emily Blunt (Camane), Colm Feore (Julius Caesar), Chris Egan (Agrippa), Michael Byrne (Cicero)

Empire was a four-hour television miniseries broadcast on the ABC network which seems to have been inspired by a desire to cash in on the success of *Gladiator* (2000) by imitating many of its elements on the small screen. As its focus, it picks a promising historical era that is rife with conflict and possibilities for high drama: the aftermath of Julius Caesar's assassination in 44 BC and the resulting power struggle between the Roman senate, Caesar's right-hand man, Mark Antony, and Caesar's teenaged grandnephew, Octavius.

Unfortunately, rather than exploiting the wonderfully rich possibilities of actual history, the filmmakers instead mingled these characters and events with a slew of improbable, and often bizarre, fictitious ones, including a ridiculously invincible gladiator named Tyrannus, a girl-power-infused Vestal Virgin, a shape-shifting master assassin "from foreign lands," a laughable PG-rated orgy, and a truly wacky sequence set in the so-called "combat dungeons of Arkham," which appear to be some sort of pseudo-Roman variant on the cinematic trope of the prison-run-by-sadists, that visually resembles Mordor from *The Lord of the Rings* crossed with a Hieronymus Bosch painting.

To tell the unlikely true story of the rise of the young Octavius from complete obscurity to one of the most important politicians in the Roman world, the miniseries emulates Shakespeare by rendering Octavius (Santiago Cabrera) as a Prince Hal–type character who, though initially a dissolute, pleasure-seeking, and vacuous young wastrel, matures into a wise and noble statesman when unexpectedly thrust into a leadership role. This is an engaging narrative arc, but it is at odds with the historical record in which Octavius from the very start seemed to possess the coldly calculating intelligence and manipulative political acumen that characterized his actions throughout his career.

In a transparent attempt to appeal to a youth audience, the filmmakers cast Octavius's role so as to transform him into a teenage heartthrob, gifting him with a tall and studly physique, a dazzling smile, and a big Jim Morrisonesque mane of sexily tousled hair. The actual Octavius is described by ancient sources as having been perpetually sickly, of a short stature, with a slight build, and possessing bad teeth, scaly skin, and a unibrow. The miniseries so enthusiastically embraces its take on Octavius as a peevish, self-obsessed, dumb-as-a-rock playboy that it becomes a complete mystery as to why anyone would possibly back him as a political leader. In the entirely on-target words of Tyrannus, this Octavius is nothing more than an "idiot brat."

In addition to the central conceit of an all-conquering gladiator who yearns to get back to his wife and child but is driven by personal integrity to become unwillingly enmeshed in politics, there are a number of direct nods to *Gladiator*, including the seemingly requisite stroll through a picturesque wheatfield while musing about "strength and honor."

On the positive side, the first ninety minutes of the show are not bad, and some of the secondary characters are well cast. Vincent Regan is an appropriately dynamic Marc Antony; Fiona Shaw is witty as his wife, Fulvia; and Michael Byrne is particularly good as an aging Cicero. Also, the miniseries was filmed in and around Rome and makes effective use of a number of actual Roman sites and historical buildings. *Empire* had a promising premise and some decent actors and settings, but it ended up being a missed opportunity.

Rome (2005–2007)

Director: Various
Producers: Bruno Heller, John Melfi, Anne Thomopoulos, John Milius, William J. MacDonald
Production Company: HBO/BBC co-production
Cast: Kevin McKidd (Lucius Vorenus), Ray Stevenson (Titus Pullo), Ciaran Hinds (Julius Caesar), Kenneth Cranham (Pompey), Polly Walker (Atia), James Purefoy (Mark Antony), Max Pirkis and Simon Woods (Octavian), Lindsay Duncan (Servilia), Indira Varma (Niobe), Kerry Condon (Octavia)

The ambitious and expensive HBO/BBC-coproduced series *Rome* has the distinction of providing viewers with one of the most accurate depictions of daily life in the capital city. It conjures an ancient Rome that is far dirtier, more crowded, more colorful, more multicultural, and more lawless than the metropolis of serene white marble monuments and stately aristocrats in many earlier cinematic representations of Rome. The series also does a good job of presenting, in a matter-of-fact way, some of the features of Roman daily life and culture that are most alien to modern sensibilities, and that most previous productions chose simply to omit. *Rome* is not without significant flaws—it takes liberties with some historical events and inserts some jarringly anachronistic behaviors—but its best moments arguably offer the most realistic rendition of Roman daily life yet to appear onscreen.

Rome is set during the turbulent final decades of the Roman Republic. The twelve episodes of the show's first season, which premiered in 2005, cover the years 52 to 44 BC and trace the struggle for dominance of Julius Caesar, his rival Pompey the Great, and the members of the Roman senate, as embodied by figures like Brutus and Cicero, who are trying to preserve their traditional power. Other important male characters include Caesar's second-in-command, Mark Antony, and Caesar's teenaged grandnephew and heir, Octavian. Obviously inspired by the scheming and manipulative Livia of the 1970s BBC miniseries, *I, Claudius*, it gives us not one but two such powerful and ambitious women: Octavian's mother, Atia, and her arch-enemy, Brutus's mother, Servilia.

Season 1 ends with the assassination of Caesar. The show was originally planned for five seasons, but it was canceled midway through Season 2, forcing the production team to condense way too much history into a handful of remaining episodes. Thus, the ten episodes of Season 2 attempt to cover the entire complicated three-way contest for power between Antony, Octavian, and the senate that unfolds over fourteen years. This struggle culminated in Octavian's victory at the Battle of Actium in 31 BC, which established him as sole ruler of the Roman world. Given the unfortunate last-minute compression of events necessary to bring the series to a conclusion, Season 2 is unsurprisingly much less successful in both historical and narrative terms than Season 1. Additionally, in Season 2, the filmmakers insert a number of unnecessarily lurid (and unhistorical) elements that further erode its quality.

The show cleverly parallels and intertwines the lives of its famous Romans with those of two lower-class protagonists who are soldiers in Caesar's army: a centurion, Vorenus, and a common legionary, Pullo. The series thus has an *Upstairs, Downstairs* sort of structure, which allows the audience to experience some of the most well-known events in Roman history from the perspectives of people at opposite ends of the social spectrum. Interestingly, Vorenus and Pullo are actually historically attested figures, being the only two ordinary soldiers mentioned by name in *The Gallic Wars*, Caesar's account of his northern conquests (5.44). In one passage, Caesar praises their battlefield bravery, but nothing is otherwise known about them, leaving considerable latitude for the show's writers to flesh out their characters.

Rome portrays them becoming fast friends, but the two men form an odd couple; Vorenus is a serious, conscientious family man with traditional values and middle-class aspirations, whereas the happy-go-lucky Pullo is gregarious, pleasure-seeking, and carefree. The writers also make Pullo into a kind of ancient version of Forrest Gump, whose blundering misadventures repeatedly and inadvertently serve as the catalyst for important historical moments. The second episode, titled "How Titus Pullo Brought Down the Roman Republic," even concocts an unlikely serio-comic chain of events by which Pullo's drunken brawl over gambling in a bar accidentally leads to the final split between Caesar and Pompey, and the outbreak of civil war.

Since the area in which the show really shines is its depiction of Roman daily life, it is worth examining a few examples of this in detail. One is its treatment of Roman paganism. Religion infused all aspects of Roman culture, from politics to entertainment, but we almost never see this portrayed in movies. Typically, paganism might be suggested by a few token references to Jupiter or presented in a highly pejorative manner to contrast with Christianity. *Rome*, however, emphasizes how religious practices and rituals are woven into the pattern of normal everyday life. It also illustrates how the vast pantheon of pagan gods were situationally invoked depending on what issue individuals were facing. Thus, when Vorenus is starting a new business, he and his family pray to a bust of Janus, the god of new beginnings; but when marital troubles arise between Vorenus and his wife, each is shown independently stopping at a street-side shrine to say quick prayers to, respectively, Venus, the goddess of love, and Magna Mater, or the Great

Mother, a deity especially popular with women. When Vorenus acquires a farm, he and his family painstakingly perform the prescribed lustration ceremony in order to purify the fields.

While we might expect such pious religious observances from the virtuous Vorenus, the more free-spirited Pullo also demonstrates piety—at least in moments of distress. In Episode 1, for example, when he is imprisoned for disobeying orders, he prays for his release to Forculus, who is, quite appropriately, the god of door hinges. Many of Pullo's prayers correctly follow the standard pagan format of offering something to a god if, in return, the god will grant his request. In Roman belief, the gods generally did not help you because they were altruistically concerned for your welfare; rather, there was a reciprocal relationship in which you gave in order to receive. Offerings often took the form of a sacrifice, which could range from something as simple as fruit or olive oil to the killing of an animal such as a sheep or a bull. In a later scene that mingles sincerity with comedy, when Pullo is yet again imprisoned and awaiting execution, he directs a heartfelt prayer to the gods for the health of his friends. However, he lacks a fitting sacrifice to accompany it. Undaunted, he makes use of the only creature available in his cell by seizing a large cockroach and messily squashing it between his hands at the conclusion of his prayer.

The show also realistically illustrates two other characteristics of Roman religion: it was a component of nearly all facets of life, including politics, and individuals differed in their degree of belief, from those who were passionately devout, to those who engaged in religious rituals mostly out of habit or to fit in socially, to those who were openly critical. Both points are driven home by Vorenus's and Mark Antony's inductions into magistracies. These political appointments were accompanied by religious rituals, but whereas Vorenus participates in his ceremony with an air of piety and humility, the skeptic Antony lounges indolently in a chair wearing a bored expression while chanting priests circle him.

Roman piety emphasized a deep reverence for one's ancestors, who were the focus of family rituals and prayers. In the foyers of their homes, members of patrician families displayed wax death masks of deceased family members, sometimes going back centuries. These masks, known as *imagines*, played a central role in many rituals, such as funerals, but almost never appear in Roman movies. Here, they are conspicuously flaunted in the homes of Atia and Servilia. These women are members, respectively, of the Julii and the Junii families, both among the oldest and most aristocratic in Roman society, so it is entirely appropriate that ancestral masks would be so prominently visible in their houses.

The series even examines those components of ancient Roman religion that we might regard as superstition or magic. Curses are employed by both upper- and lower-class characters in order to call down the wrath of gods on their enemies through ritualized invocations. One of the best and most accurate representations of this shows Servilia manufacturing curse tablets to use against her enemy, Atia, and her ex-lover, Caesar. Servilia carves the curses, along with magic diagrams, onto thin sheets of lead, then rolls these up and has them hidden in the walls of their targets' homes. Quite a few such curse tablets from antiquity have been recovered, and the procedure depicted in the show is exactly correct. Servilia's are textbook examples, including an invocation of underworld gods, the recitation of a list of the victim's anatomical parts being consigned to vengeful deities, and the promise of an offering in return for inflicting torment or misery upon the curse's victim.

Another facet of the Roman world that the show gets right is its portrayal of slavery. Too often, Roman movies attribute anachronistically empathetic attitudes to their heroes in regard to slaves, but here even the relatively "good" characters exhibit an unquestioning and callous acceptance of slavery that is probably more true to reality. In the homes of the wealthy, slaves are a ubiquitous background presence always ready to attend to their master's needs but treated by them as invisible objects. Thus, characters perform the most intimate acts in front of their slaves with no more thought than they would give to doing such things in the presence of a piece of furniture. Over the course of the series, as Vorenus moves steadily upward in status and wealth, these changes are mirrored in domestic scenes in which his household acquires more and more slaves to match his rising position.

The show also skillfully depicts the complex nature of Roman slavery as an institution exhibiting huge variations in the way that different slaves were treated and in the material conditions of their existence. The lives of agricultural slaves were frequently filled with hard labor and abuse, whereas slaves who were body servants to rich people often became their close confidants and experienced considerable luxury. We see this with the chief slave handmaids of Atia and Servilia, who are clearly their mistresses' most trusted companions and assume the role of friend, or even mother, to them. Caesar's personal clerk, Posca, is his constant companion, the custodian of his master's money, and practically the only person who regularly dares speak truth to the powerful general. It is revealing that Posca often uses the pronoun "we" when speaking, as if he were simply an extension of Caesar rather than a separate individual—which, in legal terms, he was. Freed in Caesar's will, Posca then assumes the same duties for Mark Antony. His manumission exemplifies another characteristic of Roman slavery—that the line between free and slave status was a permeable one, and there were many who crossed it in both directions.

While quite a few slaves wield surprising amounts of influence due to their proximity to their masters, the show does not whitewash the horror and dehumanization inherent in the institution of slavery. For example, during their revels, Antony and Cleopatra laughingly dress a slave in a deer hide and then drunkenly shoot arrows at the terrified man until one finally strikes him in the neck and kills him—an act that, far from provoking disapproval in the onlooking courtiers, instead elicits applause. In another scene, a slave is sadistically tortured on the orders of Atia, who exhibits a clear understanding of Roman law when she correctly notes that the testimony of a slave is only legally admissible in court if it has been obtained through torture—certainly a revealing insight into Roman attitudes toward slaves. Another dehumanizing detail is that many of the show's slaves wear small signs around their necks bearing their name and their master's name, in exactly the same way that we now put tags on our dogs to identify them as our property. While not universally used, such slave collars did exist in ancient Rome and can be viewed in archaeological museums today.

A third area in which the series is especially astute compared to most Roman movies is its portrayal of politics. The show focuses not just on the usual definition of politics in terms of formal institutions and officially elected magistrates, but also on the informal methods exploited by politicians in their struggle to gain advantages over their rivals. Aristocratic families, such as the Julii and the Junii, were constantly jockeying for position and forming and dissolving alliances with one another. For these upper-class families, marriage was not a love match, but simply a mechanism for creating or solidifying alliances. Women were political pawns, married and divorced at the command of the men in charge of their families. For example, Octavian marries his sister Octavia, against her will, to Antony to cement a temporary alliance between the two men.

Rumor and slander were other tools employed by Roman politicians, and this is also accurately illustrated in the show in a number of ways. One technique that gets a good deal of screen time is graffiti. Urban streets were coated with graffiti of all kinds, and politicians often hired professional graffiti-writers to slander opponents. The show has Caesar's enemies arrange for obscene graffiti mocking his adulterous affair to be painted throughout the city. Later, one of the factors that prompts Brutus to turn against his old friend Caesar and plot his assassination is graffiti calling upon him to live up to his family's reputation as tyrant slayers. That such graffiti influenced the historical Brutus is specifically stressed by ancient sources.

Another interesting and unusual inclusion prominently featured in Season 2 is the *collegia*. These were trade associations, somewhat like the later medieval guilds, that played a major role in both social life and politics. One of the most common types of graffiti found at Pompeii was endorsements of various politicians by different *collegia*. In the series, Vorenus becomes the head of the Aventine *collegium*, and the *collegia* are portrayed as a combination of trade organization and proto-mafia. Although their criminal activity is probably exaggerated by the show, there was indeed a persistent fear on the part of upper-class Romans that the *collegia* might serve as focal points for riots and criminality.

One other informal part of Roman society that factored into politics was the patron/client system, which tied together upper- and lower-class Romans in a complex web of obligations and exchanged favors. Several scenes of great Roman politicians receiving the petitions of clients represent this crucial but often neglected aspect of Roman culture, but when Vorenus's social status begins to rise, we also watch him becoming a smaller-scale patron to those in his local Aventine neighborhood. When Vorenus runs for election in his district, we are treated to a brief but welcome glimpse at Roman electioneering. We see him donning the *toga candida*, a special extra-white toga worn only by candidates for political office. The modern English word *candidate* actually derives from the ancient Latin term referencing the color of these togas. Garbed in his *toga candida*, Vorenus attempts an oration, but his initial efforts are amusingly amateurish. His attempts to emulate the oratorical gestures employed by Roman politicians are clumsy, and he is bedeviled by hecklers who loudly interrupt his speech. All of these details, from the toga to the gestures to the hecklers, accurately reflect the process of running for office in ancient Rome.

Public speaking was central to Roman politics, so the show is quite right to emphasize it, and the actors were trained in how to employ the stylized gestures actually used by Roman orators. Throughout the series, a public herald making announcements in the Forum utilizes a variety of these oratorical gestures, as do characters such as Cicero when delivering speeches in the senate. Other scenes featuring oratory include a law trial, during which a hostile crowd pelts one of the speakers with produce—something also attested in ancient sources. In addition, speechifying politicians are accurately depicted exhibiting a range of props in order to stir up the emotions of their audiences. Caesar displays a blood-covered Antony to his troops to incite their anger, and after Caesar's assassination, Antony in turn brandishes Caesar's bloody toga to turn the crowd against Brutus.

Another strength of *Rome* is its casting choices for a number of the major historical figures. Although James Purefoy is rather more handsome than the real Antony, the actor's characterization is spot-on, perfectly capturing both Antony's positive and negative qualities. Purefoy's Antony is charming and dynamic in an aggressively alpha-male sort of way, but he is also overconfident, vulgar, self-indulgent, and hedonistic. His performance makes it easy to understand why Antony was a successful general and highly popular with his troops. Figure 5.4.C illustrates the sort of toga worn by Mark Antony and other noblemen in the show. It is a quite realistic version of a late Republican toga, with the broad reddish stripes indicating that the wearer possessed senatorial rank. The metal arm bracers are anachronistic, however.

Figure 5.4. They Fought at Sea. (A) Legionary from the naval battle of Actium from *Cleopatra* (1963). (B) Roman admiral from *Ben-Hur* (2016). (C) Mark Antony, the loser of Actium, in a toga, from HBO/BBC *Rome* (2005). His toga is an accurate depiction of those worn at the time, and its broad stripe indicates his senatorial rank. *Illustrations by Graham Sumner.*

Rome's most inspired Basting of a historical figure, however, is Max Pirkis as the teenaged Octavian. This is an especially tough role because, unlike the bluff Antony, Octavian was a complex character and a master of propaganda, so that, even today, historians debate his true motivations. Physically, Octavian was slight of build and unimposing, but mentally, he seems to have been a brilliant manipulator. Pirkis does a fantastic job of imbuing the young Octavian with a coldly calculating intelligence—he always seems the smartest person in the room even as others discount him as being just a boy. We also see streaks of the cruelty that ancient sources attributed to Octavian—for instance, in a scene where the youth encourages Pullo to torture and kill a man and then impassively watches. So emotionless is Octavian that even the battle-hardened veteran is rather taken aback by his cool demeanor.

While there are many things to like about *Rome*, there are some real problems as well. HBO series are notorious for including heavy doses of sex and violence, and while one might assume that the historical Rome would have offered more than enough scope to satisfy this impulse, the writers apparently felt the need to up the ante by adding a number of lurid episodes that are blatantly unhistorical. For example, they invent an incestuous relationship between Octavian and Octavia. Such an incestuous liaison would have been just as shocking and taboo to the Romans as it would be today. It serves no real plot purpose and thus comes off as gratuitous, introduced purely for its shock value.

Another jarringly inaccurate element is that both ancient Rome and Egypt are represented as having a lively culture of recreational drug use. Multiple characters from both the upper and lower classes repeatedly make references to smoking and are shown inhaling hemp or opium in order to get high. Our very first view of Cleopatra has her smoking opium from a pipe, and she is portrayed as having a serious addiction to the drug. In the majority of scenes featuring her and Mark Antony, the couple is perpetually in an opium-befuddled stupor. Even the extremely level-headed and pragmatic ex-slave Posca is shown indulging in an opium pipe. At Rome, elites lounge around what looks like a nineteenth-century opium den. We even get a ludicrous scene of Roman teenagers experimenting with pot, in which, after taking a hit, one actually exclaims, "Good stuff!" Although opium and hemp derivatives were known to the Romans, there is zero evidence in the primary sources that these drugs were used recreationally, let alone that there were opium dens or a thriving drug culture. Opium was administered in small doses to treat sleeplessness, while cannabis was recommended for preventing flatulence. Additionally, the drugs were usually taken orally, and there is no mention in any source of Romans smoking them. The drug use scenes are dissonantly modern in their sensibility and seem to have been inserted solely for their shock value.

Despite these significant flaws, as well as liberties that it takes with historical facts, such as rearranging the order of some events, *Rome* is well worth watching for its gritty depiction of daily life in ancient Rome. The city is grungy and dilapidated, but also vibrantly alive. Our first look at the fabled Roman Forum reveals a densely crowded space with copious mud, hay, and excrement coating the paving stones. The buildings are majestic in scale but run-down and grubby, with faded and peeling paint. Stray dogs fossick in the muck as beggars and poor people shamble back and forth. We get the usual scenes in richly decorated villas of the aristocrats, but we also get many scenes in the dirty tenements, apartments, and slums where most of Rome's populace lived. There are mentions of the frequent floods, fires, and food shortages that plagued ancient Rome and that would have been of greater concern to its inhabitants than the public spectacles that usually monopolize our attention in Roman movies.

In describing his goals for the show's relationship to history, the show's historical advisor, Jonathan Stamp, has stated that such shows "can't be historically accurate, but . . . can be historically authentic . . . by which I mean you can try and get the details right: gesture, hair, costume, architecture, [and] color."[11] In this, *Rome* largely succeeds, and it offers a fresh, more grounded vision of what it was really like to live in ancient Rome.

The Last Legion (2007)

Director: Doug Lefler
Producers: Tarak Ben Ammar, Martha De Laurentiis, Raffaella De Laurentiis
Production Company: De Laurentiis Company
Cast: Colin Firth (Aurelius), Ben Kingsley (Ambrosinus/Merlin), Aishwarya Rai (Mira), Kevin McKidd (Wulfila), John Hannah (Nestor), Thomas Brodie-Sangster (Romulus Augustus), Alexander Siddig (Andronikos), Peter Mullan (Odoacer), Iain Glen (Orestes)

The Last Legion (2007) is one of a quartet of movies made within a brief seven-year span that are all set in Roman Britain (the others are *King Arthur*, 2004; *Centurion*, 2010; and *The Eagle*, 2011). In historical terms, *The Last Legion* is unquestionably the most ridiculous of this set, but it is also goofy fun to watch. The convoluted plot, which is partially based on a popular novel written by Valerio Massimo Manfredi, takes a kitchen-sink approach, gluing together no fewer than three major unrelated plot strands: the origin story of the mythical King Arthur and his magic sword, Excalibur; the events surrounding the deposition of the last Roman emperor in the west, Romulus Augustus; and the legend of a "lost" Roman legion that had been stationed in Britain. The cast, headed by Colin Firth as Roman general Aurelius and

Ben Kingsley as philosopher/tutor Ambrosinus, is rounded out with a large number of excellent lesser-known actors, including many who appeared in either HBO's *Rome* or *Game of Thrones*.

The film begins in AD 460 with the ascension of Romulus Augustus, a teenage boy, to the throne of the Western Roman Empire. Shortly thereafter, the Goths attack, capture the city of Rome, and imprison the boy in Tiberius's villa located on the island of Capri in the Bay of Naples, while the Gothic king, Odoacer, takes his place.[12] Romulus Augustus's deposition is often regarded as the event that marks the fall of the Western Roman Empire. All of this hews reasonably closely to history, although Romulus Augustus actually became emperor in AD 475, not 460, and he was held in the Castel dell'Ovo in the harbor of modern Naples rather than in Tiberius's villa on Capri. At this point, the actual Romulus Augustus drops out of the historical record.

This leaves room for the filmmakers to invent an exciting but completely fictitious subsequent life for him. First, a group of loyalist Roman soldiers led by Colin Firth's General Aurelius stages a daring rescue of the young emperor and his tutor Ambrosinus (Ben Kingsley) from the imposing clifftop fortress in which they have been incarcerated. This sequence seems to be channeling old World War II movies of commandos assaulting "impregnable" mountain citadels, such as *Where Eagles Dare* or *The Guns of Navarone*. The heroes are assisted in their raid by a bodyguard loaned to them by the ambassador from the Eastern Roman Empire. Fulfilling another cliché of modern Roman movies, the bodyguard turns out to be a woman super-warrior who effortlessly dispatches hordes of guards and who, in another unlikely twist, is originally from India, allowing her to deploy an array of exotic weaponry and Eastern martial arts techniques.

As luck would have it, Julius Caesar's magic sword (completely fictitious) had been stashed in Tiberius's villa and somehow remained hidden for four hundred years, yet it is miraculously and immediately discovered by Romulus Augustus. The intrepid gang then flees all the way across Europe to Britain, where they hope to find a "lost" Roman legion that is still loyal to the deposed emperor. In the process, viewers are treated to scenes of the band of heroes traversing craggy snow-covered mountains in long shots lifted directly from *The Lord of the Rings*. They are relentlessly pursued by Wulfila, the Gothic warrior who had been charged with guarding their prison. Wulfila is played by Kevin McKidd, so good in *Rome* as the centurion Vorenus, but nearly unrecognizable here under a great shaggy orange mane of "barbarian" hair. He alternates between exactly two expressions in the film—scowling and glowering—although he does both well.

In Britain, more unlikely events occur, and it is revealed that Ambrosinus was originally from Britain, his real name is Merlin, and he has been following a prophecy about a magic sword. There are more bits copied from other films, including that the British villain Vortgyn wears a gold face mask almost identical to the one worn by the villain Mordred in John Boorman's 1981 King Arthur film *Excalibur*. We get a big battle scene at Hadrian's Wall that is similar to the one found in *King Arthur* (2004). Finally, in an outrageous linkage of history and legend, we learn that Romulus Augustus will grow up to be Uther Pendragon, the father of King Arthur, and that Julius Caesar's sword will be wielded by Arthur as Excalibur.

To make all of this work, the film represents Roman emperors as constituting one unbroken hereditary succession of "Caesars" who were all related by blood, repeatedly referring to Julius Caesar as Romulus Augustus's ancestor, but in reality there was no such genetic continuity. Another distortion occurs when Romulus is being taken to Tiberius's villa and Ambrosinus tells him that it was built by "the great emperor Tiberius," who was "a man of great dignity and bearing, both of which you've inherited." Aside from the fact that Romulus Augustus and Tiberius were not of the same bloodline, describing Tiberius as a "great emperor" is quite a stretch, and his villa was best known as the site where Tiberius went to engage in debauched orgies, some of which even seem to have involved children.

As is clear by now, from a historical perspective this is a pretty silly movie, but it is saved by solid action sequences, a good cast, and by not taking itself nearly as seriously as the other three Roman Britain movies do. *The Last Legion* seems content simply to be an enjoyable popcorn flick, and on those terms, it succeeds.

Agora (2009/2010 US)

Director: Alejandro Amenábar
Producer: Fernando Bovaira
Production Company: MOD Producciones/Himenóptero/Telecinco Cinema
Cast: Rachel Weisz (Hypatia), Max Minghella (Davus), Oscar Isaac (Orestes), Michael Lonsdale (Theon), Ashraf Barhom (Ammonius), Rupert Evans (Synesius), Sami Samir (Cyril)

It is very rare for ancient historical epics to (1) feature a female protagonist, (2) be set in Late Roman Egypt, (3) center around questions of philosophy, and (4) attempt to capture the complexity of ancient religious disputes. The 2009 film *Agora* ambitiously tries to do all four of these things. It tells the story of Hypatia, a late fourth-century AD philosopher-mathematician-astronomer who lived in Alexandria, Egypt. The film, a Spanish production made with a very sizable $70 million budget, was directed by the acclaimed filmmaker Alejandro Amenábar. Rachel Weisz stars in it as Hypatia, a real person who actively taught both pagan and Christian students, and who was highly regarded by scholars of the era as possessing a top-notch intellect. However, she eventually became caught up in the political and religious conflicts of her times and was murdered by a mob of Christians.

One of the best and most historically accurate aspects of the film is its physical re-creation of late fourth-century AD Alexandria. While some CGI was employed, many of the principal sets were constructed at full scale on the island of Malta. Set designers built key sections of Alexandria, including the Agora, or marketplace, and the Serapeum, a temple complex that also contained a large library. Alexandria, a city named for Alexander the Great and founded by him on the coast of Egypt, was one of the largest and most cosmopolitan cities of the ancient world. Its location made it the crossroads of antiquity; goods from all across the Mediterranean, the Near East, and Africa flowed through its harbors. One ancient author called Alexandria "the marketplace of the world" because every product known to humankind could be bought there. Similarly, its inhabitants were a diverse mix of cultures, religions, and ethnicities. This eclecticism was reflected in the city's architecture, a mélange of Egyptian, Greek, and Roman elements with lavish public buildings representing all of these styles both singly and in combination.

The film does a terrific job of capturing this hybrid environment onscreen. For example, the Agora is adorned with a veritable forest of monuments and statuary evoking these different heritages. We see a traditional Egyptian obelisk and accurate Egyptian-style statues of the gods Anubis and Sekhmet, but also classical statues of the Greek goddess Artemis and the Greco-Egyptian deity Serapis. The space is bordered by both Egyptian buildings and Greco-Roman temples accurately sporting triangular pediments and Corinthian columns. The precinct of the Serapeum contains a forecourt that is a textbook example of that of an Egyptian temple complete with a pylon gate and an avenue lined with two rows of ram-headed sphinxes, just like those found at the Temple of Amun at Luxor. Inside the complex, however, the library is a compilation of thoroughly Greco-Roman architectural elements. Movies that take place in Alexandria often favor either the Egyptian or the Greco-Roman side of its heritage in their set design, sometimes entirely omitting one or the other, but *Agora* gets it right by highlighting both.

The production did a good job with some costuming details, in particular the hairstyles. For visual inspiration, the filmmakers claim to have drawn heavily on the Fayyum mummy portraits that survive from Egypt of this era; many of the actors resemble Fayyum portraits brought to life. The military outfits are disappointing, however, as the soldiers wear equipment that would be more appropriate to legionaries of the Roman Republic five hundred years earlier. There is an extremely well-realized re-creation of a small Roman theater with a two-story *scaenae frons*, the elaborately decorated architectural background framing the performance space. We are treated to a fine snippet of a theatrical performance complete with masked actors, a chorus, and appropriate props. When one of Hypatia's students serenades her at the theater, he plays on a nice replica of the distinctive double-tubed ancient flute called an *aulos* or *tibia*. For the library scenes, over eight thousand realistic scrolls were manufactured by hand, many with writing on them.

Alexandria of the fourth century harbored an extremely volatile mix of competing religions, including the adherents of various Greek, Roman, Egyptian, and Eastern pagan deities, several rival Christian sects, and a significant Jewish populace as well. During this period, tensions among all of these groups resulted in frequent and bloody riots. The film captures this turbulent atmosphere. Early on, there is a scene in the Agora in which two opposing soapbox orators, one representing the pagans and the other the Christians, harangue the crowd and each other. Correctly employing ancient rhetorical techniques, both speakers spice up their theological arguments with humorous put-downs in order to appeal to the crowd. Defending the human foibles of the Greco-Roman deities, the pagan speaker retorts, "If my gods eat and drink and fornicate—good for them!" When this elicits chuckles from the crowd, the Christian counters by drawing laughs of his own by pointing to a nearby statue of the god Serapis and mocking its appearance: "Who could trust a god with a flower pot for a crown?" Frequent interactions with the crowd, the use of humor, and exploiting features of the environment are all completely historically accurate rhetorical strategies that are taken straight from the advice given in ancient rhetorical handbooks, such as those written by Cicero and Quintilian.

In terms of the character of Hypatia herself, the results are more mixed, but this is largely due to the problem that none of her own writings have survived; her life and beliefs are known only through scattered references from various authors. Many of the incidents in the film—including the student who is infatuated with her, her bloody handkerchief "gift" to him, her urging him to take up music, her role as advisor to the Prefect of the city, and her interests in math and astronomy—are indeed historically attested. However, one major component of her intellectual outlook is omitted from the film, since she was known to be a strong adherent of the Neoplatonic school of philosophy. Perhaps the filmmakers decided that Neoplatonism would add one layer too many of esoteric concepts in a film that was already heavily weighted with complex cerebral ideas.

Hypatia is portrayed as a proponent of the heliocentric model of the universe and also as having deduced the elliptical movement of the planets. There is no direct evidence for her having come up with this particular insight—a fact a that is not noted in the film itself but is acknowledged by the filmmakers in the making-of documentary about the movie. Similarly, the film seems to assert that the Great Library of Alexandria was still in existence at the time of Hypatia, even though it had almost certainly been destroyed by then. This, too, the filmmakers admit in the documentary, in which they justify their inclusion of a library in the Serapeum by claiming that it is a hypothetical surviving "daughter library" of the Great Library.

While the film simplifies some of Alexandrian history during this period and sometimes attributes the actions of several different historical figures to one composite character in the film, most of the events and people are attested, including Hypatia, Prefect Orestes, Bishop Synesius, Bishop Cyril, the firewalking "miracle," the destruction of the Serapeum by the Christians, and the attacks on the Jews by the Christians. Hypatia's condemnation by Bishop Cyril and her death at the hands of a mob, perhaps led by the Parabalani, also occurred, even if some of the details are either altered or invented. One of the most notable of these changes is that her murder was in reality apparently even more brutal than depicted in the film, with her eyes being gouged out, her body dismembered, and the fragments dragged through the city streets.

The one major character that is completely invented is Davus, Hypatia's slave who eventually converts to Christianity and joins the Parabalani. The film does not, however, fall into the common pattern in most ancient movies of the protagonist holding anachronistically modern attitudes toward slavery. Even though Hypatia is acutely aware of the discrimination directed at her because she is a woman and respects Davus's intelligence, she is nevertheless completely accepting of slavery as an institution and repeatedly makes disparaging comments about slaves. While today we find such an attitude reprehensible, this is probably a far more historically accurate representation of the ancient mindset than filmmakers usually are comfortable portraying.

Another interesting aspect of the film is its depiction of the Parabalani, a semi-official organization of Christians active in Alexandria at the time, attested both as performing charitable deeds and being among the most aggressive in inciting and carrying out violent acts against non-Christians. Thus, in the movie, Ammonius, one of the main Parabalani, is shown compassionately handing out food to the poor, but he also brutally and indiscriminately murders innocent people just because they are of a different faith. Director Amenábar has stated that Ammonius was intended to represent "the best and the worst of Christianity."[13] The Parabalani are garbed in rather menacing black robes. Apparently, the film's costume designer originally based their attire on ancient sources, but, judging that the resulting outfits looked a bit silly, she redesigned them to incorporate elements copied from the clothing of modern Taliban terrorists in order to achieve the desired threatening effect.

The film caused some controversy upon its release and was accused by some critics of being anti-Christian. While it unquestionably shows Christians committing horrific acts in the name of their faith, the film has a more complex approach, since it presents them sympathetically as well. For example, the slave Davus finds in Christianity a doctrine that values his humanity in a way that the social and legal systems of the time simply do not, and the Parabalani perform both altruistic and evil deeds. The film seems more a critique of fundamentalism and extremism in any form, not just in a Christian context. Amenábar has stated that he was drawn to this particular period because he saw it as a moment when "the whole system changed from secular to theocratic" and that it illustrates the potential dangers if science and reason are completely abandoned.[14]

Two of the repeated visual motifs of the film are overhead shots that pull back until humans are reduced to little ant-like figures scurrying around below, and nighttime shots that pan up to display an endless expanse of glittering stars. Both effects emphasize another theme of the movie: set against the vast majesty of the universe, all the impassioned human squabbles over religion and science seem petty and inconsequential. As Amenábar says in the documentary, "We see we're nothing but tiny creatures." *Agora* is not always entirely successful and can be a somewhat depressing viewing experience, but it deserves credit for tackling a difficult subject and period and for doing a commendable job of portraying it in a two-hour mainstream movie.

Centurion (2010)

Director: Neil Marshall
Producers: Christian Colson, Robert Jones
Production Company: Pathé Pictures International/Celador Films
Cast: Michael Fassbender (Quintus Dias), Dominic West (Titus Flavius Virilus), Olga Kurylenko (Etain), Noel Clarke (Macros), Liam Cunningham ("Brick"), David Morrissey (Bothos), Riz Ahmed (Tarak), Dimitri Leonidas (Leonidas), Ulrich Thomsen (Gorlacon), Imogen Poots (Arianne), Paul Freeman (Agricola)

Rival film studios frequently seem to make films on exactly the same topic at the same moment. Thus, in 1954, there were two films made about Attila the Hun; in the first decade of the twenty-first century, we had two movies about the supposedly Roman origins of King Arthur; and 2010 and 2011 brought two competing films based on the legend of a "lost legion" in Roman Britain.[15] The core idea of the "lost legion" stems from some rather vague historical evidence that the Ninth Roman Legion marched into the mists of Scotland and mysteriously disappeared, apparently wiped out by savage British tribes. The Romans were then allegedly so traumatized by this catastrophe that their expansion northward came to a grinding halt, and the emperor Hadrian built his famous wall in order to keep the northern barbarians at bay. However, the actual evidence for a "Lost Legion" is extremely scanty, and many scholars are very skeptical that such a military disaster even happened. Yet millions still believe in it, and interest in this story is so substantial that it gave rise to multiple movies. How did this come about? The answer can be traced back to a piece of fiction aimed at the young adult audience.

In 1954, Rosemary Sutcliff published a novel called *The Eagle of the Ninth* intended for children and young adults that tells the heroic tale of a Roman soldier, Marcus Flavius Aquila, who is the son of the destroyed legion's commander. To redeem his family honor, he ventures beyond the wall accompanied only by a British slave, Esca, on a mission to retrieve the eagle standard lost by his father's legion. The novel was enthusiastically received and became a beloved text for several generations of young readers. Sutcliff herself went on to write dozens of other historical novels and was named a Commander of the Order of the British Empire, one of Britain's highest honors.

The slaughter of the Ninth is a good story, but it is only based on tenuous documentation. The Ninth Legion was a real legion, originally formed during the late Roman Republic, that fought in the civil wars of the first century BC. When Rome conquered Britain a century later, the Ninth was stationed there, where it participated in a number of major battles. During the great revolt led by Queen Boudica of the Iceni tribe in AD 61, the Ninth was nearly wiped out; however, it was reconstituted and, in AD 82, was one of the legions deployed by the Roman governor Agricola when he launched an invasion of northern Britain, known by the Romans as Caledonia.

The Ninth seems to have been a bit of a hard-luck legion, since, during this invasion, it allowed itself to be taken unawares by a large force of Britons, who attacked its camp at night. The Britons killed the sentries, scaled the walls, and broke into the camp. Agricola rushed to their aid with cavalry and, according to the Roman historian Tacitus, a fierce and confused fight raged within the ramparts of the camp throughout the night. Tacitus wrote, "As dawn was breaking, the standards of the [relief force] could be seen. Caught thus between two fires, the Britons were dismayed, while the men of the Ninth took heart again . . . at last the enemy was routed by the efforts of the two forces" (*Agricola* 26).

We know that the legion was still posted in Britain in AD 108, since a surviving inscription documents its participation in the construction of a major stone legionary fort at Eburacum, modern York. After this, however, its whereabouts become uncertain. Eminent nineteenth-century historian Theodor Mommsen combined their apparent disappearance from the historical record with a stray reference in a literary source to Britons killing a lot of Roman soldiers during the reign of the emperor Hadrian, in order to hypothesize that the Ninth had been annihilated by the Britons around AD 120. When this theory was repeated in Sutcliff's popular novel, Mommsen's speculation was transformed into a widely accepted "fact" among the general public. In the 1990s, however, new archaeological evidence appeared, in the form of several inscriptions, suggesting that the Ninth (or at least some elements of it) was in the Netherlands after the date of its supposed eradication in Britain.

It does seem that, by the third century AD, the legion no longer existed, leading some historians to conjecture that it was transferred to the east and then destroyed there, with Judea and Armenia among the proposed sites for its demise. There is at least one scholar who continues to believe that it was obliterated in Britain north of Hadrian's Wall, but at this point, the consensus is that the evidence is simply too sketchy for any firm conclusions to be drawn. When legions were dramatically wiped out as a result of enemy action, it usually was recorded and commented upon by multiple ancient authors. On the other hand, it was quite common for understrength legions to be combined, or even just disbanded, for a variety of reasons. Therefore, the fact that we don't know the precise moment when the Ninth ceased to exist does not prove that anything terrible happened to it. It's more likely that, rather than being massacred by barbarians, the Ninth fell victim to bureaucrats conducting a reorganization.

Whereas Sutcliff's novel follows efforts to retrieve the Ninth's eagle standard, the 2010 film *Centurion* is a prequel set twenty years earlier that imagines the circumstances in which the Ninth might have been lost. Director Neil Marshall has described the origins of the film thus: "I was sitting in a bar with a mate of mine, and he mentioned to me this legend . . . of the Ninth legion of Rome—this entire legion of Roman soldiers that marched into Scotland in 117 AD and vanished without a trace. . . . I was instantly hooked. I thought 'This is going to make a great movie.'"[16] Marshall, who had previously made a film called *Dog Soldiers* in which a squad of modern British Army soldiers goes to Scotland and encounters a pack of werewolves, initially considered giving the Ninth's story a supernatural spin: "I thought we could add some sort of fantastic element to it; they all get slaughtered by the Loch Ness Monster or something. But then I quickly thought 'That's not the road I want to go down. I'd really like to know what could've potentially happened to them.' . . . So I came up with this whole story . . . where they're battling these tribes in Scotland called the Picts, and how the Picts might have fought against the Romans in a kind of guerrilla war, and they've beaten the Romans somehow and then actually it's the Romans that create the myth as a cover-up for their own screw-up."[17]

The film opens with a night attack on a small, encamped detachment of Roman soldiers that recalls Tacitus's description of the actual major nocturnal assault on the Ninth. In this case, however, no help comes, and all the Romans are slain except for one centurion, Quintus Dias, played by Michael Fassbender. The attack is compellingly and gorily filmed; unfortunately, once atop the walls, the Picts inexplicably shoot fire arrows. Not only would such tactics have been counterproductive since the flames would have helped the targeted Romans dodge them, but it is unexplained how the Picts could have lit them. After all, had they been carrying lit torches, they could hardly have snuck up to the very walls of the fort without being spotted by the sentries. Of course, the real reason for their inclusion is the usual filmmakers' love of visually exciting pyrotechnics, but this conceit ruins an otherwise effective sequence.

After Fassbender's captured centurion manages to escape, he meets the main Roman force, the Ninth, which is marching north to punish the Picts. By the way, the term "Picts" does not appear in any ancient source until several hundred years later. The Romans probably would have referred to barbarians native to this region as Caledonians, or just generically as Britons, but this is a minor point. The commander of the Romans, named Titus Flavius Virilus, is depicted a bit unrealistically as drinking, socializing, fighting, and even arm-wrestling with the common soldiers. This wins him their affection, with one soldier commenting, "I've never seen a general so beloved of his men." Virilus is clearly intended to represent the epitome of masculinity, a point crudely emphasized by his very name, since Virilus in Latin literally means "manly."

The ambush and destruction of the Ninth in the film resembles what was perhaps the most famous defeat in Roman history, when three legions were surprised and wiped out in AD 9 by Germanic barbarians in the Teutoburg Forest. There are numerous parallels. In both cases, the Romans are led into a trap by a barbarian whom they believe is on their side, but who is really acting as a double agent. In the Teutoburg massacre, this was a German chieftain named Arminius; in the movie, this role is updated for twenty-first-century notions of gender equity as a warrior-woman of the Picts named Etain, who is pretending to be a scout for the Romans. In the Teutoburg disaster, the Romans were caught strung out while marching through heavily forested and

Figure 5.5.   Legionaries of the Lost Eagle. (A) Legionary from *The Eagle* (2011) wearing the usual leather movie version of what should be metal armor. (B) Legionary from *Centurion* (2010) wearing a more correct metal version of the same armor. Both figures' helmets, swords, and shields are reasonably accurate. (C) Tunic and trousers worn in *Centurion* (2010).   Illustrations by *Graham Sumner. Photograph and prop from the Graham Sumner Collection.*

swampy terrain. In the film, we see just such an ambush in the dense woods. In both cases, the discipline and organization of the Romans help them fend off the initial assaults, as small groups of legionaries form defensive squares behind a wall of shields. There is an effective moment when a Roman officer instructs his nervous troops, "Whatever comes out of that mist, lads, you will hold the line." This accurately reflects the emphasis on discipline at the core of the Roman military machine, and one can well imagine such words having been spoken by Roman centurions in the Teutoburg Forest.

In the Battle of the Teutoburg Forest, the Roman formations were gradually worn down over several days of continuous fighting, until the exhausted and scattered groups that remained could be picked off and slaughtered. The movie substitutes a quicker and more dramatic mechanism for Roman defeat that, once again, anachronistically involves fire. The Picts unleash a barrage of gigantic, six-foot-high flaming balls that weave through the forest, miraculously dodging all the trees while unerringly smashing into the densest concentrations of Roman troops. This improbable method of attack is completely unattested in any ancient sources but was undoubtedly inspired by the similarly invented flaming logs in the 1960 version of *Spartacus*. The remainder of the film follows the adventures of a handful of Roman survivors, including Fassbender's centurion. At first, they try to rescue their beloved commander, Virilus, who has been taken prisoner. However, when this proves to be impossible, they focus their efforts on escaping back to Roman territory, pursued the entire way by the vengeful Picts, led by the bloodthirsty warrior-woman Etain. Somewhat atypically, the casting of the Roman legionaries attempts to reflect the ethnic diversity of the Roman Empire. The veteran legionaries "Brick" and Bothos are apparently from Italy, Macros hails from Numidia, Leonidas from Greece, and Tarak the cook is originally from the Hindu Kush region.

As seen in Figure 5.5.B, the legionary equipment, such as the Gallic-style helmets and the *lorica segmentata*-type body armor, is among the most accurate to be featured in a mainstream movie. The swords and shields are also quite historical. The kit of the centurions in the film (see Figure 5.6.A) is also very well done, including the harness adorned with award disks (*phalerae*), the transverse helmet crest, the chain mail shirt, and the belt. His boots are a more modern design, however. The widespread presence on both legionaries and centurions of large metal arm guards (vambraces), which were not part of the Roman panoply, is disappointing. Compared with the costuming found in most Roman films, however, this is a relatively minor quibble. The standard-bearers are correctly shown wearing scale shirts (*lorica squamata*) and with animal pelts draped over their helmets. The reconstruction of the small Roman fort is reasonably authentic, although it is incorrectly named Inchtuthil, which is the modern name for a large legionary fortress that had already been abandoned around AD 86.

While it cannot be said that the film is a truthful depiction of historical events, it at least references or mirrors some actual episodes in Roman history. The name of the governor who wants to cover up the massacre is Agricola, a clear nod to the most famous Roman governor of Britain, who ruled over the province a few decades earlier in the 80s. The movie was filmed on location in the highlands of Scotland rather than in a studio, and it employs physical special effects instead of computer-generated ones, lending it a greater sense of authenticity. So realistic was the filming that several of the actors got frostbite, and there were almost two dozen injuries among the crew. It's a rather gory film, which consumed over fifty gallons of fake blood. Like *Gladiator*, the production made use of historical reenactors, who portrayed both Romans and Britons. A large portion of *Centurion* is basically a chase film, and overall, it is a satisfying adventure/war movie.

One final interesting bit of trivia is that Marshall has stated that another of his inspirations was the 1979 movie *The Warriors*, directed by Walter Hill, who is accordingly thanked in the credits. Much of *Centurion* concerns a small band of Roman soldiers traversing hostile enemy territory in the attempt to reach safety, while *The Warriors* relates the story of a modern New York street gang that has to cross New York City, evading other hostile gangs, in order to return to the safety of its home turf on Coney Island. What does this have to do with ancient history? *The Warriors* is itself a modernized retelling of a famous episode from classical history in which a group of Greek mercenaries, stranded deep within the hostile territory of the Persian Empire, had to fight their way back home to Greece.

The Eagle (2011)

Director: Kevin Macdonald
Producer: Duncan Kenworthy
Production Company: Toledo Productions/Film 4/DMG
Cast: Channing Tatum (Marcus Flavius Aquila), Jamie Bell (Esca), Donald Sutherland (Uncle Aquila), Mark Strong (Guern/Lucius Caius Metellus), Tahar Rahim (Seal People Prince)

Together with *Centurion* (2010), *The Eagle* (2011) is the second film to appear in just two years inspired by Rosemary Sutcliff's popular children's novel *The Eagle of the Ninth* (1954) concerning the legend of the "lost Ninth Legion."[18] Much more so than *Centurion*, this film is directly based on Sutcliff's novel. Set in AD 140, twenty years after the events of the first film, *The Eagle* focuses on the son of the commander who lost the Ninth's eagle standard. Now a centurion himself, he comes to Britain determined to redeem his family's honor. His character, played by Channing Tatum, is called Marcus Flavius Aquila. This is a less-than-subtle use of names to indicate what is important about him, since *aquila* in Latin literally means "eagle."

Director Kevin Macdonald's casting of an American actor in the main Roman role was very deliberate. As Macdonald explains, "I wanted to go against the grain. . . . The convention is that Romans are always British with posh accents because it represents the days of the empire. [My] idea is that they are meant to be Americans. He is a G.I. Everyone who is Roman in this movie is American. . . . Then [the British characters] speak with British regional accent[s]. . . . I wanted to get that difference between the two."[19] Macdonald was drawn to the project because he is one of the many who had read Sutcliff's book as a child. As he recalls, "I must have first read it when I was ten or twelve, and it was one of those books that as a young person I really liked. . . . It made a big impression on me."[20]

Like *Centurion, The Eagle* begins with a night assault on a small Roman fort—although in this iteration, the Britons more realistically spring out of the darkness without giving themselves away with flaming arrows—but they are then repulsed thanks to Aquila's alertness. The next day, they begin to execute some Roman prisoners in front of the fort's walls, so Aquila leads a sortie to rescue the captives. He orders his men into the defensive *testudo* formation often depicted in films, in which the troops create a dense rectangle with a solid barrier of shields on all sides and overhead (although under these circumstances, the *cuneus*, or wedge formation, might have been more appropriate). As the troops shuffle forward, a mob of frenzied Britons engulfs them, seeking a weak spot. The Romans are realistically shown jabbing at the surrounding tribal warriors with their short swords from behind the wall of their shields.

Though not accurate in every regard, this scene does a credible job of portraying how one of the more famous Roman battle formations could be employed against less disciplined troops. The Britons counter with an attack by chariots equipped with blades on their wheel hubs. Aquila saves his men by heroically spearing the lead driver, but he is badly wounded in the process. The Britons did use war chariots, so again, this is an accurate detail—although whether or not they had chariots with blades on the wheels is debated. The fortlet itself is well done, and various historically correct features can be observed, including the earth and timber defenses and a large mule-powered rotary grain mill. The equipment of the soldiers, in particular the Roman cavalry, is quite authentic.

Another realistic touch is that, several times, Aquila is shown praying before battle to the god Mithras, a deity who was especially popular with soldiers. One scene even portrays Aquila beside the standard Mithraic sculptural relief that depicts the god ritually slaying a bull framed by various mystical symbols and figures. Roman religious beliefs are also alluded to when, uncertain which direction to take, Aquila offers a prayer while clutching a totemic carving of an eagle. A real eagle promptly appears in the northern sky, and Aquila follows this divine omen. Augury, a form of divination based on observing the flight of birds, and especially of eagles, was an important practice in Roman paganism—a fact effectively illustrated by this scene.

Discharged from the military due to his injury, Aquila recovers at the villa of his uncle, played in an engaging cameo by Donald Sutherland. Still determined to bring honor to his family, Aquila decides to venture north of the wall in an attempt to find and recover the lost eagle standard of the Ninth Legion. As a culture, the Romans—particularly members of the hereditary aristocracy—were quite obsessed with one's family name and honor, so Aquila's fixation upon these legitimately reflects Roman values. He sets off, accompanied only by his body slave, Esca. Although Esca is the son of a chief slain by the Romans and hates them, he is bound by a debt of honor to serve Aquila. They (as well as other characters) engage in a number of debates about the Romans' presence in Britain and the nature of Roman imperialism, which neatly encapsulate opposing perspectives on this complex issue. In one scene, a character says of the Romans, "Why'd they have to come north? There's nothing here worth taking. Couldn't they have been satisfied with what they had? They always have to punish and push on, looking for more conquests and more territories and more wars." These lines closely echo similar sentiments expressed by a British chieftain leading a rebellion against the Romans as recounted by the ancient Roman historian Tacitus: "Pillagers of the world, [the Romans] have exhausted the land by their indiscriminate plunder. . . . A rich enemy excites their cupidity, a poor one their lust for power. East and west alike have failed to satisfy them. They are the only people on earth to whose covetousness both riches and poverty are equally tempting" (*Agricola* 30).

When Aquila and Esca venture beyond the wall, it is presented as if they are entering hostile territory. However, in the period when the story is set, Hadrian's Wall was no longer the edge of the empire, since the Romans had advanced into what is now southern Scotland and a new frontier had been established along what is today known as the Antonine Wall. A bust of the current emperor, Antoninus Pius, correctly appears in the headquarters building of the legionary fortress. As Aquila and Esca continue on their quest, they encounter a Roman survivor of the Ninth's final battle named Guern, who has gone native and leads them to where it took place. One idea in the book, also in the movie, is the notion that all Roman soldiers had a tell-tale chin-strap scar: this is how Aquila and Esca discover the true identity of Guern. But, as any reenactor can attest, the chin strap of a Roman helmet leaves no such permanent distinctive scar.

Figure 5.6. Centurions of the Lost Eagle. (A) Fairly accurate Roman centurion outfit from *Centurion* (2010), except for the metal forearm guards. (B) This centurion from *The Eagle* (2011) wears a metal cuirass, although a chain mail shirt would probably have been more likely. Both centurions have the correct transverse crests on their helmets. (C) Reconstruction of a centurion from the mid-second century AD. *Illustrations by Graham Sumner.*

An effectively unsettling sequence has them wandering over the site of the decades-old massacre while Guern tersely describes the slaughter. Surrounded by dark, menacing trees, they discover moss-encrusted Roman skulls, piles of bones, and armor lying half-buried among the decaying leaves on the forest floor. Guern solemnly intones, "This is the killing ground. . . . They used those stones as altars to kill the officers. They ripped their hearts out while still alive. We could hear them being sacrificed." This creepy scene seems to have been directly based on another passage from Tacitus, in which a Roman army finds the site of the infamous annihilation of three legions in the Teutoburg Forest, years after it occurred: "The whitening bones of men were strewn everywhere, or piled in heaps, as they had fled, or stood their ground. Nearby lay fragments of weapons, and limbs of horses, and also human heads, prominently nailed to trunks of trees. In the adjacent groves were the barbarous altars, on which [the Germans] had sacrificed tribunes and first-rank centurions" (*Annals* 1.61). From here onward, the film moves firmly into the territory of fiction, as Aquila and Esca are captured by the completely unattested tribe of the Seal People, experience further adventures, discover the eagle standard among the Seal People, steal it, become fast friends, manage to flee south to the Roman lines, return the eagle, and resolve their respective father issues.

The film's costumes are not quite as historically accurate as those in *Centurion* but are not bad. The legionaries (Figure 5.6.A) are equipped with leather versions of *lorica segmentata* body armor rather than metal. Although only a relatively lowly centurion, Aquila (Figure 5.6.B) wears an elaborate metal muscle cuirass more typically found on high-ranking officers. Figure 5.6.C depicts a reconstructed centurion of this period for comparison. As in *Centurion*, nearly all the Roman soldiers inaccurately sport arm guards of various designs.

For those interested in Roman Britain or the Roman army, *The Eagle* and *Centurion* are worth watching. Neither is a truly great movie, but both are entertaining adventure stories that contain some solid information about the Roman army and its tactics. More significantly, they raise important issues about the nature of Roman imperialism and the interactions between Roman civilization and the indigenous cultures of the provinces. A number of scholars and critics have noted how it is possible to interpret both films as allegories of recent historical events—in particular, American imperialism and the experiences of US soldiers in Vietnam, Iraq, and Afghanistan, where they found themselves traversing a hostile landscape inhabited by often resentful local peoples.[21] At the very least, the two films form an interesting pair and are testimony to the enduring allure of the "Legend of the Lost Legion," as well as to how compelling children's literature can be.

Spartacus: Blood and Sand, Gods of the Arena, Vengeance, and War of the Damned (2010–2013)

Directors: Rick Jacobson, Michael Hurst, Jesse Warn, and others
Producers: Steven DeKnight, Robert Tapert, Sam Raimi, Joshua Donen
Production Company: DeKnight Productions/Starz
Cast: Andy Whitfield/Liam McIntyre (Spartacus), John Hannah (Batiatus), Lucy Lawless (Lucretia), Manu Bennett (Crixus), Peter Mensah (Oenomaus), Nick Tarabay (Ashur), Jai Courtney (Varro), Erin Cummings (Sura), Lesley-Ann Brandt/Cynthia Addai-Robinson (Naevia), Dan Feuerriegel (Agron), Craig Walsh-Wrightson (Solonius), Dustin Clare (Gannicus), Craig Parker (Glaber), Viva Bianca (Ilithyia), Katrina Law (Mira), Pana Hema Taylor (Nasir), Anna Hutchison (Laeta), Simon Merrells (Crassus), Todd Lasance (Julius Caesar)

Following the success of HBO's lauded *Rome* series (2005–2007), another premium cable television network, STARZ, came out with a series of its own, this time based on the ever-popular figure of Spartacus, the gladiator who led a major slave rebellion during the late Roman Republic. The STARZ production team took a very different approach from HBO's *Rome*, however. Whereas *Rome* had garnered praise for striving to be a sophisticated and realistic "quality drama" along the lines of the acclaimed series *The Sopranos*, *Spartacus* was instead filmed in a deliberately artificial style recalling the exaggerated imagery of a graphic novel or a video game, and featured sensationalistic plots and an outrageous superabundance of cartoonish sex and violence. This style, the most prominent characteristic of which was copious gallons of CGI blood constantly spurting, splashing, and splattering, was clearly copied from Zack Snyder's 2007 film *300*, about the Spartans and their heroic last stand at the Battle of Thermopylae. Like that movie, *Spartacus* also favors unrealistic, but extremely gory, fight scenes heavily influenced by modern Asian martial arts, and legions of super-macho and hyper-muscular sweaty men clad in skimpy S&M-type leather outfits.

Perhaps in reaction to these qualities, initial critical response to *Spartacus* was fairly scathing. Their flavor is summed up by Charlie Brooker's review in the *Guardian*, which began: "If you're a 15-year-old boy, chances are *Spartacus: Blood and Sand* will strike you as the finest TV show ever made. . . . This is possibly the lustiest, goriest, most willfully red-blooded drama series the law and human decency will allow. Roughly every 30 seconds someone gets an axe or sword in the face. Roughly every 20 seconds a woman bares her breasts. Roughly every 10 seconds someone grunts a four-letter word. . . . They should have called it *Spartacus: Blood and F**king Tits*."[22] These tendencies are especially problematic in the first few episodes before enough elements of the plot kick in. In the commentary, even *Spartacus* executive producer Steven DeKnight confessed, "There's probably too much sex, too much violence, and too much cursing in those first couple of episodes, which I completely admit to."

Although it repelled some critics, the series proved popular with audiences. It ran for four seasons, earned good ratings, and spawned spin-off comics, novels, a board game, and a video game. Interestingly, however, if one strips away its distractingly lurid style and excess of sex and violence, the show is surprisingly faithful to what is known about the actual Spartacus and his rebellion. It benefits from the fact that, while at least a dozen ancient authors mention Spartacus, none of their accounts are more than a few pages long and they often contradict each other, leaving plenty of room for the makers of a forty-hour series to creatively fill in the details.

What we know from the sources is that, in 73 BC, a group of sixty to eighty slave gladiators, who were training at a gladiator school in Capua run by a man named Lentulus Batiatus, rebelled and escaped into the countryside. Their leader was a gladiator named Spartacus, who was originally from Thrace and may have served as an auxiliary in the Roman army before being enslaved and assigned to the school. Among his main lieutenants were gladiators named Crixus, Oenomaus, and Gannicus. From various bases, including Mt. Vesuvius, they raided nearby villas, freed other slaves, and increased their numbers until they were over a hundred thousand strong. They defeated a succession of Roman paramilitary forces sent against them, the first of which was led by Gaius Claudius Glaber. Growing concerned, the Romans dispatched several regular legionary armies under the command of Marcus Licinius Crassus to squash the rebellion. The slave army managed to evade them, roamed through Italy for several years, and made abortive attempts to escape over the Alps and to hire Cilician pirates to transport them to Sicily. Ultimately, one division of the slave army that was commanded by Crixus was caught and destroyed, and soon afterward, Spartacus and the main army were defeated by Crassus, who crucified six thousand captured prisoners along the Appian Way.

Every one of these major historical events and figures was incorporated into the series, as were a number of more minor ones. For example, the author Frontinus described several improbable military stratagems allegedly employed by Spartacus that feature prominently in the show, such as the rebels weaving vines into ropes to rappel down the side of Mt. Vesuvius and launching a surprise attack on Glaber, and Spartacus using the dead bodies of his own people to fill in and cross over a trench that had been dug by Crassus in order to trap him. Another notable incident accurately portrayed in the series is Crassus punishing a group of Roman soldiers who had run away during a battle by holding a decimation, a ritual in which the men draw lots and one in ten is beaten to death by his comrades. Also correctly depicted is how Pompey the Great showed up very late in the campaign and stole from Crassus much of the credit for defeating Spartacus. Viewers with a deep knowledge of Roman history will enjoy the occasional allusions to events outside the scope of the series, such as when Caesar comments that he dislikes Cilician pirates—a reference to an occasion in his youth when he was captured and held for ransom by a band of Cilician pirates—or the introduction of a character who was a victim of the dictator Sulla's proscriptions. The scriptwriters even integrated several specific phrases from ancient sources into the show, such as when Pompey the Great is several times referred to as "the adolescent butcher," and Spartacus's Thracian wife, who was a seer, prophecies that he is "destined for great and unfortunate things."

The first season, *Blood and Sand*, covers Spartacus's capture in Thrace and his experiences in the gladiator school, ending with the revolt. Tragically, after the first season was filmed, Andy Whitfield, the actor playing Spartacus, fell ill with cancer and died. To fill the gap until a replacement could be chosen, the show's producers made Season 2, *Gods of the Arena*, a prequel that delved into the previous history of the gladiator school of Batiatus before Spartacus's arrival. Season 3, *Vengeance*, then picked up the story of the rebellion and followed it through the defeat of Glaber with a new actor, Liam McIntyre, taking over as Spartacus. Season 4, *War of the Damned*, traced the remainder of the rebellion's history, with Crassus assuming the role of Spartacus's main antagonist.

The filmmakers made some interesting linguistic choices apparently to try to impart a Roman flavor to the show. First, they decided to insert a large number of untranslated Latin terms into the script, such as *lanista*, *legatus*, *medicus*, *editor*, *dominus/a*, *pulvinus*, and *ludus*. Second, all the dialogue is written in a somewhat stilted form of English that omits most definite articles and frequently includes terse declarative phrases (e.g., "Apologies," "Gratitude"). While it is initially somewhat distracting and does not offer a literal rendering of Latin grammatical constructions, this stylized diction nevertheless does effectively impart a sense of "otherness" to the dialogue.

The show also accurately depicts many aspects of Roman culture. Some examples include the equipment of the gladiators; the emphasis placed on the importance of patronage in Roman society; Roman funerary rituals, such as disheveled hair, black clothes, forgoing shaving, and the display of *imagines* (wax death masks of one's ancestors); a reference to the Roman law that if a slave kills his master, all the slaves in the household will be put to death; and that free Romans could sell themselves into slavery in order to pay their debts. Also effective is the show's general representation of the cruelty of the institution of slavery, in which slaves were regarded as objects rather than as humans and were often subjected to sexual abuse. The show additionally offers a vivid illustration of the intense social climbing and competition for status among the elites that characterized Roman society. One of the more enjoyable elements of the series is the constant scheming of Batiatus and his equally ambitious wife, Lucretia (engagingly played by John Hannah and Lucy Lawless), as they claw their way upward in Roman society by any means possible.

Some major aspects of the plot are entirely unhistorical, however. The character of Crassus's son, Tiberius, is invented; Julius Caesar was not directly involved in any way in suppressing the Spartacan revolt; the rebels did not raid and destroy the amphitheater at Capua; and the "fighting pits" that figure prominently in several episodes are a complete fabrication. While Roman attitudes toward sexuality were arguably more permissive in some respects than is typical today, the show's portrayal of nonstop orgies and unremitting debauchery is grossly exaggerated. Still, since the makers of many less accurate historical films vigorously insist that their creations are genuine history, one has to credit *Spartacus*'s filmmakers for being refreshingly honest in admitting the limits of their show's authenticity. In the making-of featurettes, producer Steven DeKnight freely acknowledges that "this is grounded in history, but none of us are saying that this is history. At the end of the day, we are making a show that is entertaining," and producer Robert Tapert states, "We don't let history stand in our way, but we also don't want to run roughshod all over it."

If ever a show so richly earned the adjective "gratuitous" in reference to its depiction of nudity and bloodshed, it is STARZ's *Spartacus*. The unrealistic, CGI-heavy, stylized visual aesthetic may not be to some viewers' taste and is so prominent and extreme that it will deter many. If, however, one is able to tune out these elements, what remains is an enjoyably pulpy story and a not wholly inaccurate historical epic.

Pompeii (2014)

Director: Paul W. S. Anderson
Producers: Paul W. S. Anderson, Jeremy Bolt, Don Carmody, Robert Kulzer
Production Company: Constantin Film/Impact Pictures
Cast: Kit Harington (Milo), Emily Browning (Cassia), Kiefer Sutherland (Corvus), Carrie-Anne Moss (Aurelia), Adewale Akinnouye-Agbaje (Atticus), Jared Harris (Severus), Sasha Roiz (Proculus)

Pompeii (2014) is a fast-paced, loud, over-the-top action-adventure film. It feels like one of those Frankenstein pastiches in which filmmakers stitch together a bunch of pieces from other movies in the belief that the resultant creature will have maximum crowd appeal. In this case, the thinking seems to have been to combine a disaster-movie scenario (exploding volcano!) with the gladiator-seeking-revenge-for-his-slaughtered-family plot of *Gladiator*. Onto this, they grafted the love story from *Titanic*, replicating not just the doomed lovers, but also the romantic triangle structure of a rich but empathetic young upper-class woman, her arrogant and aristocratic suitor, and a scrappy charmer from the wrong side of the tracks. Then they completed their monstrous creation by endowing the hero with a stunningly sculpted set of abs worthy of the Spartans in *300*.

Not only are the major elements lifted from other films, so are most of the minor ones. To give just a few examples of many: an ultra-skilled, noble Black gladiator who starts off as a rival to the protagonist becomes his friend and then sacrifices himself for him (*Spartacus*); a tragic lone survivor of an exterminated tribe (*The Last of the Mohicans*); a recurrent image of a tree festooned with slain warriors (*Excalibur*); a soundtrack featuring Lisa Gerrard-like ululations (*Gladiator* and every ancient movie that followed); a prologue in Roman Britain that recalls all four recent Roman movies set there (*King Arthur*, *The Last Legion*, *Centurion*, *The Eagle*); and the hero's special horse-whisperer talent, which plays a key role in several scenes (*The Horse Whisperer*).

From a historical perspective, the filmmakers clearly exerted some effort to make their CGI version of Pompeii resemble the layout of the actual city, although they shifted its location from inland to the shore of the Bay of Naples. They also attempted to depict the different attested stages of the eruption, from the initial warning tremors through the devastating pyroclastic flow. The background details in the street-life scenes are pretty good. Some historical misrepresentations are made for dramatic effect, such as inventing a "law" that gladiators were automatically freed after a certain number of fights, and portraying the emperor Titus as a corrupt ruler, when he actually seems to have been a reasonably decent one.

Pompeii is not a profound film, but if you are looking for some mindless entertainment and enjoy seeing a whole lot of somewhat cheesy computer-generated chaos and explosions, you will come away satisfied. Ultimately, *Pompeii* is a bit too much of a formulaic cut-and-paste job whose components borrowed from other movies fail to cohere as a unified whole, and even its makers seem aware of this. In an unconvincing attempt to explain why his movie is not just a rip-off of *Gladiator*, director Paul W. S. Anderson rather defensively begins his audio commentary by asserting, "Yes, there are gladiators in [this film], but there was no volcano in [*Gladiator*]!"

Ben-Hur (2016)

Director: Timur Bekmambetov
Producers: Sean Daniel, Joni Levin, Duncan Henderson
Production Company: Sean Daniel Company/Lightworkers Media
Cast: Jack Huston (Judah Ben-Hur), Toby Kebbell (Messala), Morgan Free-man (Sheik Ilderim), Rodrigo Santoro (Jesus), Nazanin Boniadi (Esther), Sofia Black-D'Elia (Tirzah)

One might well think that another *Ben-Hur* movie would be completely unnecessary given the multiple well-regarded and popular earlier versions, including the 1925 film starring Ramon Novarro and the 1959 one with Charlton Heston. However, Hollywood is perennially infatuated with re-makes, so in 2016, we were given the dubious gift of a new *Ben-Hur*. Despite a sizable budget of $100 million, the result is about what one might expect: a mediocre film with lots of computer-generated special effects that is popu-lated by a bunch of attractive young people with bodies plainly sculpted in modern gyms and who talk in a slangy contemporary manner ("That's low!" "Don't care." "Okay." Upon hearing Jesus preach, one character actually comments: "That's very progressive.").

As with previous productions of *Ben-Hur* the highlights are the naval battle and the chariot race. Thankfully, rather than entirely relying on CGI, the filmmakers constructed a partial circus for the race, and the scene com-bines real horses and chariots with digital effects. The result is respectable but inferior to both the 1925 and 1959 versions. While the overall dramatic im-pact of the two earlier naval battles is better, this rendition does have an inter-esting twist. It is filmed almost entirely from the limited belowdeck perspective of Judah Ben-Hur, lending the sequence an effectively disorienting and chaotic atmosphere. On the historical accuracy of these two action sequences, see the entries for the 1925 and 1959 films, which analyze them in detail. Nearly all those comments apply here.

The costuming for the film includes some odd elements. For example, the charioteer outfit worn by Messala (see Figure 2.8.C) seems to be made up of components derived from armor worn by Roman soldiers and painted a men-acing black. As the attire of a charioteer, however, this get-up is utterly unre-alistic. The one notable exception is the curved dagger, attested to have been used by drivers to cut themselves free from the reins when crashing. (For actual charioteer attire, see Figure 2.8.B.) In an early scene of marching legionaries, the men's helmets, swords, and body armor are reasonable, but their marching packs and associated equipment are a bizarre assemblage of components that seem to come from much later eras. Figure 3.1.B depicts a marching legionary from the film, while Figure 5.7 includes front and back photographs of the prop tunics, backpacks, and equipment used in this scene. As can be seen, the men carry modern-looking shovels, rather than the famous and distinctive Roman pick-axe, the *dolabra*. The rows of little leather pouches across their chests are plainly inspired by the ammo pouches carried by British soldiers in World War I and World War II rather than any authentic ancient artifact. Figure 3.1.C offers a more realistic reconstruction of a marching legionary.

The main way in which the plot of this *Ben-Hur* deviates from the previous ones is by emphasizing and expanding upon the early relationship between Judah and Messala, who this time is some sort of adopted son of the Hur family with an odd backstory about his grandfather having been disgraced due to involvement in Julius Caesar's assassination. Also, Judah's adoption by the Roman admiral is entirely left out; after the naval battle, Judah washes ashore at the camp of Sheik Ilderim. Finally, it concludes with a contrived and unconvincing happy ending in which Messala and Judah tearfully forgive one another, declare themselves once again "brothers," and blissfully wander off into the desert with their wives and a group of Christians.

With the plot condensed into a snappy two hours, the movie feels rushed and the action scenes never carry the emotional weight that they should. The film goes overboard in its depiction of the Romans as rapacious, one-dimensional imperialists, with a Roman officer characterizing the purpose of the empire as being to "crush the freedom of innocent civilizations simply because they were different." *Ben-Hur* (2016) isn't horrible, but it is completely superfluous, and it would have been nice if its $100 million budget had been spent on telling a fresh story about the Roman world.

The First King (2019)

Director: Matteo Rovere
Producers: Matteo Rovere, Andrea Paris
Production Company: Groenlandia/Gapbusters/Rai
Cast: Alessio Lapice (Romulus), Alessandro Borghi (Remus), Tania Garribba (Satnei the Vestal)

Oddly, the most recent film covered in this book is also the very earliest in terms of the time period when it is set. *The First King* (2019) is an Italian-made production about Romulus and Remus, the semi-legendary founders of Rome, who allegedly lived in the middle of the eighth century BC. This is long before most movies about the Romans take place. At this point, they were still centuries away from becoming a powerful nation with great wealth, a huge empire, mighty legions, and impressive monumental buildings. The city of Rome does not yet even exist, and the people who

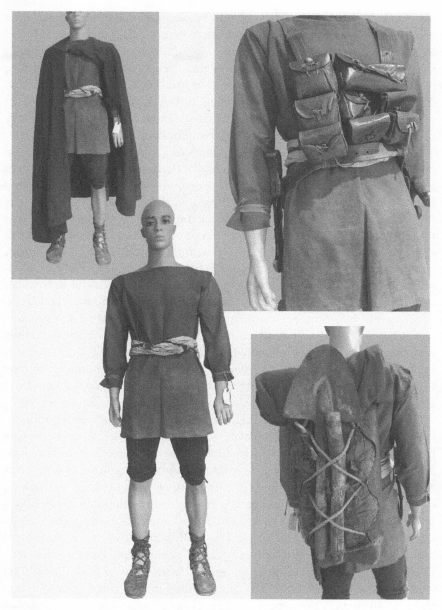

Figure 5.7. *Ben-Hur* (2016) Legionary on the March. Costumes and props used by marching Roman legionaries in *Ben-Hur* (2016), including linen tunic, wool trousers (*bracae*), wool cloak (*sagum*), boots (*caligae*), and ahistorical marching pack with pick, shovel, and knives, along with front pouches nearly identical to a WWI soldier's ammo pouches. Compare with the painted legionaries in Figure 3.1. *Photographs and props from the Graham Sumner Collection.*

will found it are just a handful of grubby outcasts blundering through the swamps of central Italy, on the run from more powerful, already established local tribes. Directed by Matteo Rovere and filmed on a $9 million budget in the actual wetlands, hills, and forests around the city of Rome, *The First King* is refreshingly original in its subject and entertaining to watch. Additionally, it incorporates some quite knowledgeable historical references, even if most of the film about this extremely poorly documented phase of Roman history consists of creative speculation rather than attested fact.

The filmmakers opted for an extreme and very gritty realism. These proto-Romans live in squalor, perpetually slathered in grime, dressed in ragged sheepskins, wielding crude weapons, and with primitive thatched huts as their most luxurious dwellings. The frequent violence in the film is also brutally realistic. Eschewing the showy, balletic, martial-arts-influenced style of fighting that seems to have taken over ancient epics in recent decades, the battles here are fast, frantic, and savage. Combatants (sometimes including women and children) gouge eyes, bite, throttle, bludgeon, and stab their opponents with the believable ferocity of individuals desperately fighting for their lives. Balanced against all the mud and blood is absolutely beautiful cinematography full of atmospheric mist-shrouded fens, nocturnal rituals illuminated by flickering torchlight, and foreboding, shadowy woods. Another uniquely realistic element is that all the dialogue is spoken in a kind of proto-Latin dialect. Linguists at La Sapienza University in Rome were enlisted to translate the script into a reconstructed version of the language that the people at that time and place may have spoken.

The Romans themselves created a number of legends about the foundation of their city, all of which date to several centuries after the events being described, and many of which contradict one another. In the most familiar one, the god Mars impregnated a Vestal Virgin, who gave birth to the twins Romulus and Remus in the city of Alba Longa, but the king ordered that they be drowned by being cast into the flooding Tiber River. Fortuitously, the floodwaters deposited the basket containing the infants safely on the slopes of the Capitoline Hill, where they were discovered and nursed by a wolf and a woodpecker (animals associated with Mars). Eventually taken in by a sheepherder, the twins grew to young adulthood as shepherds, at which time they deposed the king of Alba Longa who had tried to kill them. Gathering a small band of followers made up of outcasts from neighboring tribes, they founded the city of Rome in 753 BC on the spot where they had washed up as babies. However, they fell to quarreling over who should be the ruler of the new city, and Romulus killed his brother, thereby claiming the title of first king of Rome for himself.

The film skips over the early supernatural stages of the twins' legend, and begins with them as adult shepherds who, along with their flock, are suddenly swept away by a raging flash flood that delivers them and other unfortunates into the hands of Alba Longa's inhabitants. Forced to fight in gladiator-style combats as a form of religious sacrifice, the twins lead the prisoners in a rebellion and escape, taking with them as a captive the Vestal Virgin bearing a pot of sacred fire. The majority of the film follows their harrowing journey through hostile lands, pursued by the Albans and other foes, on their quest to reach the far side of the Tiber and establish their own community. In an effectively creepy scene, the Vestal conducts a haruspicy, examining the liver of a sacrificed lamb and proclaiming that one brother will become a great king, with the proviso that in order to fulfill this prophecy, he must slay the other. Eventually, they reach the Tiber and fend off their pursuers, but quarrel over who should lead, which results in Romulus killing his brother.

The film makes the interesting choice of presenting Remus as the more dynamic brother who incites the revolt, holds the beleaguered group together, and cares for Romulus when he is badly wounded. Remus espouses a kind of Nietzschean Übermensch philosophy in which humans create their own destiny by asserting their will, and he is skeptical of the gods, ultimately declaring his rejection of them. In contrast, the very pious Romulus is always looking to the gods for guidance, but his faith also has the effect of rendering him too passive, meekly accepting misfortune as the will of the gods, and having to be roused by his brother to escape or even eat. The film seems to present the argument that when survival was the paramount necessity, Remus's pitiless pragmatism made him the right person to lead, but these qualities soon transformed him into an egotistical tyrant. Once the city had been founded and a leader was needed who could bring the community together, Romulus's piety and attendant empathy made him the right man for the job, but first Remus had to be removed. Romulus's eventual murder of Remus is prompted less by a desire to rule than as punishment for an act of religious sacrilege committed by Remus. Several times, the film portrays the twins as if they are two halves of one whole, collectively possessing the qualities required for success.

While these plot points and characterizations are creations of the filmmakers that do not appear in the ancient sources, they are not incompatible with the lacunae in the extant accounts. While on the surface *The First King* is primarily an adventure film, the movie possesses an intriguing subtext that explores the themes of destiny versus free will and the nature of the relationship between humans and gods. With its cinematography and settings, the movie is also very effective at evoking a primeval-feeling era when the boundaries between humanity, nature, and the divine were still ambiguous. Director Rovere has stated, "The production needed to contain a universe of primordial elements. . . . A world where nature becomes not only the manifestation of the god, but also the enemy to be confronted."[23]

Although much of the film's story is invented, many of the specific set, costume, and plot details are based on archaeological or historical evidence. For example, the re-creation of the city of Alba Longa features small, oval huts constructed by driving wooden posts in the ground and weaving sticks through them. These are precisely the kind of dwellings that archaeologists have found traces of in the earliest layers of Rome, and which we also see reproduced in the form of hut-shaped Etruscan urns. The clothing, fashioned from crude homespun wool and animal skins, is quite realistic. Much of the arms and armor (such as the "Villanovan"-style pectoral plates) are derived from evidence of equipment used by the Etruscans or early Latin tribes. The interpretation of omens through the reading of internal organs, especially liv- ers, is thought to be one of the oldest rites of Roman religion, likely borrowed from the Etruscans, as is the practice of gladiator-type combats as a ritual offering. Thunder and the flight of birds, both of which occur in the film as divine omens, are other Roman augury methods of great antiquity. According to some legends, Romulus instituted the priesthood of the Vestal Virgins in order to tend the sacred flame of Rome. Even the very swampy nature of the region around Rome at this point in history is correct, since the Romans had not yet undertaken the large-scale hydrological projects that would make the region more habitable.

The First King may not please all viewers. The violence is quite graphic, the subtitles may deter some, and the setting may lack the grandeur that others expect in an ancient epic. Although admittedly speculative, it is nonetheless an engaging and well-crafted attempt to flesh out a sparsely documented legend in a realistic fashion.

~

Notes

Introduction

1. "Nero Poisons His Slaves," The Silent Film Channel, YouTube, July 4, 2020, https://www.youtube.com/watch?v=1E1zsnbgzAQ.

Chapter One

1. Annette Dorgerloh, "Competing Ancient Worlds in Early Historical Film: The Example of *Cabiria* (1914)," in *The Ancient World in Silent Cinema*, ed. Pantelis Michelakis and Maria Wyke (New York: Cambridge University Press, 2013).

2. The entire Maciste phenomenon is a fascinating topic relevant to a number of subjects in addition to cinema and ancient history. An excellent study is Jacqueline Reich, *The Maciste Films of Italian Silent Cinema* (Bloomington: Indiana University Press, 2015).

3. German critic Fritz Olimsky, *Berliner Zeitung*, October 15, 1920; Scorsese's comment made in the documentary *My Voyage to Italy* (1999).

4. On the film and its surviving fragments, see Phillip Dye, *Lost Cleopatra: A Tale of Ancient Hollywood* (Orlando, FL: BearManor Media, 2020).

5. Jon Solomon, *Ben-Hur: The Original Blockbuster* (Edinburgh: Edinburgh University Press, 2016). Many of the specific details in this paragraph were taken from Solomon's outstanding and thorough analysis.

6. On the status of rowers in antiquity, see Simon James, "The Roman Galley Slave: *Ben-Hur* and the Birth of a Factoid," *Public Archaeology* 2 (2001): 35–49.

7. Cited in Lloyd Llewellyn-Jones, *Designs on the Past: How Hollywood Created the Ancient World* (Edinburgh: Edinburgh University Press, 2018), 67.

8. Staff review of *Cleopatra*, *Variety*, December 31, 1933.

9. Cited in Llewellyn-Jones, *Designs on the Past*, 109.

10. Quoted in Robert Birchard, *Cecil B. DeMille's Hollywood* (Lexington: University Press of Kentucky, 2004), 279.

11. Quoted in Maria Wyke, *Projecting the Past* (New York: Routledge, 1977), 21–22.

12. Steven Ricci, *Cinema and Fascism: Italian Film and Society 1922–1943* (Berkeley: University of California Press, 2008), 97.

Chapter Two

1. See, for example, Martin Winkler, "The Roman Empire in American Cinema after 1945," in *Imperial Projections: Ancient Rome in Modern Popular Culture*, ed. Sandra Joshel et al. (Baltimore: Johns Hopkins University Press, 2001), 50–76.

2. "The New Pictures," *Time*, October 24, 1960.

3. Kirk Douglas, *The Ragman's Son* (New York: Simon & Schuster, 1988), 304.

4. Quoted by Martin Winkler, "Culturally Significant and Not Just Simple Entertainment: History and the Marketing of *Spartacus*," in *Spartacus: Film and History*, ed. M. Winkler (Malden, MA: Blackwell, 2007), 226.

5. Quoted by Martin Winkler, "The Holy Cause of Freedom: American Ideals in *Spartacus*," in *Spartacus: Film and History*, ed. M. Winkler (Malden, MA: Blackwell, 2007), 182.

6. Quoted by Brent Shaw, *Spartacus and the Slave Wars* (Boston: Bedford, 2001), 19.

7. Letter of Karl Marx to Friedrich Engels, February 27, 1861.

8. Howard Fast, *Spartacus*, new edition with special introduction by author (New York: Routledge, 1996), 215.

Chapter Three

1. Bosley Crowther, "The Screen: Story of the Thief Who Was Spared," *New York Times*, October 11, 1962.

2. The design process for Harrison's outfits is described by Lloyd Llewellyn-Jones in *Designs on the Past* (Edinburgh: Edinburgh University Press, 2018), 267–70.

3. Quoted in Lloyd Llewellyn-Jones, *Designs on the Past* (Edinburgh: Edinburgh University Press, 2018), 268.

4. Jeffrey Richards, *Hollywood's Ancient Worlds* (New York: Continuum, 2008), 155.

5. Quoted in Richards, *Hollywood's Ancient Worlds*, 89.

6. Quoted in Martin Winkler, "Cinema and the Fall of Rome," *Transactions of the American Philological Association* 125 (1995): 140. Winkler has written extensively on this film, including editing and contributing to an entire book of essays analyzing

it: Martin Winkler, *The Fall of the Roman Empire* (Malden, MA: Wiley-Blackwell, 2009). The ideas expressed in this entry owe much to his very insightful scholarship.

7. Quoted by Elena Theodorakopoulos, *Ancient Rome at the Cinema* (Exeter, UK: Bristol Phoenix Press, 2010), 85.

8. Richards, *Hollywood's Ancient Worlds*, 91.

9. Tino Balio, *United Artists: Volume 2, 1951–1978* (Madison: University of Wisconsin Press, 2009), 137.

Chapter Four

1. Roger Ebert, *Fellini Satyricon*, January 1, 1970, https://www.rogerebert.com/reviews/fellini-satyricon-1970.

2. Roger Ebert, *Fellini Satyricon*, July 27, 2001, https://www.rogerebert.com/reviews/fellini-satyricon-2001.

3. Dario Zanelli, ed., *Fellini's Satyricon* (New York: Ballantine, 1970), 4.

4. Alastair Blanshard and Kim Shahabudin, "Art Cinema: *Fellini-Satyricon* (1969)," in *Classics on Screen: Ancient Greece and Rome on Film* (New York: Bloomsbury, 2011), 154.

5. Zanelli, *Fellini's Satyricon*, 26.

6. Zanelli, 45.

7. Elena Theodorakopoulos, *Ancient Rome at the Cinema* (Exeter, UK: Bristol Phoenix Press, 2010), 122–44.

8. Quoted by Thomas Vinciguerra, "*I, Claudius*: Hardly a Roman Holiday," *New York Times*, November 25, 2012.

9. Quotes drawn from the documentary *I, Claudius: A Television Epic*, included as bonus material to the thirty-fifth anniversary DVD edition, Acorn Media, 2011.

10. *I, Claudius*, thirty-fifth anniversary DVD.

11. *I, Claudius*, thirty-fifth anniversary DVD.

12. Roger Ebert, "*Caligula*," September 22, 1980, https://www.rogerebert.com/reviews/caligula-1980.

13. Fred Kaplan, *Gore Vidal* (London: Bloomsbury, 1999), 491.

14. The Pythons, *The Pythons Autobiography* (New York: St. Martin's Press, 2003), 276–78.

15. Comment made by John Cleese during appearance on BBC2 show *Friday Night, Saturday Morning*, broadcast on November 9, 1979.

16. The Pythons, *The Pythons Autobiography*, 280.

17. The Pythons, 280.

18. The Pythons, 287.

Chapter Five

1. SHA, Com. 1.7.

2. Quotes taken from the filmmakers' verbal commentaries found in the special features on the deluxe edition of the film on DVD.

3. Diana Landau, ed., Gladiator: The Making of the Ridley Scott Epic (New York: Newmarket, 2000), 64.

4. Landau, 66.

5. Gladiator: The Making of the Ridley Scott Epic, ed. Diana Landau, Newmarket Press, 2000, p. 31.

6. Chris Davies, Blockbusters and the Ancient World (New York: Bloomsbury, 2019), 113–27.

7. Mel Gibson, in David Neff and Jane Struck, "Dude, That Was Graphic," Christianity Today, February 23, 2004, https://www.christianitytoday.com/ct/2004/februaryweb-only/melgibson.html.

8. Roger Ebert, The Passion of the Christ, February 24, 2004, https://www.rogerebert.com/reviews/the-passion-of-the-christ-2004. It should be noted that Ebert also gave the film four out of four stars and praised it highly. David Edelstein, "Jesus H. Christ: The Passion, Mel Gibson's Bloody Mess," Slate, February 24, 2004, https://slate.com/culture/2004/02/the-passion-mel-gibson-s-bloody-mess.html.

9. These visions were printed under the title "The Dolorous Passion of Our Lord."

10. The Roman characters' medieval/ecclesiastical style of Latin pronunciation may have resulted from the fact that most of the actors were native Italian speakers and thus used an Italianate pronunciation. It is also possible that it was a deliberate attempt to indicate the low social status of the common soldiers, since there is some evidence that lower-class Romans spoke Latin differently from upper-class ones. However, Pilate, certainly a representative of the upper classes, uses the same pronunciation as the soldiers.

11. Jonathan Stamp, in "Balancing Fact and Fiction: The Ancient World of HBO's Rome," Getty Villa, March 5, 2009, https://www.youtube.com/watch?v=H1Wu-zAdbc4.

12. The famous clifftop villa was built in the first century AD by the second Roman emperor, Tiberius.

13. Quote by Amenabar from the "Director Commentary" found as a special feature on the DVD of the film.

14. Quotes by Amenabar in the "Director Commentary" found as a special feature on the DVD of the film.

15. Attila and Sign of the Pagan (both 1954); King Arthur (2004) and The Lost Legion (2007); Centurion (2010) and The Eagle (2011).

16. Neil Marshall, in Samuel Zimmerman, "Centurion: Marshall-ing Forces," Fangoria, August 27, 2010.

17. Marshall, in Zimmerman, "Centurion: Marshall-ing Forces."

18. See the preceding entry on *Centurion* for more detailed information about the novel and the origins and historicity of the legend of the "lost legion."

19. Kevin Macdonald, in Jami Philbrick, "Kevin Macdonald Talks *The Eagle*," Movieweb, January 31, 2011, https://movieweb.com/exclusive-kevin-macdonald-talks -the-eagle/.

20. Kevin Macdonald, in Jami Philbrick, "*The Eagle* Cast and Crew Interviews," Movieweb, February 10, 2011, https://movieweb.com/exclusive-the-eagle-cast-and -crew-interviews/.

21. See, for example, Kevin Wetmore, "In the Green Zone with the Ninth Legion," in *The New Peplum: Essays on Sword and Sandal Films and Television Programs Since the 1990s*, ed. Nicholas Diak (Jefferson, NC: McFarland, 2018); the essays by Strong and McAuley in *Screening the Golden Ages of the Classical Tradition*, ed. Meredith Safran (Edinburgh: Edinburgh University Press, 2019); and several of the chapters in Chris Davies, *Blockbusters and the Ancient World: Allegory and Warfare in Contemporary Hollywood* (New York: Bloomsbury, 2019).

22. Charlie Brooker, "Charlie Brooker's Screen Burn: *Spartacus: Blood and Sand*," *The Guardian*, May 22, 2010.

23. Quote by Rovere from the "Making Of" documentary, found as a special feature on the DVD of the film.

~

Select Bibliography

For anyone wishing to learn more about films set in the Roman world, this select bibliography includes many of the key works consulted by the authors when researching and writing this book.

Augoustakis, Antony, and Monica Cyrino, eds. STARZ Spartacus: *Reimagining an Icon on Screen*. Edinburgh: Edinburgh University Press, 2018.

Blanshard, Alastair, and Kim Shahabudin. *Classics on Screen: Ancient Greece and Rome on Film*. New York: Bloomsbury, 2011.

Caprotti, Federico. "Scipio Africanus: Film, Internal Colonization and Empire." *Cultural Geographies* 16, no. 3 (2009): 381–401.

Cornelius, Michael, ed. *Of Muscles and Men: Essays on the Sword and Sandal Film*. Jefferson, NC: McFarland, 2011.

Cyrino, Monica. *Big Screen Rome*. Malden, MA: Blackwell, 2005.

———, ed. *Rome, Season One: History Makes Television*. Malden, MA: Blackwell, 2008.

———, ed. *Screening Love and Sex in the Ancient World*. New York: Palgrave Macmillan, 2013.

Davies, Chris. *Blockbusters and the Ancient World: Allegory and Warfare in Contemporary Hollywood*. New York: Bloomsbury, 2019.

Diak, Nicholas, ed. *The New Peplum: Essays on Sword and Sandal Films and Television Programs Since the 1990s*. Jefferson, NC: McFarland, 2018.

Dye, Phillip. *Lost Cleopatra: A Tale of Ancient Hollywood*. Orlando, FL: BearManor Media, 2020.

James, Simon. "The Roman Galley Slave: *Ben-Hur* and the Birth of a Factoid." *Public Archaeology* 2 (2001): 35–49.

Joshel, Sandra, Margaret Malamud, and Donald McGuire Jr., eds. *Imperial Projections: Ancient Rome in Modern Popular Culture*. Baltimore: Johns Hopkins University Press, 2001.

Llewellyn-Jones, Lloyd. *Designs on the Past: How Hollywood Created the Ancient World*. Edinburgh: Edinburgh University Press, 2018.

McCall, Jeremiah. *Swords and Cinema: Ancient Battles in Modern Movies*. Barnsley, UK: Pen & Sword, 2014.

Michelakis, Pantelis, and Maria Wyke, eds. *The Ancient World in Silent Cinema*. New York: Cambridge University Press, 2013.

Milnor, Kristina. "What I Learned as Historical Consultant for *Rome*." In *Rome, Season One: History Makes Television*, edited by Monica Cyrino, 42–48. Malden, MA: Blackwell, 2008.

Morcillo, Marta García, Pauline Hanesworth, and Óscar Lapeña Marchena, eds. *Imagining Ancient Cities in Film: From Babylon to Cinecittà*. New York: Routledge, 2015.

Paul, Joanna. *Film and the Classical Epic Tradition*. Oxford: Oxford University Press, 2013.

Pomeroy, Arthur, ed. *A Companion to Ancient Greece and Rome on Screen*. Malden, MA: Wiley-Blackwell, 2017.

———. *"Then It Was Destroyed by the Volcano": The Ancient World in Film and on Television*. London: Duckworth, 2008.

Reich, Jacqueline. *The Maciste Films of Italian Silent Cinema*. Bloomington: Indiana University Press, 2015.

Richards, Jeffrey. *Hollywood's Ancient Worlds*. New York: Continuum, 2008.

Russell, James. *The Historical Epic and Contemporary Hollywood: From Dances with Wolves to Gladiator*. New York: Continuum, 2007.

Safran, Meredith, ed. *Screening the Golden Ages of the Classical Tradition*. Edinburgh: Edinburgh University Press, 2019.

Smith, Gary Allen. *Epic Films: Casts, Credits and Commentary on More Than 350 Historical Spectacle Movies*. 2nd ed. Jefferson, NC: McFarland, 2004.

Solomon, Jon. *The Ancient World in the Cinema*. Rev. ed. New Haven, CT: Yale University Press, 2001.

———. *Ben-Hur: The Original Blockbuster*. Edinburgh: Edinburgh University Press, 2016.

Theodorakopoulos, Elena. *Ancient Rome at the Cinema: Story and Spectacle in Hollywood and Rome*. Exeter, UK: Bristol Phoenix Press, 2010.

Vishnia, Rachel Feig. "Ancient Rome in Italian Cinema under Mussolini: The Case of *Scipione l'Africano*." *The Italianist* 28 (2008): 246–67.

Winkler, Martin. "Cinema and the Fall of Rome." *Transactions of the American Philological Association* 125 (1995): 135–54.

———. *Classical Literature on Screen: Affinities of Imagination*. New York: Cambridge University Press, 2017.

———, ed. *Classical Myth and Culture in the Cinema*. New York: Oxford University Press. 2001.

———, ed. *The Fall of the Roman Empire: Film and History*. Malden, MA: Blackwell, 2009.

———, ed. *Gladiator: Film and History*. Malden, MA: Blackwell, 2005.

———, ed. *Spartacus: Film and History*. Malden, MA: Blackwell, 2007.

Wyke, Maria. *Projecting the Past: Ancient Rome, Cinema, and History*. New York: Routledge, 1997.

Index

About the Authors

Gregory S. Aldrete is professor emeritus of history and humanities at the University of Wisconsin–Green Bay. Winner of numerous national fellowships and awards as both a scholar and a teacher, his books about the ancient world include *The Long Shadow of Antiquity: What Have the Greeks and Romans Done for Us?*; *Daily Life in the Roman City*; *Floods of the Tiber in Ancient Rome*; *Gestures and Acclamations in Ancient Rome*; and *The Greenwood Encyclopedia of Daily Life: The Ancient World*. He has also made half a dozen popular educational video courses with The Teaching Company/The Great Courses/Wondrium. His research has been featured in several television documentaries and as the subject of print or online articles in *The New Yorker* magazine, *The Atlantic* magazine, *The Chronicle of Higher Education*, *U.S. News and World Report*, and *Der Spiegel* magazine.

Graham Sumner has written and illustrated publications on ancient Rome for almost forty years. His works include three successful publications on Roman military clothing for Osprey, and he has written the only standard work on Roman military dress for The History Press. He also illustrated two publications for Frontline books, one on *The Roman Soldier* and the other on *Romano-Byzantine Court Dress*. As well as being interested in the Roman army, Graham is passionate about Hollywood movies, in particular those that deal with the Roman world. He wrote a series of sixteen articles for *Ancient History* magazine analyzing how the Roman army has been depicted onscreen, and was recently a historical advisor for the film *Illyricum*. Therefore, this book combines two of his interests into something unique and very close to his heart.